STRATEGIC HRM

STRATEGIC HRM

Research and Practice in Ireland

Edited by

Brian Harney and Kathy Monks

ORPEN PRESS

Published by
Orpen Press
Lonsdale House
Avoca Avenue
Blackrock
Co. Dublin
Ireland

e-mail: info@orpenpress.com
www.orpenpress.com

Paperback ISBN 978-1-909895-19-5
Kindle ISBN 978-1-909895-21-8
ePub ISBN 978-1-909895-20-1
PDF ISBN 978-1-909895-22-5

Printed in Ireland by SPRINT-print Ltd.

Contents

Contents

About the Contributors

David Collings is Professor of Human Resource Management at Dublin City University Business School and a visiting professor at King's College London. His research and consulting interests focus on management in multinational corporations with a particular emphasis on staffing and talent management issues. His work has been published in outlets including the *Journal of World Business*, *Journal of Vocational Behavior*, *Human Resource Management* and the *Industrial and Labor Relations Review*. He is the editor of *Human Resource Management Journal* and former editor of the *Irish Journal of Management*.

Edel Conway is a senior lecturer in human resource management and organisational psychology at DCU Business School and director of the Leadership, Innovation and Knowledge (LInK) Research Centre at DCU. Edel's research focuses on employee perspectives on work, including their reactions to work intensification and organisational change. Edel has published in leading international journals, including *Work, Employment and Society*, *Human Resource Management* and *Human Resource Management Journal*. She is editor of the *Irish Journal of Management* and is a member of the editorial advisory boards of *Human Resource Management Journal* and *Personnel Review*.

Niall Cullinane is a lecturer in Queen's University Management School, Queen's University Belfast. His research interests lie in the area of industrial relations, industrial sociology, worker participation and trade unionism. He has published in a number of international academic journals, including *Work, Employment and Society*, *Economic and Industrial Democracy* and the *International Journal of Human Resource Management*.

Jean Cushen is a lecturer in human resource management at Dublin City University Business School. Jean's research interests include financialisation, human resource management, knowledge work and the labour process. Jean has published book chapters and articles on these topics in *New Technology Work and Employment, Qualitative Research in Accounting and Management, IBEC* and *People Focus.* Jean also worked for several years, both in Ireland and Canada, as a human resource consultant for Towers Watson.

Tony Dundon is Professor of Human Resource Management and Employment Relations, and head of the management discipline at the School of Business and Economics, National University of Ireland, Galway. He has published extensively on employee voice, social partnership, HRM in small to medium-sized enterprises, and non-union employment relations. Professor Dundon is editor-in-chief of the *Human Resource Management Journal.* His recent books include *Employment Relations in Non-Union Firms* (London: Routledge, 2004); *Understanding Employment Relations,* (London: McGraw-Hill, second edition, 2011); *Cases in Global Management: Strategy, Innovation and People Management* (Prahran, VIC: Tilde University Press, 2012); and *Global Anti-Unionism: Nature, Dynamics, Trajectories and Outcomes* (Basingstoke: Palgrave, 2013).

Na Fu is an Irish Research Council funded postdoctoral research fellow at Dublin City University Business School. Na's research focuses on the ways in which human resource management systems influence firm performance and she has explored this issue in the context of both professional service firms and the public sector. Her PhD was highly commended in the Emerald/EFMD Outstanding Doctoral Research Awards and she received a best paper award in the 2010 Academy of Management annual conference.

Claire Gubbins is a lecturer in human resource management and organisational behaviour at Dublin City University Business School, associate editor of *Human Resource Development Quarterly* and senior research fellow on the Enterprise Ireland funded ICMR project on tacit knowledge. She is a former Government of Ireland Scholar, received the US Academy of HRD dissertation finalist award and is published in *Organisation Studies, Advances in*

Developing Human Resources, Human Resource Development Review and the *Journal of European Industrial Training.*

Patrick (Paddy) Gunnigle is Professor of Business Studies at the Kemmy Business School, University of Limerick. A former Fulbright Scholar and current Marie Curie Exchange Scholar, his research largely focuses on industrial relations and HRM in multinational companies. His published work has appeared in many of the leading journals in the field. Paddy is an inaugural fellow of the Irish Academy of Management and chartered fellow of the Institute of Personnel and Development.

Brian Harney is a lecturer at Dublin City University Business School and an academic fellow of the Centre for International HRM, University of Cambridge. His research explores the relationship between strategy and HRM with a particular focus on the SME and higher education sectors. Brian is the co-author of three books and has published in journals such as *Human Resource Management Journal* and the *International Journal of Human Resource Management.* Brian currently serves as the Irish ambassador for the HRM division of the American Academy of Management and is a member of the editorial advisory boards of *Employee Relations* and the *International Journal of Human Resource Management.*

Margaret Heffernan is a lecturer at Dublin City University Business School. She has presented at numerous academic conferences and published book chapters and articles in journals such as the *International Journal of Human Resource Management* and the *Journal of European Industrial Training,* among others. Her research interests span the areas of strategic human resource management, organisational justice, employee experiences of HRM and psychological contracts, and non-profit sectors.

Mary Keating is an associate professor in Trinity College Dublin where she teaches human resource management in the School of Business. She is a fellow of Trinity College Dublin, research fellow of the International Institute for Integration Studies (IIIS) at TCD and a fellow of the Salzburg Seminar. She has published widely in scholarly journals, including the *Journal of Applied Behavioural Science, Journal of Business Ethics,* the *International Journal of Human*

Resource Management, Thunderbird International Business Review and *Leadership Quarterly*. She has consulting experience in the area of HRM, specifically in management recruitment and compensation.

Gráinne Kelly is a lecturer in management at Queen's University Belfast. Her research interests include understanding employee experiences of human resource management practices in knowledge-intensive firms and knowledge management processes in multinational organisations. Her work is published in journals such as the *Human Resource Management Journal*, the *International Journal of Human Resource Management, Work, Employment and Society* and *Personnel Review*.

Jennifer Kennedy is a PRTLI funded PhD scholar working with Dr Claire Gubbins and Dr Finian Buckley at Dublin City University. Her research interests lie in the areas of knowledge management, organisational citizenship behaviours and HRM. Jennifer holds a BA in Business and Economics from Trinity College Dublin and graduated with first class honours from the MSc in Human Resource Management at DCU, where she won the ESB award for best dissertation.

Jonathan Lavelle is a lecturer at the Kemmy Business School, University of Limerick. His main research interests are in the field of international and comparative human resource management with a particular interest in employment relations in multinational companies. He has presented papers at a number of leading international conferences and has published in leading international journals such as the *Industrial and Labor Relations Review, Human Relations, Human Resource Management, Human Resource Management Journal* and the *Journal of World Business,* as well as co-authoring a book and a number of book chapters.

Aoife McDermott is a lecturer in human resource management at Cardiff Business School. She previously worked as a lecturer in Dublin City University Business School, and completed her PhD at Trinity College Dublin. Her research interests concern people and change management in professional and public sector contexts. Aoife's work has been published in journals including *Human*

Resource Management, the *British Journal of Management* and the *International Journal of Human Resource Management*.

Anthony McDonnell is a reader in management at Queen's University Belfast and senior adjunct research fellow at the University of South Australia. His research interests are primarily focused on how multinational companies manage their workforces across different host environments and how organisations are engaging in talent management. He has published widely in journals such as *Human Resource Management, Human Relations, Journal of Business and Psychology, Journal of World Business* and *Human Resource Management Journal*.

Kathy Monks is Emeritus Professor of Human Resource Management at Dublin City University Business School. Her main research interest lies in understanding more about the ways in which HR systems work and her work is published in journals such as *Human Resource Management Journal, Human Resource Management,* the *International Journal of Human Resource Management* and *Work, Employment and Society*.

Sue Mulhall is a lecturer in human resource development and leadership at the Dublin Institute of Technology. Prior to joining DIT, Sue ran her own training, consulting and coaching business and was previously an HR practitioner. Her award-winning doctorate explored how personal transitions can trigger processes of critical self-reflection, thus having material consequences for a person's career experiences. Sue is a pracademic, combining theory and practice, particularly in the field of career management, and has published both nationally and internationally.

Ciara Nolan is a lecturer in human resource management at the University of Ulster. She has also worked as a human resource manager in the retail and hospitality industries, and as a human resources consultant. She is a member of the Academy of HRD, the Chartered Institute of Personnel and Development (CIPD), the British Academy of Management and the Irish Academy of Management. Her current research examines the nature and scope of HRD practices within small professional service firms in Ireland.

William K. Roche is Professor of Industrial Relations and Human Resources at the School of Business, University College Dublin and honorary professor at the School of Management, Queen's University Belfast. His research spans human resource management and industrial relations; his most recent books are *Recession at Work: HRM in the Irish Crisis* (London: Routledge, 2013), *The Oxford Handbook of Conflict Management in Organizations* (forthcoming from Oxford University Press), *Managing Workplace Conflict in Ireland*, (Dublin: Government Publications, 2009) and *Partnership at Work: The Quest for Radical Organizational Change* (Oxford: Routledge, 2006).

Tom Turner is a senior lecturer at the Kemmy Business School, University of Limerick and lectures in industrial relations and human resource management. He has published widely in international journals. His main areas of research include the integration and impact of immigrants in the labour market, trends in occupational structures, precarious work and trade union studies.

Introduction

Brian Harney and Kathy Monks

This brief introduction will set the context for this book while also providing an overview of the various chapters. It is now some fifteen years since Roche et al.'s (1998) edited volume explored strategic human resource management (SHRM) in Ireland from a research-based perspective. The intervening years have seen a significant increase in SHRM research by Irish scholars, coupled with the proliferation of specialist undergraduate and masters' level SHRM programmes (Carbery et al., 2013). In terms of the human resource (HR) profession in Ireland, the Chartered Institute of Personnel and Development (CIPD) has witnessed a dramatic 80 per cent increase in membership since the 1980s. These developments highlight the necessity for continuous theoretical reflection and empirical scrutiny of SHRM practice. The purpose of this book is to provide an integrated overview of both theory and evidence of the practice of strategic HRM in an Irish context. Broadly understood, SHRM involves a focus on linking human resource management (HRM) to business strategy, designing high performance work systems (HPWSs) and adding value through good people management in an attempt to gain sustained competitive advantage (Boselie, 2010; Delery and Doty, 1996). At the same time, SHRM is subject to multiple interpretations and sometimes contested meanings. This book therefore aims to provide empirically informed insights to illuminate current thinking around SHRM, including a critical analysis of its relevance, application and development in an Irish context. Reflecting the richness, diversity and breadth of SHRM expertise in Ireland, the book draws on the insights of twenty-one contributors representing some nine different institutions. In so doing, we believe it will prove an invaluable resource for undergraduates specialising in SHRM and masters' students requiring up-to-date knowledge about people management practices and processes, while also serving as a reflective resource for experienced executives.

Why Strategic HRM and Why Now?

It is worth drawing attention to why the task of examining SHRM in an Irish context is important and why it holds particular relevance at the current time. First is the reality that the evaluation of SHRM takes place in the context of a dramatically altered economic landscape. Commentary on the decline of the Irish economy in what has been termed 'the Great Recession' (Roche and Teague, 2013) is well rehearsed. Ireland experienced the largest compound decline in gross national product (GNP) of any industrialised economy over the 2007–2010 period (Kinsella, 2012). As a result, Ireland once again finds itself faced with the challenge articulated by pioneering Taoiseach Seán Lemass 60 years ago of ensuring the 'economic foundation of independence'. Ireland has once more returned to a labour surplus economy representing a dramatic reversal of fortunes from the 'Celtic Tiger' era, which had been characterised by an unprecedented requirement for workers and a growing reliance on immigrant labour (Turner, 2010). Specifically in employment terms, Ireland has gone from having a laudable unemployment rate of 4.6 per cent in 2007 to a rate of 14.8 per cent in 2012, the third highest unemployment rate in the Euro area, eclipsed only by Spain (21.6 per cent) and Greece (17.7 per cent) (Forfás, 2012). This reality, and the associated collapse of national level social partnership, represents a challenging economic and social backdrop for SHRM. From a HR perspective, the recession has significantly altered the basis of recruitment, the nature of pay decisions and remuneration levels, channels of employee voice and levels of employee morale. HR professionals have had to develop expertise in dealing with employee exit and downsizing decisions. In the public sector, HR professionals have had to confront the challenges presented by early retirement schemes, recruitment embargoes and third-party pressure for reform. This provides a timely reminder of the significant challenges that emanate from the contextual and institutional environment in which SHRM is enacted (Gunnigle, 1998). However, it is also important to recognise arguments that the 1980s' recession and subsequent recovery served as a key catalyst for the reinvention and renewal of HRM in Ireland (Gunnigle et al., 1994; Roche et al., 1998: 17). Recent commentary notes that a 'new people management agenda' could emerge from the context of the current recession (Roche and Teague, 2013). National survey findings highlight a greater willingness by employees to take on more responsibility, to innovate and to up-skill in addition to a greater demand for involvement in decision-making (O'Connell et al., 2010: 9). The unfolding economic and social circumstances and associated challenges and opportunities highlight the importance of reassessing the status of SHRM in an Irish context.

A second reason for exploring SHRM in Ireland concerns the growing recognition that the management of people is of strategic significance to success (Barney, 1991). Indeed, a burgeoning stream of international evidence over the last two decades has highlighted the impact that SHRM can have in shaping both organisational performance (Huselid, 1995) and employee outcomes (Takeuchi et al., 2009). As we outline in **Chapter 1**, Irish contributions have likewise evolved from exploring the nature of HRM in Irish organisations to examining its viability and assessing its contribution to key organisational and employee outcomes (Monks, 1992; Roche, 1999; Guthrie et al., 2009; Conway and Monks, 2009). The importance of developing human capital has also been at the forefront of government policy. Since the 1960s, Ireland has invested heavily in education as a pathway to future economic and social prosperity. By the 1980s, Ireland was a pioneer in purposefully drawing on this human capital base to position itself as an attractive location for foreign direct investment. A key exemplar was the Industrial Development Authority's 'We're young Europeans' campaign, which publicised Ireland's highly educated, bright and youthful workforce (MacSharry and White, 2000). Structural funds from Europe during the 1980s and economic growth in the 1990s led to increased investment in human resources (Kirby, 2010). Today, agencies such as Science Foundation Ireland assert that 'Ireland's success on the world stage cannot be based on low labour costs or mineral resources; it must be based on our human resources and our science' (Science Foundation Ireland, 2012: 8). A key differentiator in attracting foreign MNCs to Ireland has been this highly educated and skilled workforce. This has invited something of a reinforcing cycle as many of these firms, from the early arrival of Pfizer and Intel, through to the recent additions of Google and LinkedIn, are at the leading edge in terms of the development and diffusion of SHRM practice.

The changing economic circumstances and importance of developing human capital for both organisations and national competitiveness renders the exploration of strategic HRM in Ireland an important task. Allied to this is the necessity of exploring the relevance and impact of key conceptual developments in SHRM. There has long been debate over the extent of diffusion of HRM in an Irish context, evident in a discourse of 'new orders' and the 'continuity of tradition and change' (Foley and Gunnigle, 1995; Gunnigle et al., 1994; Turner and Morley, 1995). It is important to continue and update such conversations. The idea of assessing key conceptual developments via empirical scrutiny forms the core of the contemporary movement for so-called 'evidence-based HR' (EBHR). EBHR emphasises the critical importance of ensuring that HR decision-making takes place in the context of the best and most recent research evidence available (Rousseau and Barends, 2011). In bringing together leading experts in SHRM each chapter in this book carefully considers global developments and debates before specifically examining how Irish evidence reflects these developments and contributes to these debates. This is an important task in ensuring that the wealth of recent research evidence in Ireland about how HR operates and has most impact (e.g. Carbery et al., 2013) is brought to bear to inform analysis. This opens up important questions concerning the extent to which the assumptions and key arguments of SHRM, largely US in origin and based on particular types of organisations (e.g. large, private sector), can, or indeed should, hold universal relevance (Batt and Banerjee, 2012; Brewster, 2007). Both extensive global competition and a substantial MNC presence have undoubtedly shaped the nature of SHRM in Ireland. Yet, questions remain concerning the specificity of SHRM in an Irish context. Indeed, one commentator has argued that 'maybe it is time we learned to import more discerningly across the whole spectrum of ideas, societal no less than economic, and had the confidence to be more makers than takers in getting the best out of ourselves' (Lee, 2002: 300). Debate also abounds about the relevance of SHRM across different categories of workers both within and across organisational boundaries (Lepak and Snell, 2002; Marchington et al., 2004). Comparisons of international developments in the field with Irish research evidence serves as one basis to contribute to these debates.

Overall, the impact of the current economic and social context, the prospective role of SHRM in enhancing performance and competitiveness, and the importance of assessing the relevance of conceptual developments all provide a clear rationale for exploring SHRM in Ireland. Critically, these are not mutually exclusive, with developments in one domain shaping and reinforcing those in another. The current economic crisis has directed attention to the importance of restoring national competitiveness so that human capital considerations have taken on renewed significance. Associated commentary has indicated a complex terrain including an increasingly formally educated workforce, but below European averages in terms of lifelong learning (Forfás, 2012). Similarly, while Ireland continues to attract leading foreign multinational corporations (MNCs), there are also skills shortages in key growth and knowledge-based sectors (Shanks et al., 2013). Akin to the 1980s, recessionary circumstances have also fostered conceptual developments founded on how best to leverage the potential of talent. Concepts such as 'employee engagement' have emerged as important in countering potential negative effects on productivity and performance with reference made to 'the commitment, motivation, ideas and creativity of all employees as key elements in rebuilding a vibrant and competitive economy and a high-performing public service' (Fallon-Byrne, 2010: 2). Likewise, there is growing recognition of the importance of 'innovations in the organisation of work' as a basis for fostering economic recovery (Watson et al., 2010: 24).

Employee experiences have also come to the fore in recent times, not only in understanding the impact of the economic downturn, but also in terms of changing expectations. Employees are now more educated and technologically versed, with noted generational differences suggested with respect to demands in terms of career paths and development provisions (Hewlett et al., 2010). All the while, dedicated attention is required to the nature of the psychological contract employees hold with the organisation, and the important role that line managers play in balancing employee expectations with employer intentions (McDermott et al., 2013).

These changes suggest an ever-broadening range of competencies, challenges and depth of knowledge required of HR professionals (cf. Sheehan, 2002). In this vein it is clear that considering the impact of the current economic context, appreciating the prospective contribution of SHRM to enhanced performance and assessing conceptual developments are of equal and related importance in the field of SHRM. Reflecting this line of argument, the centenary CIPD conference held in April 2013 focused on three interrelated themes: retaining talent when the upturn comes, managing employee expectations and rebuilding trust. Overall, there is a consensus that Ireland's economic fortunes are inextricably bound to the management of people and their ideas at an individual, workplace and national level (Kakabadse and Moore, 2002; McWilliams, 2012). This in turn reinforces the imperative of a strategic approach to the development and nurturing of human resources as a critical foundation for success. The next section outlines how each chapter in this book sets out to provide insights in this regard.

Overview of Contributions

Progress

This book is structured around four key sections. The first section comprises two chapters which examine the broad theme of *Progress* in research and understanding of SHRM in Ireland. **Chapter 1,** by Harney, Heffernan and Monks, offers an historical overview of the emergence of HRM in Ireland before examining contemporary developments and associated Irish evidence with respect to the development of SHRM and the relationship between SHRM and performance. Key empirical developments highlighted include the gradual incorporation of employee perspectives and a better understanding of the key intermediary variables shaping the SHRM–performance linkage. Following this broad overview, **Chapter 2,** by Roche, provides a review of how HRM professionals and international scholars have considered the effects of recessions on SHRM. The chapter then draws on findings from extensive Irish research examining the impact of the recession on both private and public sector organisations. These results highlight a leaner, somewhat more influential HR function with evidence of a dual deployment of HRM practices to balance retrenchment with efforts at maintaining workforce motivation and commitment. Taken together, these two chapters provide a broad understanding of the state of play of SHRM in both steady state and recessionary circumstances, thereby setting the foundation for chapters that examine more specific HR practice.

Practice

The second section of the book examines developments in strategic HRM in terms of four specific domains of *Practice*. **Chapter 3**, by Collings, explores the nascent area of talent management (TM) by highlighting five key streams or waves of development. The chapter then examines evidence on the content, operation and impact of TM from the limited pool of research that has been conducted in an Irish context. While challenges remain, clearly TM is an area of growing significance; indeed the subtitle poses the question 'a new era for HRM?' **Chapter 4**, by Cullinane and Dundon, explores the domain of employee voice, which is noted as an enduring process, inherent to the employment relationship. This chapter documents the demand for employee voice, before unpacking its meaning and the key basis by which employee voice can be evaluated. Turning to the Irish evidence, Cullinane and Dundon highlight a tendency for more pronounced patterns of direct and non-union forms of voice, coupled with growing employer resistance to institutional and European attempts to reframe the dynamics of employee voice.

Chapter 5, by Gunnigle, Turner, Lavelle and McDonnell, examines the issue of pay and performance management in the context of MNCs, typically viewed as market leaders and innovators in this domain. The chapter begins with an overview of key debates in relation to the emergence, content and purpose of performance management systems before drawing on survey evidence from MNCs in Ireland to assess the nature of pay and performance systems in place. The findings highlight ownership and sector as key determinants of the types of systems in place, in addition to variances in application between occupational groups. **Chapter 6**, by Gubbins and Kennedy, takes on the critical domains of learning and knowledge. Five key learning orientations are presented with each one illustrated by relevant Irish research evidence. Moving to knowledge, the chapter deconstructs key definitions before providing an overview of recent Irish research which has examined key outcomes of knowledge processes. Overall, the chapter makes clear that the knowledge embedded in people and mastery of how that knowledge is shared and retained are of vital consideration in realising individual and organisational potential.

While this section on HR practice encompassing talent, employee voice, pay and performance, and knowledge and learning presents them in a standalone fashion, in reality they are likely to operate more like bundles which can either serve to be 'mutually rein-forcing' or operate as 'deadly combinations' (Becker et al., 1997: 43; Monks and Loughnane, 2006: 1926). The task of the HR manager is to understand the detail of how each practice operates, but also to interpret this from the perspective of the HR system as a whole.

Context

Section 3 continues the empirical conversation by examining SHRM in *Context*. This follows a growing recognition that SHRM originated from a limited US, private sector, large-firm standpoint so key findings may not generalise across national contexts, or to the majority of the working population, including those operating in the context of small firms or the public and non-profit sectors (Bamberger and Pratt, 2010; Batt and Banerjee, 2012). By the same token, some researchers have questioned the relevance of certain principles of SHRM when applied to an increasingly educated and knowledge-centric workforce (Chasserio and Legault, 2009). This section, therefore, explores the meaning and operation of SHRM in varying contexts.

Chapter 7, by Lavelle, McDonnell and Gunnigle, examines the topic of international HRM by exploring the role and significance of MNCs. Specifically, the chapter offers an overview of theoretical debates concerning country-of-origin versus host-country effects. The chapter then explores how this debate has been played out in an Irish context before considering more recent empirical evidence relating to the role of MNCs in Ireland. **Chapter 8**, by Harney and Nolan, moves the discussion to the often neglected context of small and medium-sized enterprises (SMEs). This chapter presents some key characteristics of SMEs before assessing the applicability of extant SHRM theory to this context. Turning to empirical evidence, the chapter draws on both national and organisational level find-ings to offer a more nuanced understanding of the nature of HRM in Irish SMEs.

Chapter 9, by Monks, Conway, Kelly and Fu, engages with the significant area of knowledge-intensive firms (KIFs). Having delineated the key concepts of knowledge work and knowledge workers, this chapter provides an overview of recent research. The chapter then offers a multi-layered overview of Irish research, examining KIFs at the level of industry, firm and employees. In so doing, the chapter highlights complexities in terms of HRM systems deployed and subsequent employee outcomes. The final chapter on context is **Chapter 10**, by McDermott and Keating, which examines HRM in healthcare, specifically the hospital sector. This chapter highlights the challenges and constraints that characterise HRM in this context before exploring recent evidence on the relationship between HR practices and performance in healthcare settings. Throughout the chapter, McDermott and Keating draw on their own research to illuminate the complexities of HR in the context of multiple, and sometimes competing, stakeholder demands.

These four chapters illustrate that while the overall principles of SHRM may hold some universal relevance, the specifics of how SHRM actually operates is likely to be heavily shaped by the immediate context in which the organisation is operating. These chapters also indicate how SHRM in each of the contexts explored is subject to its own tensions, including those of convergence versus divergence, formality versus informality, generalist versus specialist and the competing requirements of multiple stakeholders. In addition, they highlight how HRM decision-makers will need to be attentive to broader institutional backdrops in the form of legislation and wider institutional networks (Curran and Quinn, 2012; McLaughlin, 2013).

Challenges

The final section of the book picks up the themes of complexity and tension with two chapters which examine *Challenges* for SHRM. **Chapter 11**, by Mulhall, explores careers and career development. Here it is clear that traditional conceptions of career have been replaced by a variety of new career types and this will have differing implications in terms of HR understanding. The Irish evidence presented illustrates novel approaches to up-skilling and developing learning networks. In **Chapter 12**, Cushen and Harney explore the reasons why SHRM may not always work in the ways originally intended or expected. In particular, they focus on neglected issues including financialization and the inherent tensions of the employment relationship. Irish evidence is used to support the argument providing a useful empirical counter to overly simplistic claims assuming automatic benefits or outcomes as a result of SHRM interventions. Finally, in the conclusion Monks and Harney explore some key dilemmas likely to inform future theoretical and empirical conversations.

References

Bamberger, P. and Pratt, M. (2010), 'Moving Forward by Looking Back: Reclaiming Unconventional Research Contexts and Samples in Organizational Scholarship', *Academy of Management Journal*, 53(4): 665–671.

Barney, J. (1991), 'Firm Resources and Sustained Competitive Advantage', *Journal of Management*, 17(1): 99–120.

Batt, R. and Banerjee, M. (2012), 'The Scope and Trajectory of Strategic HR Research: Evidence from American and British Journals', *International Journal of Human Resource Management*, 23(9): 1739–1762.

Becker, B., Huselid, M., Pickus, P. and Spratt, M. (1997), 'HR as a Source of Shareholder Value: Research and Recommendations', *Human Resource Management*, 36(1): 39–47.

Boselie, P. (2010), *Strategic Human Resource Management*, Maidenhead: McGraw-Hill.

Brewster, C. (2007), 'Comparative HRM: European Views and Perspectives', *International Journal of Human Resource Management*, 18(5): 769–787.

Carbery, R., Gunnigle, P. and Morley, M. (2013), 'Human Resource Management Research Output in Ireland: A Retrospective', *Irish Journal of Management*, forthcoming

Chasserio, S. and Legault, M.J. (2009), 'Strategic Human Resources Management Is Irrelevant When It Comes to Highly Skilled Professionals in the Canadian New Economy', *International Journal of Human Resource Management*, 20(5): 1113–1131.

Conway, E. and Monks, K. (2009), 'Unravelling the Complexities of High Commitment: An Employee-Level Analysis', *Human Resource Management Journal*, 19(2): 140–158.

Curran, D. and Quinn, M. (2012), 'Attitudes to Employment Law and the Consequent Impact of Legislation on Employment Relations Practice', *Employee Relations*, 34(5): 464–480.

Delery, J.E. and Doty, D.H. (1996), 'Modes of Theorising in Strategic Human Resource Management: Tests of Universalistic, Contingency and Configurational Performance Predictions', *Academy of Management Journal*, 39(4): 802–835.

Fallon-Byrne, L. (2010), 'Preface' in P. O'Connell, H. Russell, D. Watson and D. Byrne (eds), *The Changing Workplace: A Survey of Employees' Views and Experiences*, Dublin: National Centre for Partnership and Performance, Research Series 7(2): 2–3.

Foley, K. and Gunnigle, P. (1995), 'The Personnel Function – Change or Continuity?' in T. Turner and M. Morley (eds), *Industrial Relations and the New Order*, Dublin: Oak Tress Press, 141–170.

Forfás (2012), *Ireland's Competitiveness Scorecard 2012*, Dublin: National Competitiveness Council.

Gunnigle, P. (1998), 'Human Resource Management and the Personnel Function' in W.K. Roche, K. Monks and J. Walsh (eds), *Human Resource Strategies: Policy and Practice in Ireland*, Dublin: Oak Tree Press, 1–23.

Gunnigle, P., Flood, P., Morley, M. and Turner, T. (1994), *Continuity and Change in Irish Employee Relations*, Dublin: Oak Tree Press.

Guthrie, J., Flood, P., Liu, W. and MacCurtain, S. (2009), 'High Performance Work Systems in Ireland: Human Resource and Organisational Outcomes', *International Journal of Human Resource Management*, 20(1): 112–125.

Hewlett, S.A., Sherbin, L. and Sumberg, K. (2010), 'How Gen Y & Boomers Will Reshape Your Agenda', *Harvard Business Review*, July–August: 71–76.

Huselid, M.A. (1995), 'The Impact of Human Resource Practices on Turnover, Productivity, and Corporate Financial Performance', *Academy of Management Journal*, 38(3): 635–672.

Kakabadse, A. and Moore, S. (2002), 'The Challenges and Paradoxes of Organisational Leadership: Strategic Climate, National Culture and Key Recommendations for Effective Leadership Development' in P. Gunnigle, M. Morley and M. McDonnell (eds), *The John Lovett Lectures: A Decade of Developments in Human Resource Management*, Dublin: Liffey Press, 127–147.

Kinsella, S. (2012), 'Is Ireland really the Role Model for Austerity?', *Cambridge Journal of Economics*, 36(1): 223–235.

Kirby, P. (2010), *Celtic Tiger in Collapse: Explaining the Weaknesses of the Irish Model*, New York, NY: Palgrave Macmillan.

Lee, J.J. (2002), 'Labour, Employment and Society in Twentieth Century Ireland' in P. Gunnigle, M. Morley and M. McDonnell (eds), *The John Lovett Lectures: A Decade of Developments in Human Resource Management*, Dublin: Liffey Press, 279–303.

Lepak, D.P. and Snell, S. (2002), 'Examining the Human Resources Architecture: The Relationships among Human Capital, Employment and Resource Configurations', *Journal of Management*, 28(4): 517–543.

MacSharry, R. and White, P. (2000), *The Making of the Celtic Tiger: The Inside Story of Ireland's Boom Economy*, Cork: Mercier Press.

Marchington, M., Grimshaw, D., Rubery, J. and Wilmott, H. (2004), *Fragmenting Work: Blurring Organisational Boundaries and Disordering Hierarchies*, Oxford: Oxford University Press.

McDermott, A., Conway, E., Rousseau, D.M. and Flood, P. (2013), 'Promoting Effective Pyschological Contracts through Leadership: The Missing Link between HR Strategy and Performance', *Human Resource Management*, 52(2): 289–310.

McLaughlin, C. (2013), 'The Role of Productivity Coalitions in Building a "High Road" Competitive Strategy: The Case of Denmark and Ireland', *European Journal of Industrial Relations*, 19(2): 127–143.

McWilliams, D. (2012), *The Good Room: Why We Ended Up in a Debtor's Prison – and How We Can Break Free*, Dublin: Penguin Ireland.

Monks, K. (1992), 'Models of Personnel Management: A Means of Understanding the Diversity of Personnel Practices?', *Human Resource Management Journal*, 3(2): 29–41.

Monks, K. and Loughnane, M. (2006), 'Unwrapping the HRM Bundle: HR System Design in an Irish Power Utility', *International Journal of Human Resource Management*, 17(11): 1926–1941.

O'Connell, P., Russell, H., Watson, D. and Byrne, D. (eds) (2010), *The Changing Workplace: A Survey of Employees' Views and Experiences*, Dublin: National Centre for Partnership and Performance, Research Series 7(2).

Roche, W.K. (1999), 'In Search of Commitment-Orientated Human Resource Management Practices and the Conditions that Sustain Them', *Journal of Management Studies*, 36(5): 653–678.

Roche, W.K., Monks, K. and Walsh, J. (eds) (1998), *Human Resource Strategies: Policy and Practice in Ireland*, Dublin: Oak Tree Press.

Roche, W.K. and Teague, P. (2013), 'Recessionary Bundles: HR Practices in the Irish Economic Crisis', *Human Resource Management Journal*, doi: 10.1111/1748-8583.12019.

Rousseau, D.M. and Barends, E. (2011), 'Becoming an Evidence-Based HR Practitioner', *Human Resource Management Journal*, 21(3): 221–235.

Science Foundation Ireland (2012), *Agenda 2020: Excellence and Impact*, Dublin: SFI.

Shanks, R., O'Neill, N. and O'Mahony, A. (2013), *Closing the Skills Gap in Ireland: Employers at the Heart of the Solution*, Dublin: Accenture Institute for High Performance, Accenture.

Sheehan, B. (2002), 'Irish Industrial Relations and HRM: An Overview of the "Lovett Years"' in P. Gunnigle, M. Morley and M. McDonnell (eds), *The John Lovett Lectures: A Decade of Developments in Human Resource Management*, Dublin: Liffey Press, 323–354.

Takeuchi, H., Chen, G. and Lepak, D.P. (2009), 'Looking through the Looking Glass of a Social System: Cross Level Effects of HPWS on Employees' Attitudes', *Personnel Psychology*, 62(1): 1–29.

Turner, T. (2010), 'The Jobs Immigrants Do: Issues of Displacement and Marginalisation in the Irish Labour Market', *Work, Employment and Society*, 24(2): 318–336.

Turner, T. and Morley, M. (1995), *Industrial Relations and the New Order: Case Studies in Conflict and Co-Operation*, Dublin: Oak Tree Press.

Watson, D., Galway, J., O'Connell, P. and Russell, H. (2010), *The Changing Workplace: A Survey of Employers' Views and Experiences*, Dublin: National Centre for Partnership and Performance, Research Series 6(1).

Section 1

Progress

CHAPTER 1

The Emergence and Status of Strategic HRM in Ireland

Brian Harney, Margaret Heffernan and Kathy Monks

Introduction

This chapter explores the emergence and current status of strategic human resource management (SHRM) in Ireland. The chapter is divided into three key parts in order to capture particular aspects of this development. The first section traces the evolution of HRM from its early roots in the welfare movement through to the emergence of personnel management. The second section moves to examine more contemporary developments concerning the status of SHRM by considering issues surrounding the nature of SHRM and associated Irish research evidence. The third section explores attempts to justify the significance and managerial relevance of SHRM interventions, most notably via debates related to the concept of high performance work systems (HPWS). The chapter concludes with an examination of the continuities and divergences in Irish research findings and proposes areas for future research and practice. In so doing we caution against simplistic assumptions of progress or staged evolution and invite more contingent explanations of the status of SHRM in Ireland.

The Emergence of HRM in Ireland: From Welfarism to Personnel Management

It is difficult to find a consensus on the origins of HRM, with international commentators suggesting anything from shortly before the First World War through to the 1980s (Kaufman, 1999). In an Irish context, Barrington (1980) indicates that a personnel function had been established in the civil service after the First World War, but its official recognition in the private sector is probably best dated from the setting up in 1937 of an Irish branch of the Institute of Labour Management, the forerunner of today's Chartered Institute of Personnel and Development (CIPD). The first meetings of the Institute of Labour Management in Ireland were held in the recreation hall attached to Jacob's biscuit factory and were attended by a small group of individuals, mainly women, who were employed as welfare supervisors in Dublin factories. These factories had strong Quaker traditions and meetings concerned issues such as the health and leisure time of employees and worker participation in recreation committees and works councils, as exemplified in Box 1.1.

Box 1.1: The Welfare Stage

The issues facing the welfare workers who were the precursors of today's HRM managers are captured in the minutes from the meetings of the Labour Management Institute. In *Labour Management* (May 1940) it was reported that Mr Julian Rowntree of Associated Chocolate Co Ltd, Dublin spoke on 'Cooperation in Industry' and recommended that employees should be given scope in running their own recreation sub-committees and encouraged in the use of their leisure time. He also put forward proposals for a works council at which all levels of management and workers should be represented. Factory inspectors were highly prized as speakers at these events and health issues were of particular importance. In many of the Quaker-owned factories, the concern with welfare issues was translated into the provision of a range of employee facilities such as sports grounds and evening classes on a range of topics.

While legislative changes such as the Industrial Relations Act of 1946 provided a foundation for improved working conditions, Ireland during the 1940s and 1950s remained a predominantly agricultural and stagnant society (Lee, 1980). A sea change occurred during the 1960s with the government of Seán Lemass and his programme of economic and industrial development, which provided the catalyst for substantial change to the personnel function. Nonetheless, a survey carried out in 1966 by the Irish Institute of Management found that only 6.4 per cent of firms with more than 500 employees actually employed a personnel manager with a professional qualification, and hardly any mentioned personnel as an area for development (Tomlin, 1966). This is reflected in the low levels of membership (150 people) of what was, by now, the Institute of Personnel Management (IPM) (Institute of Personnel Management Irish Branch, 1968).

The 1970s saw significant growth of personnel management in both the public and private sectors. This growth was very much associated with new legislation governing the employment relationship at both national and EU level. Increasingly, there was a need for someone in the organisation to become more knowledgeable with respect to legislation governing issues such as pay, holidays, equality, redundancy and employment protection. While the personnel specialist was well-placed to step into this role (Gunnigle, 1998), the status of the personnel function within organisations was not proven. For example, Barrington (1980: 90) criticised its role in the public service, stating: 'Personnel is another of those ideas, regarded as "good things", that are maintained, if not wholly for ornament, then not really for use either.' Various submissions to the Commission of Inquiry on Industrial Relations (1981) criticised the low priority given to personnel issues in many Irish firms and the lack of authority of personnel officers.

During the 1970s and 1980s, industrial relations (IR) was the predominant personnel activity. This was reflective of a long-standing tradition of low-trust industrial relations and a reliance on adversarial collective bargaining (Roche, 1999). Indeed, MacNeill (1980: 58) considered that trade unions 'had a virtually uncontested right to bargain on any matter affecting people at work, to regulate what they will do, how they will get it and what they will get for doing it'. However, by the end of the 1980s, the picture had altered with a notable 'reassertion of management control' as a key outcome of the high levels of unemployment during the decade (Gunnigle, 1992). This was also evidenced in the increase of non-union multinational corporations (MNCs) operating within Ireland. Overall, the 1980s witnessed a notable shift in the core focus of personnel activities, away from the management of industrial relations towards a more direct and individualistic approach to the management of employees (Sheehan, 2002). The economic difficulties of the 1980s were reflected in the themes of the IPM's annual conferences, which included 'Survival Management' (1983) and 'the Uncertain Future' (1986). Yet by the 1990s the economic climate was improving. Signalling the emergence of a new strategic-centred discourse, the 1990 CIPD conference was entitled 'The 1990s Workforce: Committed or Controlled?', with speakers explicitly addressing topics of competition, performance and change. The next section describes the development of this strategic approach to HRM before examining empirical evidence of its status in Ireland.

Strategic Human Resource Management

The normative logic of strategic HRM (SHRM) stresses the importance of directly aligning HRM with organisational strategy, while also paying dedicated attention to securing appropriate behaviours from employees (Schuler and Jackson, 1987). This strategic discourse found true significance in the context of intensive global competition, most notably from Japan, and the emergence of more people-intensive service and knowledge-based industries. Increasingly, attention was directed to the role of internal organisational processes in generating competitive advantage. It was noted that successful organisations exhibited a clear consistency between their organisational objectives and human resource (HR) activities (Arthur, 1994). This consistency combined both horizontal and vertical integration, whereby HR activities are mutually supportive of each other and fit with the strategic direction of the organisation. One of the key proxies for the extent of strategic integration is the extent of HR representation at corporate board level (Lengnick-Hall et al., 2009). Overall, a SHRM approach acknowledged that managers exercise strategic choice when making decisions in key areas of HR such as rewards, employee relations, training and performance management, culminating in an overall philosophy towards employees.

In an Irish context, the growing significance of SHRM aligned neatly with favourable macro-economic conditions which saw the realisation of fast-paced economic development, coupled with the emergence of educational and labour market institutions and value systems particularly favourable to the workings of SHRM (Horgan and Mühlau, 2006). The stability provided for by centralised pay bargaining and social partnership also contributed to an alleviation of many IR and administrative demands on the HR function. At the same time, the influence of United States (US) MNCs in promoting the ideals and ideology of SHRM cannot be understated (Carbery et al., 2013). Survey research has consistently shown that ownership and size are strong predictors of HR practices, with MNCs deploying much more advanced and sophisticated HR practices relative to indigenous Irish firms (Geary and Roche, 2001; Lavelle et al., 2009; Monks, 2002). A stream of research also explored the compatibility between new, more strategic HRM practices and trade union influence (Roche and Turner, 1998; Turner et al., 1997), including the influence of specific SHRM practices such as performance-related pay and the individualisation of the employment relationship (Gunnigle et al., 1998; Roche, 2001).

A number of studies have specifically examined the extent of the strategic orientation of HRM in Ireland. Early work revealed evidence of HRM practices emerging in some Irish organisations, as gauged by attention to strategy, employee commitment and devolution to line management (Kelly and Brannick, 1988). By the early 1990s there was evidence of several models of personnel/HRM operating in Ireland, ranging from the traditional welfare- or industrial-relations-focused approaches to more innovative models that encompassed a range of sophisticated practices associated with SHRM (Monks, 1992). Associated with the latter was a heightened unitarist outlook manifest in opposition to union recognition, and the emergence of a strong non-union sector (Gunnigle, 1992). The University of Limerick/Cranfield surveys offered some encouraging signs that Irish HR practitioners were adopting a more strategic role through their position in the top management team which might allow them to integrate HRM concerns into the formulation of business strategy (Foley and Gunnigle, 1994). Nonetheless, research still reported that much HRM adoption was characterised by its 'piecemeal or fragmented manner' (Roche and Turner, 1998: 76) with O'Brien (1998: 454) arguing that 'while there is evidence of a wide range of HRM-type initiatives being developed in organizations, the evidence of a link between business strategy and HRM is far more limited.' Little seems to have changed over time. A recent study examining 169 of the *Business & Finance* top 1,000 performing firms in Ireland finds few organisations have business strategies which are fully cascaded down into HR strategies with specific outputs and deliverables. In addition, while 72 of these firms had a HR presence at the level of the board of directors (or equivalent), over a quarter of these reported having little or no involvement in corporate strategy development (Heffernan et al., 2008).

Despite the fragmented and complex diffusion of SHRM in Ireland, Irish evidence has found some support for the argument that the strategic integration of HRM enhances effectiveness. In Roche's (1999) analysis, those firms exhibiting high strategic integration were twenty times more likely to adopt high commitment practices. Heffernan et al. (2008) found that those organisations exhibiting integration *and* pursuing a high-road differentiation strategy were more inclined to adopt sophisticated SHRM and exhibit more organisational innovation relative to those pursuing a low-road, cost-focused strategy. Integration clearly plays an important role, as does the relationship between SHRM and organisational performance. The latter has emerged as a particularly important development in recent SHRM research and one with which Irish researchers have also extensively engaged.

Strategic HRM and Performance

The past twenty years have produced numerous studies which claim to demonstrate that sophisticated SHRM practices are positively related to organisational performance. Some of the labels that have been attached to SHRM from this research indicate these linkages, for example best practice SHRM, high performance work systems (HPWS) and high commitment management (HCM) (see Wall and Wood, 2005). In the case of HPWS, these have been defined as 'systems of human resource practices designed to enhance employees' skills, commitment and productivity in such a way that employees become a source of competitive advantage' (Datta et al., 2005: 135). In this definition and others there is a widely held view that SHRM impacts upon organisational performance through practices that promote and nourish employee autonomy, skills and discretionary behaviours. These typically include sophisticated recruitment and selection techniques, appraisal, training, teamwork, communications, empowerment, performance-related pay and employment security (Wall and Wood, 2005). Collectively, these individual practices are seen to operate as a bundle of mutually reinforcing, synergistic HR practices which help to facilitate employee commitment and involvement and subsequent organisational performance. By examining practices as a holistic bundle, an index has been used to capture the use of a *system* of high performance work practices and the extent of HPWS coverage (Huselid, 1995).

A stream of empirical evidence has emerged to support the promise of HPWS. A meta-theoretical review of data from 92 studies, covering a total of 19,319 organisations, indicates that 20 per cent of the utility available from predicting performance differences among organisations is attributable to HPWS (Combs et al., 2006). However, this research has not been without criticism, including the fact that organisational outcomes are too distal from SHRM practices for the impact of SHRM interventions to be adequately captured, that employee insights and experiences have been neglected, and that line managers' roles have been insufficiently explored. Methodological criticisms include the use of single respondents and lack of clarity regarding choice of HR practices within the HPWS. There has also been limited theoretical explanation of how and why SHRM performance impacts occur, with this explanatory gap generally referred to as the 'black box' (see Guest, 2011). Irish research has engaged with, and contributed to, debates on the SHRM–performance relationship by examining the diffusion of sophisticated SHRM in Ireland, the impact of HPWS on performance, and the mechanisms by which HPWS operate. Each of these issues is now examined in turn.

The Diffusion of Sophisticated SHRM in Ireland

In terms of diffusion, early studies in Ireland examined important changes in the domains of work design and team-working, noting these as 'central to the development of a high performance approach to work' (Morley, 1995: 83; see also Geary, 1999). Roche (1999) explored commitment-orientated HRM practices, finding limited full diffusion of such practices, save for an elite 5–10 per cent of organisations. McCartney and Teague (2004) explored high performance employment practices across three industries (food/drink/tobacco, electronics, and banking and finance) and found significant evidence that Irish workplaces were experimenting with workplace innovation. More recent research has directly explored the diffusion of HPWS of the type specified by Huselid (1995). The general picture that emerges is one of a rather moderate to low take-up of the full-blown HPWS model. Indeed, Irish research has been relatively consistent in reporting a score of mid-40s out of a possible 100 on the HPWS index (Guthrie et al., 2009; Heffernan et al., 2008). This is consistent with international evidence, with Datta et al. (2005) reporting the take-up of HPWS among US firms to be 49.58. Box 1.2 documents the breakdown of HPWS diffusion across specific practices in the Irish context.

Box 1.2: The Diffusion of High Performance Work Practices in Ireland

Research by Heffernan et al. (2008) provides an overview of the diffusion of high performance work practices in 169 top performing firms in Ireland. Findings indicate a high usage of practices such as employee induction programmes and company-specific training. In line with the logic of the resource-based view of the firm (Barney, 1991), this suggests that top-performing firms recognise the critical role of socialisation in the organisation. Likewise, they are much more likely to invest in skill sets which are unique to the firm (78 per cent) as opposed to those that are more generic in nature (38 per cent) and thus more easily transferrable across organisations. However, less than one-third of firms surveyed used validated employment tests (as per earlier research by Heraty et al., 1994), had a skill- or knowledge-based pay system, paid a premium wage or administered employee attitude surveys on a regular basis.

High Performance Work Practices in Ireland

Employee Resourcing	
Structured/standardised interviews	64%
Validated employment tests	24%
Formal job analysis	36%
Exit interview	49%
Performance Management and Remuneration	
Routine formal appraisals	62%
Formal performance feedback from more than one source	31%
Compensation partially contingent on *individual* merit or performance	44%
Compensation partially contingent on *group* merit or performance	36%

Option for shares of organisation's stock	18%
Paid a premium wage in order to attract and retain them	28%
Training and Development	
Formal induction	86%
Training in company-specific skills	78%
Training in generic skills	39%
Involved in total quality management programme	30%
Communication and Involvement	
Programmes designed to elicit participation and employee input	35%
Provided relevant financial performance information	53%
Provided relevant strategic information	61%
Regular attitude surveys	31%
Grievance/complaint procedure	91%
Organised in self-directed work teams	40%
Work–Life Balance	
Covered by family-friendly policies or work–life balance practices	52%

The Impact of HPWS on Performance

Irish research has also directly explored the impact of HPWS on performance. Flood and colleagues (Flood and Guthrie, 2005; Guthrie et al., 2009) provided methodologically robust evidence for the SHRM–performance linkage through their utilisation of objective productivity measures whilst also drawing on matched HR and general manager survey responses from 165 companies. They were able to convert the SHRM and performance linkage into more concrete, monetary terms, stating that 'if a firm were to increase its relative use of the set of high performance HR practices from "average" to "above average" it would increase employee sales productivity by 15.61%. For the median firm in the sample, this represents an additional €50,032 in revenue per employee' (Flood and Guthrie, 2005: 6). In addition, they found that where HR managers report higher utilisation of HPWS, general managers perceive their HR departments as having more strategic value (Guthrie et al., 2011). Drawing on the same data, Armstrong et al. (2010) extended the HPWS argument by demonstrating that diversity and equality management systems (including diversity training and monitoring recruitment, pay and promotion across minority and disadvantaged groups) contributed to firm performance over and above the effects of a traditional HPWS. Performance impact in this instance included higher labour productivity, workforce innovation and lower voluntary employee turnover.

The Mechanisms by which HPWS Operate

Irish research has moved beyond simple counts of practices to offer valuable insights into the mechanisms by which SHRM may impact performance, paying particular attention to both employee and line manager perspectives. At an employee level, research by Conway and Monks (2008) found that the HR practices valued by employees that are related to a range of employee-related outcomes are very different to those proposed in the lists of HR practices found in the high performance literature. Another employee survey examining high commitment management in three financial service firms found that there were varying routes to commitment and retention, which were contingent on employee expectations and values (Conway and Monks, 2009). These findings suggest that there may be divergence between what is touted as best practice in fostering high employee commitment and what actually works in practice.

With respect to line managers, Harney and Jordan (2008) provide case study evidence from a call centre in Ireland where, despite HRM being imposed by a dominant supplier, line managers' interventions ameliorated some of the negative aspects of work tasks. This included the introduction of practices which resonated with those prescribed by HPWS, including efforts at improving morale and creating a sense of involvement and a better atmosphere among telesales representatives. The result was that while employees exhibited the low commitment characteristic of the sector, they also demonstrated significant organisational citizenship behaviours manifest in discretionary efforts to go beyond what was required of the immediate task on hand. More recently, Roche and Teague (2012) have demonstrated that proactive line manager engagement in conflict management is positively related to organisational outcomes and that this relationship is further enhanced by the presence of HPWS types of HR practices (Teague and Roche, 2011). Finally, there is evidence of theoretical approaches which bring together both employee and line manager perspectives to offer accounts of the social climate within the firm and its role in bridging intended and enacted HR practice (Cafferkey, 2011). Research by Heffernan and Dundon (2012) has illuminated the importance of the perceived fairness of the HR system in attempting to understand the true effect of the actual HPWS system on employees' attitudes and behavioural outcomes such as job satisfaction, affective commitment and work effort. Box 1.3 provides some case evidence highlighting the critical intermediary role of organisational justice.

Box 1.3: HPWS, Line Managers and Organisational Justice at Prof Co

Prof Co. is a professional services firm employing over 2,000 workers in Ireland. It has made a significant investment in high performance work systems. Perceived fairness in the outcomes of HR decisions has emerged as particularly important in performance management and reward decisions. One manager argued that equity rules of distributive justice could 'be applied more rigorously in terms of the contribution or effort that people make in terms of what they actually get'. One employee acknowledged that the impact of an unfair outcome such as a performance appraisal rating or pay increase can be demotivating to other employees 'as someone can actually be crap and still get a 15 per cent bonus.' Issues of voice, consistency and bias also emerged from the employee interviews to highlight the importance of procedural fairness when enacting HR practices. One senior manager acknowledged that although they try to ensure procedural justice is to the forefront of decisions, the degree to which these policies are applied 'is reasonably open to the discretion of the manager'. In particular, the perception of voice during HR decisions emerged as a key theme with one employee acknowledging the importance of 'being able to speak up and tell my manager if I feel I haven't scored fairly in my performance appraisal'. The interpersonal treatment of employees appeared as a final theme. According to one employee, 'it falls back to dignity at work ... we're here to do a job but we're all human beings.'

Source: Heffernan and Dundon (2012)

Emergence and Status of SHRM in Ireland: Analysis and Insights

This chapter has charted a steady progression with respect to both the content and scope of research on SHRM in Ireland. (More recent efforts capturing the impact of the recession are the subject of **Chapter 2** by Roche). In general, research has expanded its reach and significance, moving from early descriptive accounts attempting to capture the nature of HRM practices towards more recent attempts to understand how SHRM works and impacts upon employees. A number of observations can be made. First is the constant finding that while firms have gradually invested in HR practices, they typically remain significantly short of adopting a singular, sophisticated approach. Instead there is consistent evidence of the existence of a wide variety and combination of SHRM practices, including a co-existence or dualism between new and old workplace practices (Monks, 2002; Roche, 1999; Watson et al., 2010). This suggests the value of research which does not simply assess the nature of SHRM practices by way of a supply-side model (e.g. a list of best practices), but instead moves to explore the diffusion and organisational demand for HR practices (Kaufman, 2010). By this logic, the notion of a HPWS may represent something of a normative ideal as opposed to reflecting an organisational reality.

This also suggests the importance of examining the value of certain types of SHRM in certain sectors, or for certain groups of employees (see **Section 3** of this book). Industrial sector, capital intensity and the expectations of employees are likely to heavily inform the type of SHRM that will be viable. It is not unsurprising, therefore, that research has shown that industries such as financial services, high technology and pharmaceuticals invest heavily in HPWS relative to agriculture and manufacturing (Heffernan et al., 2008; Guthrie et al., 2009). Likewise, SHRM has been shown to have particular value in fostering knowledge sharing and relational coordination in contexts such as professional service firms (Fu et al., 2013).

A final point concerns methodology. Evidence provided in this chapter suggests that Irish research is addressing many of the methodological criticisms frequently levelled at SHRM research. Work by Conway and Monks (2008), for example, showed there was a disconnect between the HR practices that are perceived by employers as important and those that appear to be valued by employees. Consequently, they warn against rushing to implement sophisticated HR without first getting the basics of the employment relationship right. Other work suggests that understanding the true impact of HPWS often hinges on the nature of the interpersonal relations that exist not only between general managers and HR managers (Guthrie et al., 2011) but also between managers and employees (Harney and Jordan, 2008; Heffernan and Dundon, 2012).

Conclusions

This chapter has traced the evolution of SHRM from its origins in the welfare tradition through to its more recent preoccupation with performance. While the lack of empirical evidence on the extent of investment in HRM in an Irish context was once lamented (Gunnigle, 1998: 12), it is clear much has been done to address this deficiency. This is reflected in the emergence and status of SHRM as a specialist academic field and its prominence in the teaching and research activities of business schools in Ireland today (Carbery et al., 2013). The professionalisation of SHRM is evidenced in CIPD membership numbers, which have grown from 672 in 1981 to over 5,500 in 2012. Yet academic and professional progress should not be read simplistically as implying success without challenge or tension. There is still much scope for continued discussion around such areas as the extent of diffusion of sophisticated SHRM practices and their costs and benefits to organisations. Recent emphasis on employees is to be welcomed, although frequently lacking is an appreciation of how many of the decisions that are beneficial for business strategy or the HR function may not necessarily be beneficial for employees. There is also still potential to explore the vital role of SHRM in the management of change, the interface between technology and SHRM, and also the continually evolving role of the HR function. Much of this research would benefit from longitudinal insights that are rarely present in studies.

From a practice perspective there is the constant need to understand and develop the skill set required by the HR profession to manage such challenges. This also draws attention to the significant, but oft neglected, role of factors shaping the implementation of HR systems (Huselid and Becker, 2011), including acknowledging and dealing with legacy systems and path dependency (Monks and Loughnane, 2006). SHRM from this viewpoint would benefit from a broader and more inclusive definition, including the understanding that the significant contribution of the HR function stems from its ability not to offer universal blanket solutions, but to proactively anticipate and manage challenges. Overall, SHRM clearly offers value in contributing to organisational success. Its role in sustaining that success and thereby sustaining its value will come not only from exploring linkages with innovation and change, but also through practising continuous innovation in the way SHRM is researched, understood and disseminated.

References

Armstrong, C., Flood, P., Guthrie, J., Wenchuan, L., MacCurtain, S. and Mkamwa, T. (2010), 'The Impact of Diversity and Equality Management on Firm Performance: Beyond High Performance Work Systems', *Human Resource Management*, 49(6): 977–999.

Arthur, J. (1994), 'Effects of Human Resource Systems on Manufacturing Performance and Turnover', *Academy of Management Journal*, 37(3): 670–687.

Barney, J. (1991), 'Firm Resources and Sustained Competitive Advantage', *Journal of Management*, 17(1): 99–120.

Barrington, T.J. (1980), *The Irish Administrative System*, Dublin: Institute of Public Administration.

Cafferkey, C. (2011), 'Unlocking the "Black Box" of HR and Performance: An Examination of the Potential Mediating Role of Organisational Climate', Unpublished PhD thesis, National University of Ireland, Galway.

Carbery, R., Gunnigle, P. and Morley, M. (2013), 'Human Resource Management Research Output in Ireland: A Retrospective', *Irish Journal of Management*, forthcoming.

Combs, J.G., Ketchen, D., Hall, A. and Liu, Y. (2006), 'Do High Performance Work Practices Matter? A Meta-Analysis of Their Effects on Organisational Performance', *Personnel Psychology*, 59(3): 501–528.

Commission of Inquiry on Industrial Relations (1981), *Report of the Committee of Inquiry on Industrial Relations*, Dublin: The Stationery Office.

Conway, E. and Monks, K. (2008), 'HR Practices and Commitment to Change: An Employee-Level Analysis', *Human Resource Management Journal*, 18(1): 72–89.

Conway, E. and Monks, K. (2009), 'Unravelling the Complexities of High Commitment: An Employee-Level Analysis', *Human Resource Management Journal*, 19(2): 140–158.

Datta, D., Guthrie, J. and Wright, P. (2005), 'Human Resource Management and Labor Productivity: Does Industry Matter?', *Academy of Management Journal*, 48(1): 135–145.

Flood, P. and Guthrie, J. (2005), *High Performance Work Systems in Ireland – The Economic Case*, Forum on the Workplace of the Future Research Series No. 4, Dublin: National Centre for Partnership and Performance.

Foley, K. and Gunnigle, P. (1994), 'The Personnel/Human Resource Function and Employee Relations' in P. Gunnigle, P. Flood, M. Morley and T. Turner (eds), *Continuity and Change in Irish Employee Relations*, Dublin: Oak Tree Press, 39–57.

Fu, N., Flood, P., Bosak, J., Morris, T. and O'Regan, P. (2013), 'Exploring the Performance Effect of HPWS on Professional Service Supply Chain Management', *Supply Chain Management: An International Journal*, 18(3): 1–18.

Geary, J.F. (1999), 'The New Workplace: Change at Work in Ireland', *International Journal of Human Resource Management*, 10(5): 870–890.

Geary, J.F. and Roche, W.K. (2001), 'Multinationals and Human Resource Practices in Ireland: A Rejection of the "New Conformance Thesis"', *International Journal of Human Resource Management*, 12(1): 109–127.

Guest, D. (2011), 'Human Resource Management and Performance: Still Searching for Some Answers', *Human Resource Management Journal*, 2(1): 3–13.

Gunnigle, P. (1992), 'Human Resource Management in Ireland', *Employee Relations*, 14(5): 5–22.

Gunnigle, P. (1998), 'Human Resource Management and the Personnel Function' in W.K. Roche, K. Monks and J. Walsh (eds), *Human Resource Strategies: Policy and Practice in Ireland*, Dublin: Oak Tree Press, 1–23.

Gunnigle, P., Turner, T. and D'Art, D. (1998), 'Counterpoising Collectivism: Performance-Related Pay and Industrial Relations in Greenfield Sites', *British Journal of Industrial Relations*, 36(4): 565–579.

Guthrie, J., Flood, P. and Liu, W. (2011), 'Big Hat, No Cattle? The Relationship between Use of High Performance Work Systems and Managerial Perceptions of HR Departments', *International Journal of Human Resource Management*, 22(8): 1672–1685.

Guthrie, J., Flood, P., Liu, W. and MacCurtain, S. (2009), 'High Performance Work Systems in Ireland: Human Resource and Organisational Outcomes', *International Journal of Human Resource Management*, 20(1): 112–125.

Harney, B. and Jordan, C. (2008), 'Unlocking the Black Box: Line Managers and HRM Performance in a Call Centre Context', *International Journal of Productivity and Performance Management*, 57(4): 275–296.

Heffernan, M. and Dundon, T. (2012), 'Researching Employee Reactions to High Performance Work Systems in the Service Sector: The Role of Organisational Justice Theory', Paper presented at the 16th International Labor and Employment Relations (ILERA) World Congress, 2–5 July, Philadelphia, PA.

Heffernan, M., Harney, B., Cafferkey, K. and Dundon, T. (2008), 'People Management and Innovation in Ireland', CISC Working Paper, 27(1): 1–26.

Heraty, N., Morley, M. and Turner, T. (1994), 'Trends and Developments in the Organisation of the Employment Relationship' in P. Gunnigle, P. Flood, M. Morley and T. Turner (eds), *Continuity and Change in Irish Employee Relations*, Dublin: Oak Tree Press, 82–102.

Horgan, J. and Mühlau, P. (2006), 'Human Resource Systems and Employee Performance in Ireland and the Netherlands: A Test of the Complementarity Hypothesis', *International Journal of Human Resource Management*, 17(3): 414–439.

Huselid, M.A. (1995), 'The Impact of Human Resource Practices on Turnover, Productivity, and Corporate Financial Performance', *Academy of Management Journal*, 38(3): 635–672.

Huselid, M.A. and Becker, B. (2011), 'Bridging Micro and Macro Domains: Workforce Differentiation and Strategic HRM', *Journal of Management*, 37(2): 421–428.

Institute of Personnel Management Irish Branch (1968), Minutes of Annual General Meetings, 1937–1968.

Kaufman, B.E. (1999), 'Evolution and Current Status of University HR Programs', *Human Resource Management Review*, 38(2): 103–110.

Kaufman, B.E. (2010), 'A Theory of the Firm's Demand for HRM Practices', *International Journal of Human Resource Management*, 21(5): 615–636.

Kelly, A. and Brannick, T. (1988), 'The Management of Human Resources: New Trends and Challenges to Trade Unions', *Arena*, August: 4–6.

Lavelle, J., McDonnell, A. and Gunnigle, P. (2009), *Human Resource Practices in Multinational Companies in Ireland: A Contemporary Analysis*, Dublin: The Stationery Office.

Lee, J.J. (1980), 'Worker and Society since 1945' in D. Nevin (ed.), *Trade Unions and Change in Irish Society*, Dublin: Mercier Press, 2–30.

Lengnick-Hall, M.L., Lengnick-Hall, C.A., Andrade, L. and Drake, B. (2009), 'Strategic Human Resource Management: The Evolution of the Field', *Human Resource Management Review*, 19(3): 64–85.

MacNeill, H. (1980), 'Management View' in D. Nevin (ed.), *Trade Unions and Change in Irish Society*, Dublin: Mercier Press.

McCartney, J. and Teague, P. (2004), 'The Diffusion of High Performance Employment Practices in the Republic of Ireland' *International Journal of Manpower*, 25(7): 598–617.

Monks, K. (1992), 'Models of Personnel Management: A Means of Understanding the Diversity of Personnel Practices?', *Human Resource Management Journal*, 3(2): 29–41.

Monks, K. (2002), 'Personnel or Human Resource Management: A Choice for Irish Organisations?' in P. Gunnigle, M. Morley and M. McDonnell (eds), *The John Lovett Lectures: A Decade of Developments in Human Resource Management*, Dublin: Liffey Press, 1–26.

Monks, K. and Loughnane, M. (2006), 'Unwrapping the HRM Bundle: HR System Design in an Irish Power Utility', *International Journal of Human Resource Management*, 17(11): 1926–1941.

Morley, M. (1995), 'Current Themes in Organisational Design and Work Structuring' in P. Gunnigle and W.K. Roche (eds), *New Challenges to Industrial Relations*, Dublin: Oak Tree Press and Labour Relations Commission, 63–86.

O'Brien, G. (1998), 'Business Strategy and Human Resource Management' in W.K. Roche, K. Monks and K. Walsh (eds), *Human Resource Strategy: Policy and Practice in Ireland*, Dublin: Oak Tree Press, 409–458.

Roche, W.K. (1999), 'In Search of Commitment-Orientated Human Resource Management Practices and the Conditions that Sustain Them', *Journal of Management Studies*, 36(5): 653–678.

Roche, W.K. (2001), 'The Individualization of Irish Industrial Relations', *British Journal of Industrial Relations*, 39(2): 183–206.

Roche, W.K. and Teague, P. (2012), 'Do Conflict Management Systems Matter?', *Human Resource Management*, 51(2): 231–258.

Roche, W.K. and Turner, T. (1998), 'Human Resource Management and Industrial Relations: Substitution, Dualism and Partnership' in W.K. Roche, K. Monks and J. Walsh (eds), *Human Resource Strategies: Policy and Practice in Ireland*, Dublin: Oak Tree Press, 67–108.

Schuler, R.S. and Jackson, S.E. (1987), 'Linking Competitive Strategies with Human Resource Management Practices', *Academy of Management Executive*, 1(3): 207–219.

Sheehan, B. (2002), 'Irish Industrial Relations and HRM: An Overview of the "Lovett Years"' in P. Gunnigle, M. Morley and M. McDonnell (eds), *The John Lovett Lectures: A Decade of Developments in Human Resource Management*, Dublin: Liffey Press, 323–305.

Teague, P. and Roche, W.K. (2011), 'Line Managers and the Management of Workplace Conflict: Evidence from Ireland', *Human Resource Management Journal*, 22(3): 235–251.

Tomlin, B. (1966), *The Management of Irish Industry*, Dublin: Irish Management Institute.

Turner, T., D'Art, D. and Gunnigle, P. (1997), 'Pluralism in Retreat? A Comparison of Irish and Multinational Manufacturing Companies', *International Journal of Human Resource Management*, 8(6): 825–850.

Wall, T. and Wood, S. (2005), 'The Romance of Human Resource Management and Business Performance, and the Case for Big Science', *Human Relations*, 58(4): 429–462.

Watson, D., Galway, J., O'Connell, P. and Russell, H. (2010), *The Changing Workplace: A Survey of Employers' Views and Experiences*, Dublin: National Centre for Partnership and Performance.

CHAPTER 2

HRM in the Recession:
Managing People in the Private and Public Sectors[1]

William K. Roche

Introduction

The prescriptive and academic literature in human resource management (HRM) focuses in the main on normal or steady-state commercial and economic conditions. This is understandable but begs the question as to how HRM is conducted in circumstances of deep and lasting recession. This question is the subject of this chapter, which reviews the conduct of HRM in Ireland in the context of the international and professional literature on the conduct of HRM in recessionary conditions. The chapter begins by outlining how HRM professionals and scholars have considered the effects of recessions on HRM. It then examines the conduct of HRM in the Irish recession. This began to affect many firms and also the public service during 2008.

Perspectives on HRM in Recessions

The professional and academic literature on the impact of recessions on the conduct of HRM can be divided into accounts of human resource (HR) practices appropriate to handling reductions in business demand or other commercial setbacks (for example, pay freezes, pay cuts, short-time working and redundancies) and interpretations of the implications of recession for the nature of and direction of HRM practice. Here the focus will be on the second type of accounts, as such a focus provides a better understanding of what the recession may mean for both the short-term and longer-term conduct of HRM (see Roche et al., 2010: 29–40 for a detailed discussion of different HR practices used in recessions and of their implementation).

Two broad understandings of the effects of recession on HRM can be identified in the international literature. These have been informed in the main by previous serious recessions during the 1980s, especially in the United States (US) and the United Kingdom (UK), and by the reflections of professionals and scholars on the effects of the 'Great Recession' that affected much of the developed world following the international financial crisis and severe contraction in economic activity that began in 2007.

One approach claims that recessions are transformative, fundamentally altering HRM and work and employment practices more generally. The exponents of this approach, however, disagree on the nature or direction of the transformations they claim that recessions bring about. One perspective, heavily influenced by an interpretation of the 1980s recession in the US, is that recession acts as a catalyst for the emergence and spread of a 'market-driven' model of HRM in which, in addition to a pervasive rise in the incidence of downsizing, employment security for those who remain in their jobs undergoes permanent decline, the psychological contract between firms and employees comes to pivot around utilitarian or economic calculations of short-term advantage, firms become more prone to hiring rather than to investing in developing talent and neither firms nor their employees any longer expect long-term career progression to be a standard feature of HR arrangements. Firms also become more prone to considering whether they need to retain an internally resourced HRM function, or indeed whether they require any specialist HR function at all.

The paradigmatic contribution along these lines is Peter Cappelli's *The New Deal at Work: Managing the Market-Driven Workforce* (1999a; and see Cappelli, 1999b). While the starting point for Cappelli's work was the US recession of the 1980s, strong echoes of this perspective are to be found in more recent work on the effects of the Great Recession. Some international consulting firms claim that the outsourcing and off-shoring of HRM has accelerated in the recession and that HR functions have been more affected by these developments than other management functions such as information technology (IT). This putative trend implies a non-recoverable loss in specialist HR jobs within firms (The Hackett Group, 2009a and 2009b). Other commentators have claimed that there has been an acceleration during the recession in the prevalence within firms of a so-called 'new employment deal'. Reflecting the new deal at work, employees no longer expect career progression within their current firms, have come to rely on themselves for career advancement and have become subject to more 'personalised' arrangements with respect to rewards, talent management and human resource development (HRD) (Towers Watson, 2010).

While wedded to the notion that recession is transformative for HRM, other commentators hold an alternative view of what transformation involves. David Ulrich (as reported in Brockett, 2010: 11; and in *Personnel Today*, 2008) has proposed that increasing numbers of HR leaders are seizing the opportunity presented to them by the recession to become business partners and to position their organisations for the long term by investing in skills and in the creation of positive organisational cultures. A similar view has been put forward by Cary Cooper (2009), who claims that the recession has presented an opportunity to HR managers to demonstrate their capacity to manage talent and to create organisational cultures that motivate employees in a period of uncertainty. Outside the realms of HR 'gurudom', scholars like Mohrman and Worley (2009) also suggest that case studies of HR in leading US firms show that the recession is acting as a catalyst for more fluid organisational structures and more intensive and strategic ways of harnessing the talent and creativity of employees in pursuit of business objectives. The views of contributors like Ulrich, Cooper, and Mohrman and Worley seem to point implicitly or explicitly in the direction of the Great Recession as a catalyst for the more intensive or pervasive adoption by firms of a high commitment model of HRM, allied with the pursuit of efficiencies and cost reductions in the operation of HR systems and with more stringent approaches to performance management. All of these developments are seen to be powered by strategic HR leaders and business partners who persuade firms to look over the horizon of recessionary conditions and position firms and their HR strategies for recovery and return to growth.

If one perspective on the effects of recession on HRM points towards transformation or disjuncture, other contributors are more measured and more empirically orientated in their assessment of how recession impacts on HRM. Critics of apocalyptic claims about the effects of 1980s recessions have taken writers like Cappelli severely to task for misinterpreting changes that were in essence cyclical and therefore transient in nature for changes of a permanent nature in work and employment arrangements (Jacoby, 1999a, 1999b; McGovern et al., 2007). These contributors have emphasised continuities in work and employment patterns that are not greatly or permanently altered by recessionary episodes. A number of commentaries on the effects of the Great Recession chime with these assessments by presenting measured and cautious reviews of recent developments. It has been noted that firms in the UK have tried to buffer or preserve employment as much as possible during the recession and have often also sought to preserve a philosophy which treated human resources as assets rather than costs (Brown and Reilly, 2009). The imperative for HR managers to 'stick to the knitting' during the recession by preserving established HR polices has also been urged by some HR consultant commentators (Griffin and Smith, 2010). Reviews of developments in industrial relations have noted that the picture emerging is full of contradictions, complexities and challenges (Acas, 2008 and 2009).

To this measured strand of analysis and commentary can be added empirically informed commentaries on the effects of the recession on trends in employment in HRM. A survey in the UK by the Chartered Institute of Personnel and Development (CIPD) found that while HR jobs were being lost, one in five firms intended to recruit additional staff in their HR departments to cope with the burden of managing redundancy and other recessionary measures. There was also an expectation on the part of HR professionals that the balance of HR activity would change in a more strategic direction and that fewer would be engaged in transactional HR work (Phillips, 2008). Public service organisations in the UK were found to have engaged in cutting back HR numbers to ratios more comparable with the private sector and to be seeking efficiencies through shared service provision and the creation of inter-agency centres of excellence (Pickard, 2010).

In this second perspective on the effects of recessions, contributors therefore avoid thinking in terms of transformations – in whatever direction – and point instead to a more complex picture involving many changes, some of which may abide and others of which may be transitory, but also involving strong elements of continuity with pre-recession HR practices and arrangements. The overall pattern of change is not understood in terms of any consistent or coherent shift towards a new set of work and employment arrangements or a new HR paradigm.

The Recession and the Conduct of HRM in Ireland

Developments in HRM in the Irish recession can be examined and assessed against the background of international commentary and debate. The recession that began in Ireland in 2008 is the most serious economic downturn in the history of the state and Ireland is among the developed economies that have been most seriously affected by the deep and prolonged international downturn in economic activity and trade. From 2007 to 2011 Ireland's gross domestic product (GDP) declined by nearly 7 per cent, having initially collapsed by 11 per cent between 2007 and 2009. Company insolvencies rose sharply in a context of waning demand and slackening consumer sentiment. While the exporting sector, dominated by high technology foreign-owned multinationals, revived quickly, the domestic sector has remained deeply depressed. Unemployment rose from 4.6 per cent in 2007 to 14.8 per cent in 2012, and net emigration switched from minus 67,000 people in 2007 to plus 34,500 in 2010. The collapse of Irish-owned banks was warded off by the virtual nationalisation of the financial system and through extensive bank recapitalisation by taxpayers. In November 2010 Ireland was forced to resort to a rescue package from the 'Trokia' of the European Union, the European Central Bank and the International Monetary Fund. The rescue package tightened the austerity programme already in place and contributed to a sharp squeeze on public spending, coupled with tax increases. The decision to rescue and recapitalise the banks meant that bank debt became sovereign debt. The provision of finance for the banks and public spending commitments led Ireland's debt–GDP ratio to rise to more than 100 per cent in 2011.

Given the depth and longevity of the recession, the period since 2008 has witnessed wide-ranging changes in the conduct of HRM in firms and public service agencies. While the main focus of this chapter is on developments in the commercial sector, developments in the public service are considered later in the chapter. This chapter draws on a survey of nearly 450 managers responsible for human resources in the private and commercial state-owned sectors conducted in 2010 and on a series of focus groups involving 30 HR managers in firms across a diverse range of sectors and 17 trade officials from unions with membership spread across the economy. It also draws on case studies of six firms that responded to the recession by introducing progressive HR programmes; these are the financial services firm Irish Life and Permanent, the estate agent Sherry FitzGerald, the Dublin Airport Authority, which manages the main Irish airports, the US medical devices manufacturer Medtronic, the retailer Superquinn and the information and communications technology firm Ericsson. The focus groups and case studies were also conducted in 2010.[2]

HRM in the Commercial Sector

Considering the scale of the economic and fiscal setbacks since 2008, it is not surprising that nearly nine out of ten firms surveyed indicated that the recession had severe or very severe commercial effects. Table 2.1 outlines the main HR measures that firms adopted since the onset of the recession. Sizeable numbers of firms implemented pay freezes or cuts for some or all staff. Significant numbers introduced curbs on bonuses and lower entry rates for new staff. Changes to pension arrangements were also introduced by significant minorities of firms.

Table 2.1: HR Practices Adopted by Firms in the Recession
(N = 444 Firms)

HR Practices	% Firms
Pay Adjustment Measures	
Cut wages and salaries for all staff	33.9
Cut wages and salaries for some staff	15.6
Froze wages and salaries for all staff	60.4
Froze wages and salaries for some staff	10.7
Introduced lower pay/pay scales for new staff	22.5
Cut bonus for all staff	38.1

(Continued)

Table 2.1: (*Continued*)

HR Practices	% Firms
Cut bonus for some staff	16.2
Introduced proportionally higher cuts in bonus for senior staff	11.5
Changed pension arrangements for existing staff	20.8
Changed pension arrangements for new staff	13.9
Employment Adjustment Measures	
Introduced compulsory redundancies	48.3
Introduced voluntary redundancies	29.9
Introduced early retirement	7.6
General recruitment frozen	51.2
Undertook recruitment for certain grades only	19.6
General promotions frozen	14.6
Promotions to some positions only	13.3
Staff redeployed to new positions or product lines within the business	43.4
Introduced 'in-sourcing' (i.e. brought back into the business work that had previously been outsourced)	5.4
Reduced use of part-time staff	6.0
Increased use of part-time staff	32.0
Reduced use of contract staff	14.5
Increased use of contract staff	21.0
Reduced use of agency workers	10.1
Increased use of agency workers	5.0
Reorganisation of Working Time	
Introduced career breaks	9.3
Introduced short-time working	42.6
Reduced overtime	63.3
Introduced flexible working hours to better match staffing levels with peaks and troughs of the business	25.5
More Rigorous Management Systems	
Staff performance managed more rigorously	47.2
Tightened discipline, time-keeping and attendance requirements	47.8

(*Continued*)

Table 2.1: (*Continued*)

HR Practices	% Firms
Training and Talent Management	
Training and development budget reduced	50.6
Staff trained for new roles in the business	40.4
The firm undertook specific talent management measures to retain high performance or high potential staff	20.7
Communication and Engagement	
Communicating the demands of the business to staff has gained greater importance #	89.2
Introduced proportionally higher cuts in pay for senior staff responding to the recession	24.5
The business has undertaken specific employee engagement measures #	52.3
The firm has actively engaged with unions in developing HR options for responding to the recession #	61.6
By agreeing measures to respond to the recession unions have gained greater access to financial information #	23.8
By agreeing measures to respond to the recession unions have gained support for organising or representing members in the business #	7.3
Unions have secured 'claw-backs' for their members when business conditions improve #	5.6

Note: # Item reported is the combined percentages responding 'agree' or 'strongly agree'. Items on aspects of union involvement restricted to firms where unions were recognised.

Reductions in employment or headcount were also common, as were partial or complete freezes on recruitment and promotion. People were redeployed within firms on a significant scale. More firms increased than reduced forms of contingent employment, which included part-time, contract and agency work. Both sets of changes reflected firms' search for flexibility in conditions of high uncertainty. Changes in working-time arrangements were focused on reducing overtime and on introducing short-time working. More flexible working-time regimes, geared to better balancing labour supply and demand in the recession, were introduced in about a quarter of all firms. Nearly half of all firms stated that they had managed staff performance more rigorously and tightened up on discipline, time-keeping and attendance.

In addition to the widespread use of many such 'hard' HR practices, focused on cutting payroll costs, firms claim also to have adopted an array of 'soft' HR practices concerned with maintaining motivation and commitment. What stands out in this area is the greater importance assigned to communicating with staff about the challenges faced by businesses. Measures such as higher cuts in pay and bonuses for senior managers, sometimes seen as contributing to increased organisational cohesion in a recession, were far less pervasive but had still been introduced in significant minorities of firms. More than half of all firms reported having actively engaged employees in their responses to the recession or having adopted specific employee engagement measures (for example, retraining staff in new business objectives and processes following lay-offs and restructuring). Talent management measures were thinner on the ground, having been adopted by about a quarter of firms.

Firms fell into two broad categories with respect to the manner in which they deployed sets or bundles of HR practices in response to the recession. About half of all firms combined a series of HR practices that comprised pay freezes or cuts, headcount reductions, short-time working and overtime restrictions, among other measures. The other half of firms responded to the recession in the main through pay freezes and curbs on overtime. Not surprisingly, firms implementing multi-stranded HR retrenchment programmes were in general more seriously affected by the recession and were more likely to be Irish-owned than foreign-owned multinationals. More or less all firms claimed to have combined payroll cost reduction measures with measures aimed at sustaining motivation and commitment.

HR Managers

Developments in the HR function are portrayed in Table 2.2. Nearly one in three firms reduced the number of people working in their HR departments since the start of the recession, compared with about seven in ten firms that claimed to have reduced their overall headcount levels. The HR functions of 15 per cent of firms had been restructured – for example, through centralisation at HQ level, or the creation of centres of excellence in different areas of HR practice – as compared with more than six out of ten firms that claimed to have engaged in business restructuring of some kind in response to the recession. Based on both these comparisons, HR specialists, though patently often affected by the recession, appear to have been spared the worst of the staffing reductions and restructuring activities caused by the recession. More than four out of ten HR departments made less use of consultants, though significantly fewer than that reduced the costs of HR policies or processes like employee assistance programmes or staff facilities. In summary, the picture that emerges is of HR functions having become 'leaner' and having to do more with less resources but not commonly having been radically reconfigured.

Table 2.2: The Recession and the HR Function: Leaner but More Influential (N = 295)

Measure	% Firms
Fewer staff in the HR department	32.0
Less use made of external consultants	43.0
The cost of HR policies and processes reduced	17.0
The HR department has been restructured	15.0
The business role of HR has been strengthened	69.0

If HR had become 'leaner', the dominant viewpoint among managers responsible for handling human resources is that the business role of HR had at the same time been strengthened as a consequence of the recession. The HR managers who participated in the focus groups were strongly of the view that they had become more influential in management decision-making during the recession and had been integrally involved in senior management discussions of how to frame and implement appropriate HR responses. They also experienced a higher degree of reliance on their knowledge and expertise by line managers with little experience in handling redundancy programmes or other changes required by the recession. These developments were commonly articulated by HR managers themselves as bringing them more influence and a new status as 'business partners'. The following comments from HR managers in the focus groups illustrate their greater influence in business decision-making during the recession. Remarking that HR had in the past been a 'bit detached from the day-to-day realities of the business', one HR manager said that it had now become 'central to 'every step of every change that needed to be taken'. Another HR manager remarked that 'whereas previously at quarterly [management] updates or meetings the HR update might be at the end of the agenda, over the last year we've seen suddenly it's the talking point.' The reason why HR had assumed such new importance was clear-cut. Firms had become more dependent on the professional knowledge and expertise of HR specialists as they struggled to implement downsizing programmes and often to revise terms and conditions of employment.

It is important to stress that much of the newfound influence of HR managers involved the provision of guidance and support on short-term measures for responding to the recession. In this sense HR managers had become business partners by knowing how to 'work the pumps' as firms struggled to avoid going under in very inclement conditions. The new influence of HR managers and their role as business partners had not, however, commonly translated into strategic leadership or into wide-ranging influence over medium-term concerns, such as how human resources might need to be reconfigured and HR strategies changed to support recovery and growth. By and large HR managers were so busy working the pumps that strategic considerations of these kinds were not prominent in their work or priorities during the recession. Box 2.1 illustrates the kinds of activities and priorities that were foremost in leading firms as they sought to cope with the recession. The underlying emphasis in HR programmes for the most part was on preserving pre-recession HR strategies as much as possible.

Box 2.1: Working the Pumps and Preserving Pre-Recession HR Arrangements – Case Examples

Detailed research was undertaken into how six organisations responded to the recession. All were chosen because they had succeeded in securing or strengthening their businesses by finding an accommodation between employee interests and necessary changes to their operations, work practices, and terms and conditions of employment.

The six were financial services plc Irish Life & Permanent; residential and commercial estate agent chain Sherry FitzGerald; Dublin Airport Authority (which also operates Cork and Shannon airports); Superquinn, the grocery retailer, with 23 stores; the Galway manufacturing facility of US medical devices manufacturer Medtronic; and Ericsson, the global telecoms company with operations in Dublin and Athlone.

Few instances were reported in the six case studies of HR managers being active in positioning HR practices, systems or processes to support business revival over the medium or long term. Where such an instance was identifiable, for example in the Ericsson case study, the strategic focus of the HR function preceded the recession.

For the most part, changes and response programmes in the firms in which case studies were undertaken sought to preserve pre-recession HR strategies and reflected long-established relationships between the parties. Thus the innovative agreement at Dublin Airport Authority, linking the future possible reversal of pay cuts with the attainment of business and financial targets, reflects a heritage of stable industrial relations and significant past innovation. Changes in HR arrangements in the newly opened Terminal 2 at Dublin Airport reflected less the immediate effects of the recession than the stipulations of the Aviation Regulator regarding conditions that had to be met for the awarding of the contract to manage the new facility.

Management and unions at Medtronic reached agreement on the company's international pay freeze policy by postponing a previously agreed rise from 2009 to 2010. This agreement reflected pre-existing good industrial relations and a shared awareness of the need to cooperate to protect and extend the subsidiary's mandate from the parent company.

Tiered salary reductions at Sherry FitzGerald reflect an organisation that has traditionally valued staff cohesion and commitment as key brand attributes. The survival and partnership agreements negotiated at retailer Superquinn reflect a tradition of good, if paternalistic, industrial relations extending back to the company's previous owner. The pivotal HR competencies programme implemented in Ericsson's Irish operations preceded the recession and has been retained in the Irish subsidiary even while job losses took place, triggered by global restructuring.

The picture emerging from the research therefore is of firms focusing more on trying to preserve pre-recession HR, work and employment arrangements through the recession, rather than on using the recession as a means of bringing about transformation.

Concession Bargaining with Trade Unions

The progressive degeneration of social partnership from the autumn of 2008 and its eventual collapse in December 2009 meant that firms and unions have conducted industrial relations without an overarching national pay agreement for the first time in more than twenty years. Collective bargaining, however, was decentralised in an orderly manner through agreement reached between the

Irish Business and Employers' Confederation (IBEC) and the Irish Congress of Trade Unions on a 'protocol' to guide pay bargaining at firm level and to resolve any disputes that might arise. The level of industrial conflict has remained at historically low levels and most of the conflict that has occurred has surrounded firms' closure plans or the terms of redundancies. Table 2.3 outlines trends in pay fixing in the commercial sector, as mainly revealed in surveys of IBEC member companies. Pay freezes and pay cuts have predominated during the recession, with minorities of firms awarding pay increases to their workforces.

Table 2.3: Trends in Pay Fixing in the Commercial Sector

Trends in Earnings 2009–2010
(Average Hourly Earnings)
Private sector: -0.3%
Pay trend in SME sector 2008–2010: -5%

Source: Earnings trend CSO, March 2011. Data pertain to Q4 2009 to Q4 2010. SMEs: ISME survey cited in the *Irish Times*, 28 March 2011.

Trends in Pay 2010 – Employers	Trends in Pay in 2009 – Employers
Pay increased: 13%	Pay increased: 12%
Pay frozen: 72%	Pay frozen: 54%
Pay cut: 11%	Pay cut: 22%
Trends in Pay in 2011 – Employers	**Pay Intentions for 2012 – Employers**
Pay increased: 18%	Pay likely to be increased: 27%
Pay frozen: 72%	Pay likely to frozen: 64%
Pay cut: 7%	Pay likely to decrease: 5%

Source: For 2009–2010, Earnings trend CSO, March 2011. Data pertain to Q4 2009 to Q4 2010. SMEs: ISME survey cited in the *Irish Times*, 28 March 2011. IBEC *Business Sentiment Report, Q1 2011.* Based on a survey of 400 IBEC member firms. IBEC Business Sentiment Survey 2010. *Business Sentiment Report, Q3 2011.*

As these trends imply, the emphasis in dealings between employers and unions shifted from bargaining over gains to concession bargaining. In concession bargaining firms take the initiative and look for changes in pay levels and structures, benefits packages, working practices and working time in return for more or less explicit pledges that such concessions will contribute to employment security. Concession bargaining was widespread during the recession. Union officials in the focus groups were clearly of the view that firms often sought concessions quickly, with little prior notice, and that they had often insisted on shorter bargaining cycles for agreeing measures to reduce pay-bill costs. Firms sometimes sought to persuade unions that existing collective agreements no longer remained relevant and made clear, as well, their intention to institute unilateral changes if concessions could not be agreed. Employers' insistence on revising the rules of collective bargaining, combined with their bargaining power in recessionary conditions and union members' reluctance to resort to industrial action, meant that union influence declined significantly in many firms. Only very occasionally were unions able to persuade firms to change their plans with respect to HR retrenchment programmes, and they most commonly sought to moderate or ameliorate the measures announced by firms.

In the survey reported in Table 2.1, six out of ten firms recognising unions claimed to have actively engaged with them in developing HR options for responding to the recession. There is no indication in these data or in the focus groups that firms have sought to launch any general onslaught on unions. But other than pledges of increased employment security, unions only very occasionally obtained 'institutional concessions' from firms in return for agreeing to changes in pay, conditions and work practices. Access to financial information had been conceded in 14 per cent of firms. Otherwise unions gained few concessions in such areas as instituting reviews of depleted pay and conditions or mechanisms for the restoration of pay (commonly known as 'claw-back' arrangements) when business revived. Few supports to organisation or representation were also achieved. Union density declined or stagnated during the recession across most areas of the private sector, with the exception of finance, insurance and real estate services. However, density had been in general decline across the private sector for many years prior to the recession and the rate of decline has not accelerated during the recession in most sectors.

During 2011 and 2012 a confined pay round emerged in some export-oriented parts of the economy, less seriously affected by the recession, in particular pharmaceutical and medical devices firms and also in food manufacturers. During 2012 and 2013 pay rises of about 2–3 per cent began to emerge and spread to other employers, in particular retail multiples. These trends pointed to renewed pressure on pay as the economy revived. An IBEC survey on employers' pay intentions for 2013 were in line with these trends, indicating that 39 per cent of employers expected to increase pay during that year – the highest proportion signalling pay increases since the onset of the recession. In early 2014 the Services, Industrial, Professional and Technical Union (SIPTU) announced its intention to lodge pay claims across the private sector. These developments suggest that pockets of bargaining over pay rises will occur in parallel with a continuation of concession bargaining in the short to medium term. Overall developments in pay fixing since the recession have meant that pay levels in Ireland have undergone 'competitive devaluation' relative to trading partners without cuts in nominal pay for the great majority of employees.

HRM in the Public Service

The fiscal crisis accompanying the recession forced the government to make deep cuts in spending (as well as to increase taxation). The current deficit increased sharply and the level of public debt spiralled. Successive governments' approaches to fiscal consolidation have been underpinned by the Troika. In the decade preceding the crisis, public service organisations and agencies had gained progressively more flexibility and discretion in various aspects of the management of human resources. For example, under 'administrative budgeting' arrangements departments were allowed to configure grading structures to match their mandates up to the grade of principal officer. Agencies were also empowered to conduct their own recruitment and selection processes and became responsible for human resource development. Line managers were expected to assume formal responsibility for the conduct of human resource management. A greater variety of employment contracts came to be used, with agencies using external recruitment to term contracts for appointments to areas of specialist competence in short supply within the public service. Pay and staffing remained under the control of the Department of Finance, and a uniform grading system was preserved across different parts of the public service.

The fiscal crisis led to the recentralisation of human resource management, as a recruitment embargo was initially imposed across the public service in conjunction with micro-level controls over staffing under a new 'employment control framework'.

Following the general election of 2011, responsibility for HRM in the public service was transferred to the newly created Department of Public Expenditure and Reform, headed by a cabinet minister, Brendan Howlin. Pay cuts were introduced for top-level public servants. Managers in quasi-independent public agencies, such as universities, were asked to accept voluntary pay reductions, with varying levels of success. A referendum in 2012 permitted the government to cut the pay of the judiciary. A performance-related pay system that had been introduced for senior management grades in the civil service, local government, the army and Gardaí was halted in 2009 in a series of measures to reduce public spending. The system had faced considerable criticism for failing to rigorously tie the award of bonuses to different levels of performance, for lack of clarity with respect to the manner in which bonuses were decided and for failing to adequately improve performance management. A performance management and development systems (PMDS) for all public service grades had been introduced initially in the civil service and subsequently extended to other areas. PMDS had come under sharp criticism for restriction of range and leniency and for failing to address chronic under-performance (Comptroller and Auditor General, 2011). With a view to reforming the operation of PMDS the government decided in 2012 to hold senior managers directly accountable for the effective conduct of performance management within their agencies and to increase the rating that public servants needed to qualify for incremental pay rises. A two-tier salary structure was introduced, with new entrants hired at significantly lower salary levels than established employees. Career average pensions also replaced final salary related pensions for new entrants.

The Top-Level Appointments Committee (TLAC), responsible for nominating candidates to senior public service posts, was reformed to increase the number of members from outside the public service and to allow for the use of a wider range of executive recruitment practices, such as headhunting. Appointments to top-level posts in government departments with an economics mandate now appeared to favour public servants with private sector experience. A 'senior public service' has been instituted, with a view to developing strong executive leadership competencies and common public service values. In future internal top-level appointments will be made from the senior public service cadre.

A 2008 Organisation for Economic Co-Operation and Development (OECD) review of the Irish public service had complained that the prevailing 'career system' model of public service employment had fragmented through the creation over time of career 'silos' within different parts of the public service. In consequence, public servants tended to remain within the areas to which they had been appointed with little mobility between the civil service, local government and the health service (Organisation for Economic Co-Operation and Development, 2008). Attempts have been made to facilitate greater mobility across the public service, in part by removing anomalies in conditions of employment between different areas of the public service.

Prior to the fiscal crisis, partnership structures and arrangements intended to foster cooperative industrial relations had been created across much of the public service. In practice, issues of low priority for unions and management were dealt with through partnership in most public service agencies. Partnership working and arrangements appear to have been largely displaced or further marginalised during the crisis, as unions and public service employers have opted in the main to confine the conduct of industrial relations to traditional collective bargaining.

HR Managers and Strategy

In spite of a great deal of commentary on the need for a more strategic approach to HRM in the public service, various reviews conducted on the state of play before the advent of the crisis concluded that strategic human resource management had yet to emerge to any significant degree (MacCarthaigh, 2010; McGauran et al., 2005; Organisation for Economic Co-Operation and Development, 2008; O'Riordan, 2004, 2011). While multiple constraints accounted for the non-emergence of strategic HRM, including overly rigorous central controls and weak and reluctant leadership and engagement by public service managers, it was also clear that specialist human resource managers and departments were seldom capable of acting strategically, lacking both the competence and stature needed. Public service union officials in the focus groups conducted in early 2008 spoke of HR officers 'just picking up the pieces' as the employment control frameworks took effect. They also observed that 'HR isn't valued ... it's basically a troubleshooting role, it's a penance that people have to put up with during the course of their public service careers.' HRM in the public service was, in any event 'driven by government' rather than by any decisions it may want to take itself (see Roche et al., 2010).

The main reforms of the HR function since the advent of the crisis have involved the creation of shared services arrangements covering payroll and related areas, undertaken to reduce HR administration costs. The key architects of HR reforms in the Department of Public Expenditure and Reform have private sector HR experience and government proposals to reform the appointment process to the public service have identified HR as one of the areas of expertise that might be more effectively sourced from outside the public service.

It is hardly surprising that priority in the HR reform process during the crisis would be attributed to achieving payroll savings and tackling weak or dysfunctional HR practices and systems. However, the often repeated claim that things cannot return to how they were and that radical reform of public service management needs to be undertaken poses the question of the strategic direction of HRM in the public service. Other than it being clear that HR practices and systems will converge to a greater degree on private sector norms, there are few indications of any new blueprint for public service HR strategy. The 2011 Public Service Reform Plan repeats the abstractions that have been to the fore in reform documents since the mid-1990s, for example creating a 'high-performance culture', fostering 'engagement' and delivering 'customer-focused' services (Department of Public Expenditure and Reform, 2011). But the plan and its architects remain silent on key strategic areas like the future of pay fixing and rewards systems, the character of career systems, the latitude agencies will enjoy in undertaking HRM and the conduct of collective bargaining and dispute resolution.

Concession Bargaining and the Croke Park and Haddington Road Agreements

The government's initial response to the mounting fiscal crisis was to suspend the public service pay agreement renewed in social partnership talks in September 2008. In early 2009 spending on the public service pay bill was cut by the imposition of a 'levy' on public service pensions. This was followed by unilateral pay cuts in 2010. The combined effect of these measures was to reduce public service pay levels by an average of about 14 per cent. Unions' immediate reaction to these developments was to mount a one-day work stoppage across the public service in November 2009, followed by a programme of rolling and selective industrial action in early 2010. The Department of Finance also countenanced a more robust approach to industrial relations that would have involved rescinding the automatic deduction of trade union subscriptions from salaries and imposing curbs on time off for public servants engaged in union representation and training activities. In the event, the parties reached accord on a public service pay and reform agreement in March 2010. The agreement, known as the 'Croke Park Agreement', is due to run until 2014.

The Croke Park Agreement amounts to a concession bargaining framework agreement that has guided local concession bargaining across different areas of the public service, where a series of rolling 'sectoral action plans' have been implemented. Under the terms of the Croke Park Agreement, unions are committed to a series of reforms in the areas of staff mobility, working time and work practices in return for a pledge by government that no further pay cuts and no compulsory redundancies will be imposed. Whether public service allowances, which make up a significant part of the pay of some groups of public servants, constitute protected pay under the Croke Park Agreement remains disputed between the government and public service unions and represents a potential flashpoint in industrial relations.

The Croke Park Agreement has been aptly portrayed as a 'mechanism for the managed contraction of the public service' (Harbor, 2011: 16). The agreement has permitted a significant reduction in public service employment, a fall of 10 per cent having occurred in the years up to 2012. Voluntary severance and incentivised early retirement schemes have been introduced, with major resulting savings in the public service pay bill. More modest savings have been made in non-pay expenditure associated with the delivery of public services. The Croke Park Agreement and the procedure for dispute resolution agreed between the parties have also contributed to industrial peace in the context of the most significant reductions in headcount, level of reorganisation and changes in work practices in the history of the public service. While public service unions have faced unprecedented challenges, trade union density has continued to rise during the recession across the public service, in 2011 reaching 51 per cent in health, 64 per cent in education and 81 per cent in public administration. This represents a modest increase in the pre-recession trend and reflects how deeply embedded union recognition, representation and collective bargaining are in the public service, as well as the pivotal role assigned to the public service unions in the delivery of local concessions under the Croke Park Agreement and indeed in the governance and oversight of the agreement through the National Implementation Body.

In early 2013 negotiations began in the public service on a successor to the Croke Park Agreement. Although the agreement had been due to run until 2014, the government announced its determination to achieve further savings in the public service pay bill owing to acute fiscal pressures. Amid considerable turbulence among public service unions proposals were presented for a new agreement in the spring of 2013. These proposals, which involved pay cuts for those on higher salaries, increased working hours, reductions in pay premia and allowances, and the retention of the reforms and redeployment concessions in the Croke Park Agreement, were roundly rejected by most public service unions. Following intensive conciliation activity with unions representing 28 categories of public service unions, a marginally revised set of proposals were presented for ratification in the Haddington Road Agreement. As unions deliberated on the revised proposals, the government passed emergency legislation to impose pay cuts and changes in conditions of employment on categories of staff whose unions rejected the Haddington Road Agreement. The new agreement was eventually ratified by virtually all public service unions. In return for a continuation of the government's pledge that there would be no compulsory redundancies nor further pay cuts, public service unions accepted the revised deal. This involved most of the original proposals presented to union members in the spring, although sometimes, as in the case of freezes or changes in the payment schedules of service increments, the original proposals had been diluted. Allowances were also to be reviewed. The Haddington Road Agreement cut public service salaries of €65,000 and over by percentages rising progressively from 5.5 per cent to 10 per cent. Working hours were also increased for people working fewer than 39 hours per week. The PMDS system is to be made more robust. The agreement also contained measures to integrate lower salary scales for new entrants since 2011 into standard salary arrangements. The Croke Park and Haddington Road Agreements have allowed for significant reductions in headcount and in the public service pay bill and for sizeable gains in productvity without the industrial conflict or civil disorder evident in other 'bailout' countries and even in some countries that have not had to resort to financial assistance programmes.

Conclusion

The concluding section returns to the bearing of developments in Ireland on the different views of the effects of the recession on HRM considered earlier. To take the commercial sector first, it is clear that the recession has led to significant changes in HR practices in firms as they have often struggled to respond to the commercial challenges unleashed. The dominant picture is one of retrenchment, with firms implementing a variety of practices in different combinations or bundles to reduce payroll costs, while simultaneously trying to maintain motivation and commitment on the part of their workforces. Relations with unions have been dominated by concession bargaining, where firms have traded pledges of improved employment security in return for pay freezes or reductions, changes in working time and work practices, and sometimes redundancies for some staff.

HR functions have commonly become 'leaner' but also have frequently become more influential. No clear-cut change or disjuncture in work and employment arrangements, whether in the direction of the 'market-driven workforce'/'new employment deal', or in the direction of a high commitment model, is evident in the Irish experience. Although HR managers have often become more influential 'business partners', their newfound influence has been confined in the main to decision-making on measures for responding to immediate or short-term pressures. Their focus, like that of peer managers, has been on 'working the pumps'. They have not commonly used their new leverage to reposition HR in any radical way, either in response to the recession, or for recovery and growth – to some extent because the pressure of immediate challenges has allowed little time to focus on this. This was illustrated by the case study firms, selected for study because their approaches to managing HR in the recession were widely admired by professional peers and commentators. In these firms the main focus of senior HR executives has been on responding to immediate challenges and for the most part on seeking to preserve pre-recession HR strategies and arrangements.

Overall, therefore, the pattern of response of Irish firms seems consistent with that perspective in the international literature that views firms in the recession as concerned in the main with implementing essentially pragmatic practices, geared to meeting current challenges, rather than with responding to recessionary conditions or opportunities by transforming or reconfiguring work and employment arrangements.

The picture in the public service is consistent with this perspective. A series of changes have been made to weak and dysfunctional HR practices and systems and HR managers have responded to the recession largely in fire-fighting mode. Concession bargaining, as provided for in the Croke Park and Haddington Road Agreements, has facilitated significant reductions in headcount and payroll cost savings, changes in work practices and improved staff mobility. While there is clear evidence that private sector thinking and experience is being brought to bear on the public service reform process, there is – at least as yet – no clearly articulated blueprint for the transformation of HRM in the public service.

Notes

[1] The author would like to acknowledge the contribution of Paul Teague, Anne Coughlan and Majella Fahy to the research study on which this chapter draws. Research funding provided by the Labour Relations Commission is also acknowledged with gratitude.

[2] For full technical details of the research see Roche et al. (2010).

References

Acas (2008), *Lay-Offs and Short-Time Working*, London: Acas.

Acas (2009), 'The Recession: What the Future Holds for Employment Relations', *Acas Policy Discussion Papers*, June: 1–16.

Brockett, J. (2010), 'See HR as a Professional Services Firm, Says Ulrich' *People Management*, 25 March: 11.

Brown, D. and Reilly, P. (2009), *HR in Recession: What Are the Prospects and Priorities for HR Management in 2009?*, London: Institute for Employment Studies.

Cappelli, P. (1999a), *The New Deal at Work: Managing the Market-Driven Workforce*, Boston, MA: Harvard Business School Press.

Cappelli, P. (1999b), 'Career Jobs Are Dead', *California Management Review*, 42: 146–166.

Comptroller and Auditor General (2011) *Report of the Comptroller and Auditor General*, Volume 1, Dublin: Government Publications.

Cooper, C. (2009), 'The Recession Could Be the Making of HR', *HR Magazine*, 3 February, available from: <http://www.hrmagazine.co.uk/hro/features/1016812/this-recession-hr>.

Department of Public Expenditure and Reform (2011), *Public Service Reform Plan*, Dublin: Department of Public Expenditure and Reform.

Griffin, E. and Smith, G. (2010), 'Recession: A Shot in the Arm for HR', *Strategic HR Review*, 9(1): 17–22.

Hackett Group, The (2009a), 'Offshoring of Back Office Jobs Is Accelerating; Global 1000 to Move More than 350,000 Jobs Over the Next Two Years', The Hackett Group research alert and press release, 6 January, available from: <http://www.thehackettgroup.com/about/alerts/alerts_2009/alert_01062009.jsp>.

Hackett Group, The (2009b), 'Extended Jobless Recovery Likely for Back Office; 1.4 Million Jobs in IT, Finance, Other Areas Face Elimination by 2010', The Hackett Group research alert and press release, 3 December, available from: <http://www.thehackettgroup.com/about/alerts/alerts_2009/alert_12032009.jsp>.

Harbor, B. (2011), 'Union Responds to Consultants' Critique of Public Sector', *Industrial Relations News*, 40(3): 15–17.

Jacoby, S. (1999a), 'Are Career Jobs Headed for Extinction?', *California Management Review*, 42(1): 123–145.

Jacoby, S. (1999b), 'Reply: Premature Reports of Demise', *California Management Review*, 42(1): 168–179.

MacCarthaigh, M. (2010), *Non-Commercial State Agencies in Ireland*, Dublin: Institute of Public Administration.

McGauran, A.-M., Verhoest, K. and Humphreys, P. (2005), *The Corporate Governance of Agencies in Ireland*, Dublin: Institute of Public Administration.

McGovern, P., Hill, S., Mills, C. and White, M. (2007), *Market, Class and Employment*, Oxford: Oxford University Press.

Mohrman, S. and Worley, C.G. (2009), 'Dealing with Rough Times: A Capabilities Development Approach to Surviving and Thriving', *Human Resource Management*, 48(3): 433–445.

Organisation for Economic Co-Operation and Development (2008), *Ireland: Towards an Integrated Public Service*, Paris: OECD.

O'Riordan, J. (2004), 'Developing a Strategic Approach to HR in the Irish Public Service', Dublin: Institute of Public Administration CPMR

Discussion Papers, No 26: 1–103, available from: <http://www.ipa.ie/pdf/cpmr/CPMR_DP_26_Developing_Strategic_Approach_to_HR_inthe_CS.pdf>.

O'Riordan, J. (2011), *Organizational Capacity in the Irish Civil Service*, Dublin: Institute of Public Administration.

Personnel Today (2008), 'Ulrich Calls on HR to Use Recession to Scrap Jobs', *Personnel Today*, 12 September: 3.

Phillips, L. (2008), 'Firms Plan to Hire More HR Staff Despite UK Job Cuts', *People Management*, 21 February: 9.

Pickard, J. (2010), 'A Cut Above', *People Management*, 6 May: 18–21.

Roche, W.K., Teague, P., Coughlan, A. and Fahy, M. (2010), *Human Resources in the Recession: Managing and Representing People at Work in Ireland*, Dublin: Government Publications.

Towers Watson (2010), *The New Employment Deal: How Far, How Fast and How Enduring: Insights from the Global 2010 Workforce Survey*, New York, NY: Towers Watson.

Section 2

Practice

CHAPTER 3

Talent Management in Ireland:
A New Era for Human Resource Management?

David G. Collings

Introduction

With the publication of a McKinsey report titled 'The War for Talent' in the late 1990s, the topic of talent management (TM) entered the managerial lexicon and became a key driver of human resource management (HRM) practice (Cappelli, 2008; Lewis and Heckman, 2006). Since then the rhetoric of talent and talent management has become one of the most pervasive themes in debates around the practice of HRM. While the academic community was initially sceptical of the topic (Pfeffer, 2001), over the past number of years our understanding of talent management from an academic perspective has advanced significantly. However, with some notable exceptions (cf. Garavan, 2012; McDonnell et al., 2010; Whelan et al., 2010), the topic of talent management has been largely unexplored in the Irish context.

In this chapter I set out to introduce the topic of talent management through presenting some of the key debates in the extant literature and provide some evidence of the nature of TM in the Irish context. I conclude by reflecting on the prospects for talent management from the perspectives of research and practice in Ireland.

Talent Management: A Potted History

As noted above, the topic of talent management was brought to the fore when a group of McKinsey consultants coined the term 'the war for talent' to capture the challenges which United States (US) organisations were facing in terms of attracting and retaining key employees in the context of the tightening labour market conditions within which they were operating at that time (Michaels et al., 2001). Given their relatively simple and intuitive message and the potential which the war for talent had to reinvigorate the human resource (HR) function and bring HR issues to the fore for corporate executives, it is not surprising that the original McKinsey ideas quickly gained traction and influenced debates around the role of people management in organisations. High-profile executives such as General Electric's Jack Welch reinforced the message, through their public pronouncements, in regular newspaper columns and other outlets, of the centrality of talent to their organisation's success.

However, as the academic community became interested in the topic a counterbalance to the practitioner hype quickly emerged. Academic commentators were quick to point to the potential drawback of overly focusing on individual talent (see Pfeffer, 2001) and the ambiguity around the conceptual and intellectual boundaries of talent management became a key point of criticism (see Lewis and Heckman, 2006; Scullion et al., 2010). Indeed, over recent years significant effort has been devoted to unpacking these boundaries and establishing a working definition of talent management.

A key point of departure in this regard was Lewis and Heckman's (2006) review of the field, which identified three key streams of thinking or approaches to talent management within the literature. The first key body of literature placed a significant emphasis on the management of star or 'A' employees. This literature argued for top-grading and posited that all roles in the organisation should be filled by 'A' players and that 'C' players should be managed out of the organisation. The second stream represented little more than a rebranding of HR. Functions and roles that were previously titled 'HR' were now titled 'talent'. Indeed, there remains a tendency for this to happen in both research and practice and one needs to be cautious of the contribution of such rebranding exercises. The third stream focused on the development of talent pools, which emphasised 'projecting employee/staffing needs and managing the progression of employees through positions' (Lewis and Heckman,

2006:140). Building on traditional succession literatures, this stream represents an important reframing of the succession issues (see, for example, Cappelli, 2008). Collings and Mellahi (2009) subsequently identified a fourth stream of literature which placed the identification of key roles or pivotal positions at the centre of the talent debate (see, for example, Becker and Huselid, 2010; Boudreau and Ramstad, 2007; Huselid et al., 2005). This approach argues that not all roles require 'A' players and that such talent can often be underutilised if deployed in non-strategic roles and represents an important change in emphasis in thinking on talent management.

More recently, a fifth stream of literature which focuses on the use of data and analytics to inform decisions around talent and talent deployment has advanced our understanding of the potential of talent management. Data analytics applied to talent facilitates more strategic decisions around talent and moves talent decisions beyond the more subjective decision-making, which has arguably had a disproportionate impact on talent decisions heretofore (Cascio and Boudreau, 2010; Vaiman et al., 2012) (see Box 3.1).

Box 3.1: Resolving High Turnover in Pivotal Organisational Teams

PHARMA is a large multinational in the pharmaceutical sector. As part of a large organisational effort to transform the organisation into a globally efficient and effective operation, information technology was viewed as a key enabler (potential savings: US$60 million). Thus a number of highly competent IT teams were established to put the IT framework and infrastructure in place. However, these teams were not delivering at the levels expected. Employee turnover was one of the key issues. Exit interviews confirmed salary was a key issue as employees were earning salaries $5,000–$9,000 below what competitors were willing to pay. However, historically generous stock options had represented a key retention mechanism. Given the importance of the project the chief executive officer wished to raise the pay of all IT people to resolve the issue. The HR Department resisted and requested five weeks to fully unpack and understand the issue before acting.

While the detail of the process undertaken is beyond the scope of this case vignette, the application of effective data analytics to the turnover data unearthed a far more nuanced understanding of the underlying issues which were leading to the turnover. Specifically, key drivers of turnover included inadequate career paths for company employees. This was amplified as employees hired as the company ramped up for the major project generally came in on higher salaries and to higher positions than extant employees, further reducing potential for advancement amongst extant

---

employees. Similarly, the vesting periods for stock options provided were correlated with turnover. The analysis provided management with clear flags for the issues to watch out for in proactively managing retention and in building a retention intervention. It turned out that salary was only a small part of the equation, with career progression (or lack thereof) a far more significant predictor of turnover.

Source: Adapted from Hoffmann et al. (2012).

Indeed, Michael Lewis' (2003) analysis of how data analytics transformed how players are valued, and indeed influenced playing tactics, in professional baseball in the US provides an excellent illustration of how data analytics can transform talent systems. In this context, Lewis showed how traditional assessments of player potential were over-reliant on scouts who based their assessments on gut instinct and outdated data points. Data analysis provided a much stronger grounding for teams to base their talent decisions upon and early adopters of this technique enjoyed significant successes (see Wolfe et al., 2006). Overall, this stream is important in helping decision-makers make more informed decisions around talent and in framing talent issues in language that senior organisation leaders are more comfortable with.

The preceding review points to the diversity of opinion on what precisely talent management means; while we remain some way from a consensus on definitions of talent management, one of the more influential definitions is Collings and Mellahi's (2009: 304). They define strategic talent management as:

> … activities and processes that involve the systematic identification of key positions which differentially contribute to the organisation's sustainable competitive advantage, the development of a talent pool of high potential and high performing incumbents to fill these roles, and the development of a differentiated human resource architecture to facilitate filling these positions with competent incumbents and to ensure their continued commitment to the organisation.

In line with the pivotal position approach outlined above, Collings and Mellahi (2009) argue that talent systems should begin by identifying the roles that have the greatest potential to contribute to the sustainable competitive advantage of the organisation. Such roles tend to be highly dependent on human capital and there tends to be significant potential for variability in performance within the role (Becker and Huselid, 2010). For example, the potential for differential performance between an average and a superstar software designer may be significant (see Oldroyd and Morris, 2012). In contrast, there are some roles where performance is tightly defined by procedure or legislation and there is very little room for a top performer to perform better than an average employee. An example might be an airline pilot whose role is very tightly prescribed by procedure, schedule (such as air traffic control) and legislation. Thus organisations should begin by focusing on those positions that have the greatest potential to differentially impact on the performance of the organisation.

Thereafter, they advocate the development of talent pools of high performing and high potential employees to fill those pivotal positions when they become available. While recognising that there may be situations where recruitment from the external labour market is appropriate, in general organisations should prioritise the development of internal talent wherever possible. Indeed, there is a large body of research which confirms the challenges of orientating and socialising key talents, often referred to as 'on-boarding', when they join organisations from the external labour market and the performance challenges which these talents face in maintaining performance levels when they do transfer (Groysberg, 2010). The development of talent pools facilitates a more flexible approach to leadership succession than more traditional methods which identified particular individuals as successors for specific roles. In contrast, Collings and Mellahi (2009) advocate the development of talent in the generic context of the organisation rather than specific roles. This facilitates the development of high performing and high potential leadership talent who fit well with company culture and values, and who can be deployed to a particular role, with their skill set tweaked appropriately, as required. Many organisations also have multiple talent pools representing both technical and leadership employees (see Box 3.2).

Box 3.2: Talent Pools at Computerco

Computerco is a large US headquartered, Fortune 500 organisation operating in the information and communications technology sector. It employs some 400,000 employees globally and 3,500 in Ireland. Computerco operates three talent pools in its Irish operation. The first, the Executive Resource Pool (ERP), is global in its orientation with only twenty Irish employees. It consists of the highest-level executives in the organisation and those who are considered very close to reaching this level. Their careers and development are managed at corporate (HQ) level. It is also quite formalised. The second talent pool, the Top Talent Pool (TTP), is a more generic talent pool consisting of approximately 10 per cent of global employees who are considered to have the potential to move into managerial roles. Although career paths are monitored at a corporate level, the pool is managed largely at a local level. This pool operates more informally and lacks the formal development programmes evident in the ERP. Those in the TTP could potentially progress to the ERP but this is not a given. Finally, the Technical Resource Pool (TRP) represents the third talent pool. As the name suggests, this pool focuses on top technical talent as opposed to those with pure leadership potential. The pool comprises the highest performing members of the organisation's technical talent in key areas of Computerco's business and is organised at a local level. There is a parallel career track for those very high performing members of this pool who may ultimately become 'distinguished engineers'. These are the elite technical contributors in the organisation and the title is considered a real accolade.

Source: Adapted from McDonnell et al. (2011).

Finally, the strategic TM approach recognises the potential differential contribution of different employee groups (see Lepak and Snell, 1999; Hornung et al., 2010) and argues that given their centrality to organisational success, talent pools should be managed differentially. This is not to suggest that others are treated poorly, in HR terms – indeed on balance one would expect that the baseline level of HR in many high performing firms would be relatively competitive – but rather that the talent pool has a HR system adapted to reflect their centrality to the organisation. Specifically, Collings and Mellahi (2009) advocate the deployment of commitment-orientated HR practices for this cohort of employees.

Having considered the broad debates around the nature of talent management, we now turn to unpacking the empirical research on talent management in the Irish context.

Talent Management in Ireland

While there is a significant tradition of research on human resource management in Ireland, unsurprisingly, given the relatively recent acceptance of talent management as a legitimate field of study (Scullion et al., 2010), the research base on talent management in Ireland is rather limited. While acknowledging the important contributions which Irish scholars have made to international debates on talent management at a conceptual level (Collings, 2014; Collings and Mellahi, 2009; Garavan et al., 2012; Mellahi and Collings, 2010; Scullion et al., 2010; Scullion and Collings, 2010; Farndale et al., 2010), this paper focuses on empirical evidence on talent management in the Irish context.

Given the historical prevalence of foreign multinational enterprises (MNEs), particularly of US origin, in diffusing new and innovative HR practices to Ireland (Gunnigle, 1995), it is not surprising that the multinational sector is to the fore in empirical research on talent management in Ireland (Burbach and Royle, 2010; Garavan, 2012; McDonnell et al., 2010). Much of this literature has focused on understanding the nature of talent management practice in the MNE sector.

For example, based on their large-scale study of employment practice in MNEs in Ireland, McDonnell et al. (2010) explored the incidence and nature of talent management in indigenous MNEs and foreign-owned subsidiaries. Their specific focus was on understanding the extent to which these firms engaged in formal global succession planning and management development programmes for high potential employees and the nature of management development practices in these firms. Additionally, they explored the extent to which MNEs have formal global succession planning and management development programmes in place for their high potentials. This study confirmed a relatively high level of adoption of global succession planning and high potential development programmes. Indeed, some 46 per cent of firms employed both practices in tandem. Large firms with a global HR policy formation committee were most likely to utilise both. Indeed, the importance of such global committees was reinforced in Garavan's (2012) study of the multinational pharmaceutical sector in Ireland. However, Burbach and Royle's (2010) case study of a US subsidiary provides some insights into the operation of such policy formation committees. In their case firm, talent management strategy was decided by a so-called 'Human Resource Council' (HRC). This council consisted of ten senior vice-presidents from different functions. Interestingly, there was a sole European representative on the council who is selected on a rotating basis. This limited representation created a real scepticism amongst key European stakeholders around the operation of the HRC. This points to the importance of the composition of such policy committees in ensuring their acceptance by local stakeholders in the MNE context. Indeed, the role of position in the multinational network and other challenges which subsidiary level talent experienced in entering the global talent pool have been recognised in the literature (Mellahi and Collings, 2010).

However, McDonnell et al.'s (2010) study also confirms that in a significant percentage of firms, global talent management practices remain informal and *ad hoc*. This suggests that the diffusion of global talent management practices to the MNE sector might not be as deep as may be expected. This also perhaps indicates that the rhetoric of talent management has outpaced the development of management practice, as alluded to in Lewis and Heckman's (2006) review.

Turning to the operation of talent management systems, McDonnell et al.'s (2011) case study of the subsidiary of a US Fortune 500 MNE in Ireland provides some insights into the operation of the talent pool strategy. The case firm had a segmented approach to talent management and operated three distinct talent pools as part of its talent strategy. The company differentiated between the talent pools based on their impact and importance to corporate strategy. For example, the top-level pool was focused on those employees with the potential to assume senior executive roles in the organisation. The study reinforced the emphasis on the generic development of talent in line with the organisational context as opposed to development toward a particular role, as was common under more traditional succession planning systems (Cappelli, 2008; Collings and Mellahi, 2009). The talent pool strategy also emerged as an important element of talent management systems in the pharmaceutical sector (Garavan, 2012). Indeed, Garavan's (2012) study reinforced the importance of technical talent pools in addition to leadership talent pools in ensuring organisational success. Theoretically, Collings and Mellahi (2009) and others advocate the importance of identifying those pivotal roles which provide the greatest potential for sustaining competitive advantage in a particular organisational context. Such an understanding helps organisations to think beyond overly focusing on leadership talent in their talent management processes.

As alluded to above, a talent pool approach is more appropriate in a dynamic business environment where the requirements of a particular role may evolve rather rapidly, limiting the utility of static succession planning systems. McDonnell et al.'s (2011) study also points to the potential difficulty which emerges when a talent pool strategy results in an oversupply of talent, whereby those identified as talent do not have the opportunities they might expect owing to a lack of open positions in the organisation. Clearly, a key challenge for organisations that do operate open talent systems, where members of the talent pool are informed of their status as talent, is managing these talents' career expectations, particularly in light of flattening organisational structures which limit hierarchical promotion opportunities. Career counselling and horizontal job rotations must be utilised to facilitate the development of these talents. Equally, the management of the careers of those outside the talent pool emerges as an important concern in the case study.

Garavan's (2012) study of the pharmaceutical sector in Ireland provides some important insights into the impact of the global financial crisis on talent management practices in this important sector. Interestingly, of the nine firms studied only two firms had reduced their 'commitment to and investment in talent management' over the previous two years. Indeed, three of the nine firms had increased their commitment and investment. This finding is perhaps not surprising in the pharmaceutical sector, given that the relatively long development cycles and relatively high margin products might mean that these firms take a longer-term perspective than firms in other sectors. Respondents to the study identified concerns about attracting top talent combined with the challenges of retaining top performers, the requirement for a leadership pipeline and, most importantly, the requirement to maintain business growth as central to this continued investment. A stark finding in the study is that those firms that failed to maintain their investment in talent management failed to react quickly enough to the global economic climate owing to technical and leadership deficiencies, an overreliance on traditional ways of doing things and disjointed global talent strategies.

A further key contribution of this research on management of talent in the MNE sector concerns the standardisation and global transfer of TM policies and practices. For example, Burbach and Royle (2010) point to the importance of stakeholder involvement and top-level support, micro-political exchanges, and the integration of talent management with a global human resource information system (HRIS) in explaining the success of the transfer of corporate talent management systems and processes to subsidiary operations. Similarly, Collings et al. (2010) identified the importance of global HRIS in the identification of subsidiary-level talent and their transfer to other operations in the MNE. The role of the corporate HR function is also identified as key in managing global talent (Collings et al., 2010; Garavan, 2012; McDonnell et al., 2010). In this regard, Farndale et al. (2010) have developed a theoretical model of the corporate HR role in global talent management (GTM). Specifically, they identify four key roles which HR can play in GTM. First, as *champions of process* corporate HR focuses on the horizontal coordination of tools, techniques and process for talent management across internal functions. This calls for the development of effective global expertise networks and a champion of process to monitor the implementation of TM strategy on a global scale. Second, as *guardians of culture*, corporate HR emphasises the implementation of global values and systems, in the context of developing a talent culture and employer brand across the global organisation. Third, in *network leadership and intelligence*, corporate HR plays an important role in facilitating coordination across the MNE. This role emphasises the development of social capital both across and beyond the organisation's boundaries. Finally, as *managers of internal receptivity*, corporate HR plays an important role in facilitating employee mobility globally across the organisation. Indeed, corporate HR has been criticised for its lack of engagement with global mobility as an important element of MNEs' global talent systems.

A second key stream of literature and research on talent management in Ireland focuses on the integration of talent management and knowledge. Largely driven by the work of Eoin Whelan (Whelan et al., 2010; Whelan and Carcary, 2011), this work provides some important insights into the nature of the talent management of knowledge workers and the role of social networks in talent systems. A key contribution of this stream of literature is advancing our understanding of the role of social networks and social network analysis in supporting talent management initiatives in knowledge-intensive settings. Specifically, Whelan (2011) illustrates how social network analysis can provide important insights in terms of talent positioning (having the right people, in the right place, at the right time). This work also helps to understand the impact of key talents' networks on their performance in the workplace and reinforces the notion that talents can generally not perform to a high level without appropriate support (see also Groysberg, 2010). For example, it is rare for any single individual to possess all of the talents necessary to effectively acquire and disseminate new external knowledge which is central to innovation in knowledge industries (Whelan et al., 2010). Building on Tom Allen's notion of the technological gatekeeper, Whelan et al. (2010) provide important insights into the competencies required by those who acquire new knowledge externally and those who successfully disseminate it internally. They also point to a limited number of gatekeepers who possess the rare competencies to do both. Social network analysis helps to identify these individuals and to ensure that research and development (R&D) groups have members with the skills to acquire and disseminate new knowledge to maximise innovation within R&D teams.

The knowledge perspective also provides insights into how organisations can mitigate the negative impact of the turnover of star R&D performers. Turnover of this nature often results in a significant decline in collaboration throughout the R&D team. Whelan (2011) illustrates how social network analysis can usefully identify individuals with the requisite networks to resolve the void left by the departure. All-in-all, social network analysis provides rich insights into the importance of networks in R&D settings. It also provides a useful input into the management of key knowledge employees. More broadly, the integration of insights from knowledge management and talent management facilitates the management of knowledge talent in five important ways: identifying key knowledge workers, knowledge creation, knowledge sharing, developing knowledge competencies and knowledge retention (Whelan and Carcary, 2011).

Taking a more critical approach, Cushen (2009, 2011) has studied the notion of employer branding, a concept which is strongly linked with talent management. The employer brand is the external representation of an organisation as an employer and organisational culture and values are often central elements of employer brands. Cushen (2009) conceptualises employer branding efforts as a form of normative control, through the socialisation of employees into organisational cultural values and market realities. Her study points to the importance of employee identity moulded by the employer brand in attempting 'to seduce employees into delivering extra functional, discretionary effort without offering anything in return' (Cushen, 2009: 111). She concludes that efforts to extend normative control and resistance are alive and well. Her study also shows that the employees who experience such efforts at normative control are fully aware of the intentions behind such practices and are often sceptical of them. Indeed, the integration of employees as *brand recipients* (Cushen, 2011) is an important contribution of this work. Work on talent management has heretofore largely neglected the perceptions of those who experience talent management practices and the integration of employees' perspectives, particularly from a critical perspective, certainly provides a useful counterbalance to the extant literature, which is largely managerial in its orientation.

The above review highlights the diversity of research being undertaken on talent management in the Irish context. In addition to the strong conceptual and theoretical contributions of Irish-based scholars, Irish research also provides useful insights into the management of talent in the MNE, the integration of knowledge management and talent management and, to a lesser degree, a more critical understanding of the management of talent. Given the relatively early stage of development of the field the volume and quality of research is relatively significant.

Conclusion

Although talent management is a relatively recent introduction to management practice, there is little doubt but that it has quickly gained mainstream acceptance as an important contemporary management practice. Although there is as yet no empirical evidence to confirm the linkage between talent management and organisational performance, there is little doubt that framing key HR issues in theories from the talent literature offers an important development for the HR function. First, the development of talent analytics offers a key means of framing HR issues in models and language that senior organisational stakeholders are conversant with. At a minimum this will provide a greater degree of exposure to talent issues among senior organisation decision-makers. Equally, models and theories of talent management can facilitate

HR in identifying the pivotal roles in their organisations with the potential to generate the greatest potential returns to the organisation. This involves a fundamental shift in terms of how roles were evaluated and ranked in traditional job-ranking systems which tended to emphasise inputs required to do roles (Gunnigle et al., 2011). The talent approach advocated by Boudreau and Ramstad (2007), Becker and Huselid (2010) and Collings and Mellahi (2009), amongst others, brings the potential output of positions to the fore. Equally, the talent pool approach assists organisations operating in more dynamic and fluid environments where the requirements of particular roles may evolve quite rapidly in a way which challenges traditional linear approaches to succession planning (cf. Gunnigle et al., 2011).

As the field matures, researchers are faced with a number of challenges and opportunities which should drive the research agenda on talent management moving forward. The first key challenge is reaching a consensus on the conceptual and intellectual boundaries of the field (Collings and Mellahi, 2009; Lewis and Heckman, 2006; Scullion et al., 2010). Given a lack of consensus over the precise meaning (or meanings) of talent management there is currently a degree of dispersion in the academic study of the area. Second, research efforts could concentrate on demonstrating the linkages between investment in talent management programmes and performance outcomes. Finally, it is important that the views and perspectives of employees or those who experience talent management are included to a greater degree in research in the field.

References

Becker, B.E. and Huselid, M.A. (2010), 'SHRM and Job Design: Narrowing the Divide', *Journal of Organisational Behavior*, 31(2–3): 379–388.

Boudreau, J.W. and Ramstad, P.M. (2007), *Beyond HR: The New Science of Human Capital*, Boston, MA: Harvard Business Press.

Burbach, R. and Royle, T. (2010), 'Talent on Demand? Talent Management in the German and Irish Subsidiaries of a US Multinational Corporation', *Personnel Review*, 39(4): 414–431.

Cappelli, P. (2008), *Talent on Demand: Managing Talent in an Age of Uncertainty*, Boston, MA: Harvard Business School Press.

Cascio, W.F. and Boudreau, J.W. (2010), *Investing in People: Financial Impact of Human Resource Initiatives*, London: Financial Times Press.

Collings, D.G. (2014), 'Talent Management' in D.E. Guest and D. Needle (eds), *The Wiley Encyclopaedia of Management*, third edition, Volume 5, Human Resource Management, Oxford: Wiley-Blackwell, 377–378.

Collings, D.G., McDonnell, A., Gunnigle, P. and Lavelle, J. (2010), 'Swimming Against the Tide: Outward Staffing Flows from Multinational Subsidiaries', *Human Resource Management*, 49(4): 575–598.

Collings, D.G. and Mellahi, K. (2009), 'Strategic Talent Management: A Review and Research Agenda', *Human Resource Management Review*, 19(4): 304–313.

Cushen, J. (2009), 'Branding Employees', *Qualitative Research in Accounting & Management*, 6(1/2): 102–114.

Cushen, J. (2011), 'The Trouble with Employer Branding: Resistance and Disillusionment at Avatar' in M.J. Brannan, E. Parsons and V. Priola (eds), *Branded Lives: The Production and Consumption of Meaning at Work*, Cheltenham: Edward Elgar Publishing, 75–89.

Farndale, E., Scullion, H. and Sparrow, P. (2010), 'The Role of the Corporate HR Function in Global Talent Management', *Journal of World Business*, 45(2): 161–168.

Garavan, T.N. (2012), 'Global Talent Management in Science-Based Firms: An Exploratory Investigation of the Pharmaceutical Sector During the Global Downturn', *International Journal of Human Resource Management*, 23(12): 2428–2449.

Garavan, T.N., Carbery, R. and Rock, A. (2012), 'Mapping Talent Development: Definition, Scope and Architecture', *European Journal of Training and Development*, 36(1): 5–24.

Groysberg, B. (2010), *Chasing Stars: The Myth of Talent and the Portability of Performance*, Princeton, NJ: Princeton University Press.

Gunnigle, P. (1995), 'Collectivism and the Management of Industrial Relations in Greenfield Sites', *Human Resource Management Journal*, 5(3): 24–40.

Gunnigle, P., Heraty, N. and Morley, M. (2011), *Human Resource Management in Ireland*, Dublin: Gill & Macmillan.

Hoffmann, C., Lesser, E. and Ringo, T. (2012), *Calculating Success: An Analytic Approach to Managing Talent*, Boston, MA: Harvard Business Press.

Hornung, S., Rousseau, D.M., Glaser, J., Angerer, P. and Weigl, M. (2010), 'Beyond Top–Down and Bottom–Up Work Redesign: Customizing Job Content through Idiosyncratic Deals', *Journal of Organisational Behavior*, 31(2–3): 187–215.

Huselid, M.A., Beatty, R.W. and Becker, B.E. (2005), '"A Players" or "A Positions"? The Strategic Logic of Workforce Management', *Harvard Business Review*, 83(12): 110–117.

Lepak, D.P. and Snell, S.A. (1999), 'The Human Resource Architecture: Toward a Theory of Human Capital Allocation and Development', *Academy of Management Review*, 24(1): 31–48.

Lewis, M. (2003), *Moneyball: The Art of Winning an Unfair Game*, New York, NY: W.W. Norton and Company.

Lewis, R.E. and Heckman, R.J. (2006), 'Talent Management: A Critical Review', *Human Resource Management Review*, 16(2): 139–154.

McDonnell, A., Hickey, C. and Gunnigle, P. (2011), 'Global Talent Management: Exploring Talent Identification in Multinational Enterprises', *European Journal of International Management*, 5(2): 174–193.

McDonnell, A., Lamare, R., Gunnigle, P. and Lavelle, J. (2010), 'Developing Tomorrow's Leaders—Evidence of Global Talent Management in Multinational Enterprises', *Journal of World Business*, 45(2): 150–160.

Mellahi, K. and Collings, D.G. (2010), 'The Barriers to Effective Global Talent Management: The Example of Corporate Élites in MNEs', *Journal of World Business*, 45(2): 143–149.

Michaels, E., Handfield-Jones, H. and Axelrod, B. (2001), *The War for Talent*, Boston, MA: Harvard Business Press.

Oldroyd, J.B. and Morris, S.S. (2012), 'Catching Falling Stars: A Human Resource Response to Social Capital's Detrimental Effect of Information Overload on Star Employees', *Academy of Management Review*, 37(3): 396–418.

Pfeffer, J. (2001), 'Fighting the War for Talent Is Hazardous to Your Organisation's Health', *Organisational Dynamics*, 29(4): 248–259.

Scullion, H. and Collings, D.G. (eds) (2010), *Global Talent Management*, London: Routledge.

Scullion, H., Collings, D.G. and Caligiuri, P. (2010), 'Global Talent Management', *Journal of World Business*, 45(2): 105–108.

Vaiman, V., Scullion, H. and Collings, D.G. (2012), 'Talent Management Decision Making', *Management Decision*, 50(5): 925–941.

Whelan, E. (2011), 'It's Who You Know Not What You Know: A Social Network Analysis Approach to Talent Management', *European Journal of International Management*, 5(5): 484–500.

Whelan, E. and Carcary, M. (2011), 'Integrating Talent and Knowledge Management: Where Are the Benefits?', *Journal of Knowledge Management*, 15(4): 675–687.

Whelan, E., Collings, D.G. and Donnellan, B. (2010), 'Talent Management in Knowledge Intensive Settings', *Journal of Knowledge Management*, 14(3): 486–405.

Wolfe, R., Wright, P.M. and Smart, D.L. (2006), 'Radical HRM Innovation and Competitive Advantage: The *Moneyball* Story', *Human Resource Management*, 45(1): 111–145.

CHAPTER 4

Employee Voice

Niall Cullinane and Tony Dundon

Introduction

The term 'employee voice' has become fashionable currency in studies of human resource management (HRM) in recent years. However if we understand the term as referring to the ability of workers to have a say about aspects of their working lives, then it is easy to appreciate that this dynamic has always been inherent to employment relationships. During the Industrial Revolution, for example, it was not unknown for disenfranchised workers to raise grievances through assorted means: combining in unions, sabotaging employers' machinery or simply being absent from work (Pollard, 1963). As the centuries progressed, the way workers articulated their voice has taken on many different forms, some more substantive in character than others. Ultimately, changing social and economic dynamics have tended to shape both the demand, and the desire, for different types of employee voice practices amongst employers and workers.

In this chapter we begin by conceptualising 'employee voice' in terms of why it is important, not simply as some recent appendage to the battery of fashionable HRM ideas, but as an enduring process mediating employment outcomes. Having established this, we then show how interpretations of the term can oscillate through time between variants of voice as 'participation' and voice as 'involvement'. This is followed by a review of the methods used to evaluate the degrees of influence voice can have on decision-making outcomes. We then consider the dynamics with reference to developments in Ireland and associated research evidence. The chapter concludes with a general summative assessment of the role of voice and its status in Irish HRM.

Conceptualising Employee Voice

Why Do Workers Want Voice?

The practice of employee voice has been central to considerations of work and employment long before the advent of HRM. That this is the case should be no surprise. The employment relationship, by its nature, is characterised by an exchange whereby a worker sells their labour power to an employer, which the latter then utilises in the process of producing commodities. However this exchange is not unproblematic for either party: for a start, there will be disputes over the distribution of rewards between workers and employers and what can frequently be a gain for workers, in terms of increased wages for example, can be a loss for employers, in the form of a reduction of profit. Given that wages are vital to the workers' livelihood, not to say a source of social status and har-binger of general life chances, it is not difficult to see why workers will necessarily want a say on these matters. But this desire for a voice extends not just to matters of income distribution, but also to the very fabric of day-to-day work relations. When the employer purchases labour power, it is difficult in advance to specify how much work, and of what sort, shall be expended at what time and in what ways, for a given wage. However detailed a set of rules and instructions might be in a contract of employment for example, the employer cannot foresee every eventuality and cannot describe exactly what must be done. Even the most routine of tasks involves the application of the worker's abilities and knowledge of how the job should be done. That is to say, there is an *indeterminacy* to the employment relationship when managers seek to translate labour power into actual work tasks. How labour power is realised within the labour process is likely to be a potential source of disagreement amongst employers and workers. A brief inspection of contempo-rary industrial relations affairs provides ample evidence that each side is likely to hold very different conceptions of what a 'fair day's work for a fair day's pay' constitutes. Like in the case of income distribution, workers will likely need to articulate their voice over how their labour power is translated into productive labour.

Of course it is true to say that this 'wage–effort bargain', as Baldamus (1961) notably called it, illustrates only why workers might, for immediately instrumental ends, want voice over aspects of their working life. In fact, the necessity for 'employee voice' might also be rationalised on more philosophical grounds. If the claim that we live in democratic societies is to pass muster, then it is difficult to see why democratic rights cannot extend from the political to the economic sphere of production, to give workers a substantial say over aspects of their working lives (Archer, 2010). Indeed, this has long been one strain of thinking on employee voice, exemplified in such diverse practices as worker directorships on the boards of Irish semi-state companies to more radical formulas like the nineteenth-century Ralahine cooperatives in County Clare (Geoghegan, 1991). Again, such agendas are not unproblematic; employers often counter these initiatives with arguments for their 'innate' property or managerial rights, even if such arguments have been demonstrated to hold dubious legitimacy (Marglin, 1974; Cohen, 1988).

The Meaning of Voice

In establishing why employee voice might be an inherently necessary or desirable feature of the employment relationship, it is worth pointing out that the way voice might be understood is far from obvious and meanings and interpretations change over time and space. For example, the 1960s and 1970s saw a desire for what was termed 'worker participation' as a way to address a (then) widely perceived problem of employee alienation across industry. But worker participation was interpreted in widely different ways: for some, it was aligned with 'job enrichment' and enhanced worker motivation to enable employers to overcome the anomic tendencies of Fordist production (Davis, 1971). For others, participation was interpreted as 'industrial democracy', based not on solving problems of alienation but as a source of power-sharing between workers and employers in the making of joint decisions (Sorge, 1976). In Ireland, this was heralded by the passing of the Worker Participation (State Enterprises) Act 1977, which introduced board-level participation to seven semi-state companies, which in time was later extended to other companies like Irish Steel and Aer Rianta.

The meanings shaping the patterns of voice were driven in part by the changing social and economic context of the time: increasing worker militancy, industrial conflict and 'profit squeeze' led many to look for alternatives to the slowdown in capital accumulation and stagflation of the 1970s. By the 1980s and 1990s however, as the context became characterised by wage repression, declining union influence and resurgent employer power (Harvey, 2011), the tone of debate shifted to considerations of 'employee involvement' rather than 'worker participation', with a distinctive aim of improving labour productivity and efficiency. Against a background of diminishing union power, definitions of employee voice became colonised by a new managerial lexicon in which voice needed to demonstrate commercial value. Thus voice became interpreted as securing workers' cooperation for achieving the employer's profit objective. Academic analysis reflected this trajectory as new forms of managerialist thinking, encapsulated in the fashionable ideologies of 'best-practice' HRM and 'high commitment management', emphasised voice as something which improved the profitability of the firm through tapping into workers' knowledge (Thompson, 2011). In Ireland, such practices were often introduced by the high-tech sector, namely United States (US)-owned, non-union firms like Digital, Apple and Amdahl, but also in some semi-state companies like Bord na Móna.

Overlapping with the mantra of high performing workplaces has been a conceptualisation of employee voice under the rubric of 'partnership'. Taking its cue from heterogeneous sources, like American scholarship on 'mutual gains' and European social policy, this has sought to carve out a place for workers to have a say in a much more collaborative rather than adversarial manner (Ackers and Payne, 1998). In the context of union marginalisation, social democratic thinkers believed that unions could only survive if they moved away from the traditional adversarial model of bargaining shrouded in conflict to an integrative approach, exploring common ground and seeking cooperation. Thus, workers and their representatives were advised to jointly address employment relations problems with their employer and develop mutually beneficial solutions. Ireland saw some experimentation in this regard at two related levels: national- and enterprise-level partnerships. At the national level, faced with severe economic recession and mass emigration in the early 1980s, Ireland opted for a corporatist-style national partnership model. Since 1987 eight uninterrupted national-level partnership agreements provided a degree of indirect worker voice. Some of the better known exemplars of enterprise partnerships were established in Aughinish Alumina and Waterford Crystal, among others (Dobbins and Gunnigle, 2009). Indeed the Irish government established a National Centre for Partnership and Performance (NCPP) to promote the diffusion of such arrangements across Irish industry. In many respects, this approach was a synthesis of the voice distinctions noted above between 'participation' and 'involvement' approaches: partnership espoused both the commitment of workers to improvements in productivity and the acceptance by employers of workers as stakeholders with rights and interests to be considered in the context of major decisions affecting their employment.

Evaluating Voice

Whilst recognising that meanings of participation and involvement can occasionally overlap, they remain useful ways to categorise voice by showing tendencies that are likely to prompt different degrees of power-sharing when workers articulate their voice. Thus writing in the institutional–pluralist tradition, Marchington and Wilkinson (2005) note that employee voice, in its different guises of involvement and participation, might be understood in terms of the *depth*, *scope*, *level* and *forms* that they engender (see Figure 4.1).

By *depth*, it is meant the extent to which workers (or their representatives) share influence with management in decision-making. Shallow voice occurs where workers have little or no say over managerial actions whereas, in contrast, deep voice enables workers to meaningfully contribute to the final decision-making outcome in some way. *Scope* expresses the range of issues addressed within a particular voice arrangement; a process which is narrow on this dimension allows management to define certain matters as reserved for their prerogative, ensuring that only minor issues are available for employee influence. In contrast, voice with a wide scope would have few restrictions or reserved issues with worker influence extending to input on strategic matters like the introduction of new

Figure 4.1: The Depth and Scope of Employee Voice

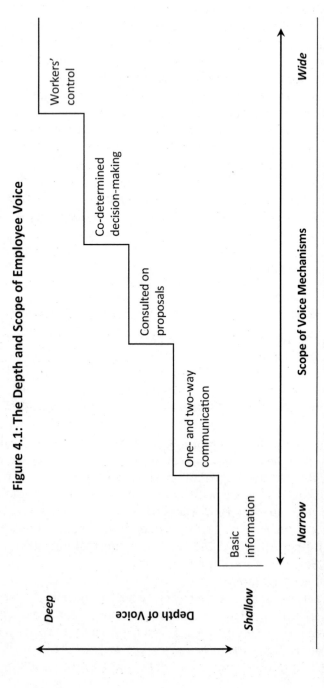

Source: Adapted from Wilkinson and Dundon (2010: 174), based on Marchington and Wilkinson (2005: 401) with permission from Wiley-Blackwell

technology or corporate investment plans. The *level* of employee voice concerns the hierarchical position within the firm at which voice is articulated: ranging from high (such as the company board room) to low (such as team or individual task level on the production floor). Finally, *form* refers to the actual methods used to enable voice and are typically thought of as being either direct or indirect. The former refers to instances where the contact is between individuals or small groups of employees and their immediate manager, whereas in the latter instance that exchange is mediated through an employee representative such as a shop steward who acts as an agent for a larger group of workers. Of course the use of such a framework is not without limitation. For example informal, spontaneous types of voice may not be captured by such a schema (see Box 4.1).

Box 4.1: Sabotage and Informal Employee Voice

In 'Mini Steel', a factory examined by Dundon (2002), it was found that not all forms of voice can be fully captured by the escalator schema in Figure 4.1. Workers at this particular steel plant articulated their voice about their concerns through a rogue employee known as the 'Scarlet Pimpernel', who engaged in guerrilla-style graffiti. The union also adopted innovative tactics to disseminate their message that Mini Steel was an anti-union employer. The company's personnel director was portrayed on 15-foot posters as Arnold Schwarzenegger in his role in *The Terminator*. We should be mindful therefore that some forms of employee voice are not easily explicable in the context of the above theoretical framework.

Source: Dundon (2002).

The Practice of Employee Voice in Ireland

Context: From Union Voice to Non-Union Voice

Historically, the practice of employee voice in an Irish context was characterised by trade-union-based arrangements or, in the terms of the above framework, indirect voice. This was evident by the high levels of union density and the associated reliance on collective bargaining at industry and workplace level. Indeed, collective bargaining remained the principal vehicle for employee voice in Ireland for much of the last century, with employers, workers and unions remaining largely disinterested in other participative forms.

However, in line with international trends elsewhere, a significant decline in union-based voice was experienced from the 1980s onwards. As capital moved production to cheaper locations abroad or reinvested in new lines of commodities, much of the traditional, highly unionised sectors, like manufacturing, declined, typically to the detriment of union voice. Newer industries, like private services and high technology manufacturing, tended to be more union averse. The opportunities and threats engendered by this new context encouraged employers to become steadily antipathetic towards trade union recognition. In Ireland, much of this dynamic was considered with reference to the role of multinationals, particularly those of American origin, as harbingers of a new non-unionism, often making comparisons with Irish employers. Geary and Roche (2001) found that foreign-owned firms were no longer adhering to what they maintained to be the traditional voice norms in Ireland, i.e. favourable to collective bargaining as the single mode of employee voice. Foreign-owned firms, particularly American, were found to place greater emphasis on internally driven HRM practices in providing for voice and much more likely to have single union recognition deals or to simply avoid unions altogether through pre-emptive strategies of union substitution. A corrective to this view however was provided by Turner et al. (1997). Their results indicated no significant difference in the probability of union recognition between US- and Irish-owned firms, pointing to a broader diffusion of a non-union preference amongst indigenous employers and viewing this as paradigmatic of trends within 'globalisation'. Research by Gunnigle et al. (2001) found a trend amongst newer workplaces in Ireland to move away from traditional union voice arrangements to non-unionism. More recently, scholarship has pointed to the practice of double-breasting, where there is the simultaneous use of union voice in one location or company plant, with non-union voice at a different site, or where a previously unionised organisation establishes a new site that it purposely operates with non-union voice arrangements (Cullinane et al., 2012) (see Box 4.2).

Box 4.2: Double-Breasting Voice in Ireland

BritCo is a large, British-owned multinational that employs 3,000 workers across the island of Ireland. In Northern Ireland (NI), BritCo has always recognised trade unions for employee voice, with extensive collective

---

bargaining and over 90 per cent union density among workers. This remains the same today in its NI operations. In the Republic of Ireland (RoI) however, BritCo opted for a non-union voice regime. In short, BritCo has 'double-breasting' voice with union representation in NI and non-union involvement in RoI. The reasons for this dual employee voice approach are complex and varied, although much has to do with opportunistic circumstances rather than rational strategic choice. To begin with, BritCo in RoI is the result of a series of corporate mergers which heralded the arrival of the multinational in Ireland. In this light, the non-union firms acquired had their non-union voice status maintained. This was made easier as there is no statutory union recognition legislation in the RoI that is comparable to union recognition laws in NI. In addition, the minimalist way the Irish government transposed the European Employee Information and Consultation Directive provided the scope to design a non-union employee representative forum along with direct individualised employee voice mechanisms. Indeed, while there was a union organising drive at the company, the use of the company non-union forum, known as *Vocal*, helped managers avoid union recognition. However, when the union threat subsided, employee satisfaction with the non-union side of the double-breasting voice arrangement waned. Management interest in the committee became less and, as a result, employee enthusiasm diminished. The type of issues considered by employees at the *Vocal* forum also reduced in scope to minor rather than the more substantive employment relations concerns.

Source: Cullinane et al. (2012)

The Growth in Direct Forms of Voice

In the absence or decline of union voice, an increase in the use of direct voice methods seems to have emerged. In the mid-1990s, Gunnigle (1995) and Roche and Geary (1996) observed how quality circles, communication schemes and attitude surveys were widely used in foreign-owned firms. This was held to be underpinned by an employer preference for dealing directly with workers rather than through any representative structure. Indeed, Gunnigle (1995) proposed that the use of these direct communications in non-union companies was an attempt on the part of employers to 'individualise' the employment relationship and ensure their union-free status. Williams et al. (2004) also noted a high presence amongst private sector companies of direct involvement arrangements, whilst Gunnigle et al. (2001) and Geary and Roche (2001) pointed towards the increasing use of autonomous work groups, briefing groups, attitude surveys and suggestion schemes, particularly within non-union companies. Consistent with this trend was Dundon et al.'s (2006) finding from a cross-section of firms which found a strong employer preference for direct communication and information channels rather than consultative-type mechanisms.

How do direct methods fare as channels for employee voice? As an instrument of employee voice, direct communications, particularly if of the 'one-way' formula, are often shallow in depth and narrow in scope (see Figure 4.1). Indeed, it is probably inaccurate to label them as a form of voice at all since they do not allow workers to have a say and their growing popularity may have more to do with their usefulness for employers rather than as a genuine form of employee voice. Autonomous work groups are perhaps the most imprecise of direct voice mechanisms. Since many of these groups tend to deal mostly with immediate, work-related matters, they are essentially a method of direct involvement. Moreover, they can be very narrow in scope and shallow in depth, and have little to do with the sharing of power or decision-making in the firm. The same might be said of attitude surveys and suggestion schemes: in Pateman's (1970) terms they represent *pseudo participation*, because they fall short of allowing employees a full voice while at the same time leaving the power structures of a firm untouched. Such criticisms of course do not imply they have no benefit; it is not implausible that they can foster a degree of bottom-up decision-making on particular problems and issues and this could release some of the creative talents of employees that may sponsor a more positive psychological exchange.

The Decline in Indirect Forms of Voice

It might be interpreted that the emergent trend of non-union, direct forms of voice simply reflects the preference of the modern Irish worker. It is not unsurprising that this is an argument some Irish employers are apt to make (Irish Business and Employers' Confederation, 2003). Yet the argument that workers in Ireland are disinclined towards union voice is not particularly convincing. Geary (2007) reported data from over 6,000 Irish employees which found that in non-union workplaces, the willingness amongst non-union workers to join a union was highly robust, and was especially marked in situations where employers offered their support for union voice. In such circumstances, almost two-thirds of respondents (64 per cent) indicated they would join a union if asked. However, this figure dropped substantially to 28 per cent in situations where the employer was not prepared to support a union role for employee voice. Overall, Geary's (2007) analysis highlighted a significant voice gap in Irish workplaces, with many employers establishing new operations that are at best indifferent, and at worst hostile, to union forms of voice. In such circumstances, many employees do not feel secure in seeking union representation and many can fear managerial power.

Further evidence of this dynamic is apparent in the work of D'Art and Turner (2005), where a study of union officials' experiences of organising non-union workplaces uncovered a number of typical employer actions. The majority of reported employer responses were claimed to be actively hostile to union organising. More than half were claimed to have resisted initial union approaches for recognition by denying officials access to the workplace or claimed to have actively discouraged workers opting for union membership. Employers in these instances were also claimed to frequently brief workers against unions, victimise union activists and hire union-avoidance consultants. Also, in the aftermath of a recognition campaign, union officials reported that many employers moved to discourage further attempts at unionising by establishing either a union substitute, such as an in-house participation scheme, or by improving pay and conditions to minimise worker concerns. Employers were also reported to adopt more coercive approaches, either by threatening closure or by acting illegally and sacking union activists.

Whilst legislation was developed to enable unionised workers in non-union workplaces to exercise voice over the terms and conditions of their employment in the form of the Industrial Relations (Amendment) Act 2001 and Industrial Relations (Miscellaneous Provisions) Act 2004, its effectiveness has been hamstrung by employer resistance and problematic legislative loopholes (O'Sullivan and Gunnigle, 2009). As such, it is not so surprising that some employers exhibit such distaste for union forms of voice. Of all the voice mechanisms discussed, union voice, through collective bargaining, is most likely to be the most extensive form in terms of depth, scope and level. It offers employees a degree of independence and power not found with other voice forms. Thus, it is with some validity that it has been argued to be an extremely practical form of democracy applied to the workplace (Clegg, 1974).

Opportunities for Indirect Voice?

Despite the collapse of national-level partnership in Ireland, as noted earlier, the practice of workplace partnership might offer a new platform for indirect employee voice under the agenda of 'mutual gains'. However, the scope of formal workplace partnership seems rather disappointing given recent Irish evidence. In surveys for the National Centre for Partnership and Performance (NCPP), only 16 per cent of private sector employers reported the presence of 'formal partnership committees' in 2009, with 34 per cent saying they have some 'informal' partnership arrangement at enterprise level. Meanwhile, with regard to the NCPP employee survey conducted in 2009, just over 21 per cent of all employees reported the presence of formal partnership institutions at their workplaces. Such partnership committees were much more common in the public sector, where over 40 per cent of employees reported their presence, than in the private sector, where only 16 per cent report their presence. The findings show that employees are more likely to be involved in formal partnership committees in large organisations, with such practices much more common within the public sector. Employees are least likely to be involved in partnership committees in hotels and restaurants, financial and other business activities, construction, and small firms. Overall, only about 4 per cent of all employees are personally involved in such forms of employee representation (O'Connell et al., 2010). (See Box 4.3 for a study of formal partnership representation.)

Box 4.3: Employee Disillusionment with Enterprise Partnership

Manufacturing Inc has always had a healthy union–management relationship. It is a company that has grown over the Celtic Tiger years, now employing around 1,600 people. There is strong union membership and the two unions that represent workers – the Services, Industrial, Professional and Technical Union (SIPTU) and the Technical, Engineering and Electrical Union (TEEU) – have always had access to senior managers when bargaining over employee issues. The company decided to follow the policy wishes of the Irish state by seeking to replicate national partnership at the workplace level. Several new staff forums and employee focus groups were created, along with a partnership committee. However, when the company wanted to alter the terms of the pension scheme, workers felt the new deal was significantly inferior to what had previously been negotiated. When employees wanted to complain, they felt the issue had been closed off to

---

them as managers initially suggested the pension scheme was not appropriate for the partnership agenda. In response the workers insisted that the union take a stand. After threats of strike action and numerous unsatisfactory discussions with management, the issue was eventually referred to the Labour Court. It was not long before the workers at Manufacturing Inc became very disillusioned with the idea of an integrative partnership voice system. Manufacturing Inc demonstrates that, even with partnership, there are inevitably some issues that are conflictual in the employment relationship that a new partnership approach may not be capable of resolving. The union continues to represent workers' interests through adversarial collective bargaining, and management seems happy for things to remain that way.

Source: Rittau and Dundon (2010)

Given the decline in union membership, the limited diffusion of enterprise partnership arrangements and the collapse of national-level social pact agreements, it might be argued that representative voice is no longer dependent on trade unions. Indeed, it can be mooted that indirect voice exists in other situations that do not involve unions, for instance in European Works Councils (EWCs) and non-union company committees. There is a tendency to view representative non-union voice as shallow and ineffective, without fully evaluating the scope, level and depth of such voice mechanisms. However, the evidence is nonetheless usually disappointing. One study of a non-union employee representation scheme in Ireland (Donaghey et al., 2012) concluded that such structures are likely to be ineffectual unless supported by legislation; left to their own devices many employers introduce weak forms of employee voice, of which workers in turn may be sceptical. This chimes with international evidence, which finds, on balance, that the depth and scope of non-union representative voice is at best variable, and at worst little more than a form of indirect employee involvement (Butler, 2005).

European Influences on Employee Voice

Whilst mention was made of legislation relating to union voice, there is also a raft of European directives affecting Irish legislation about employee voice, such as collective redundancy laws, transfer of undertakings, European Works Council requirements in large European Union (EU) multi-site firms, and employee information and consultation rights and obligations. Although it is beyond the scope of this chapter to detail every European development in relation to employee voice, one possible development worth acknowledging is the Employees (Provision of Information and Consultation) Act 2006. This legislation arose from European Directive EC/14/2002, which required member states of the EU to establish a permanent and statutory framework for employees to receive information and to be consulted on matters affecting them at work. Formally, the implications of the framework had potentially far-reaching consequences when first announced, as Ireland had no existing statutory framework for employee voice. The directive thus provided Irish workers with a legal right to be informed and consulted on business and employment matters. The scope, depth and level of required voice is potentially extensive arising from the legislation, detailing three specific areas in which managers can be obliged to consult workers: the economic situation of the firm; the structure and probable development of employment; and decisions likely to lead to changes in work organisation or contractual relations.

However, the requirement for an employer to inform and consult does not happen automatically and there is a trigger mechanism for these legal rights to be enacted, either through a formal request by at least 100 employees in the firm (or 10 per cent of the workforce), or by an employer notification to start the process and negotiate a new information and consultation agreement. Nor is the legal right a universal one, as it can only be triggered by workers who are employed in firms with 50 or more employees. In other words, those employed in very small or micro firms are excluded. A further problem with these employee voice regulations is the disjuncture between Directive EC/14/2002, which states that the form in which information and consultation takes place should be of an indirect nature by specifying the existence of employee 'representatives', and the Irish legislation which allows for direct 'individualised' voice methods. In other words, communication memos, quality circles or team-based voice mechanisms could be used to serve as an information and consultation (I&C) forum when the European intention was clearly to support mechanisms for deeper collective-type consultation.

The extent of the change arising from the European directive in Ireland has not been as far-reaching as might have been anticipated had the legislation provided for automatic and universal rights for employee voice. It appears that many employers have been ideologically opposed to collective and stronger forms of legal voice. Given that groups of workers have to trigger the rights contained in the Act, and that the law also provides substantial scope for direct methods of information and consultation, a continuation of what is already happening in the employment relations sphere in Ireland can more or less be expected. Meanwhile, unions in Ireland have been unsure whether to view I&C bodies as an opportunity or a threat to the existing channel of union representation through collective bargaining, a factor exacerbated by their disenchantment with the current legislation and what they see as its minimalist nature.

Conclusion

As argued at the start of this chapter, 'employee voice' is an enduring feature of work and employment relationships. Nonetheless, how voice is interpreted can oscillate over time between variants of voice as 'participation' and voice as 'involvement'. These different variants can further impact the scope, depth, level and form of voice in actual practice. The evolution of employee voice in an Irish context was considered and shown to be punctuated by a historical shift away from indirect, union forms of voice to a more pronounced pattern of direct, non-union forms. Much of the research evidence has examined multinational behaviour as innovators in this regard, although there is clearly a predilection amongst Irish employers to follow a similar trajectory. Employer resistance to robust forms of employee voice appears to lie at the very heart of the debate on voice in the Irish context. Indeed, the developments that we have seen in this field appear to have been conducive to creating a 'voice gap' in Irish workplaces. Notably, attempts to re-pattern the process of voice dynamics in Ireland, whether in the form of workplace partnership or through European-inspired directives, have had a rather tepid, if not negligible, impact. Furthermore, national-level partnership collapsed in 2009 amidst global economic pressures. This has had practical implications for the exercise of employee voice, at least in unionised environments: with the end of national partnership deals, local bargaining has become more important. Unions at workplace level have had to respond to this dynamic and revitalise their structures for members' voice (Millar, 2012). The success of unions in regenerating local level voice structures and any attendant implications for employers would seem a pertinent issue for further research investigation. Ultimately, the future of Irish employee voice will remain an arena of contention and controversy. This should not be unexpected, for as long as the indeterminate relations between workers and their employers continue to prevail, then the processes and methods for employee voice will remain an area fraught with tension.

References

Ackers, P. and Payne, J. (1998), 'British Trade Unions and Social Partnership: Rhetoric, Reality and Strategy', *International Journal of Human Resource Management*, 9(3): 529–550.

Archer, R. (2010), 'Freedom, Democracy and Capitalism: Ethics and Employee Participation' in A. Wilkinson, P.J. Gollan, M. Marchington and D. Lewin (eds), *The Oxford Handbook of Participation in Organizations*, Oxford: Oxford University Press, 590–608.

Baldamus, W. (1961), *Efficiency and Effort: An Analysis of Industrial Administration*, London: Tavistock Press.

Butler, P. (2005), 'Non-Union Employee Representation: Exploring the Efficacy of the Voice Process', *Employee Relations*, 27(3): 272–288.

Clegg, H.A. (1974), 'Trade Unions as Opposition which can Never Become a Government' in W.E. McCarthy (ed.), *Trade Unions*, Harmondsworth: Penguin, 142–170.

Cohen, G.A. (1988), *History, Labour and Freedom*, Oxford: Oxford University Press.

Cullinane, N., Donaghey, J., Dundon, T. and Dobbins, T. (2012), 'Different Rooms, Different Voices: Double-Breasting, Multichannel Representation and the Managerial Agenda', *International Journal of Human Resource Management*, 23(2): 368–384.

D'Art, D. and Turner, T. (2005), 'Union Recognition and Partnership at Work: A New Legitimacy for Irish Trade Unions', *Industrial Relations Journal*, 36(2): 121–139.

Davis, L.E. (1971), 'The Coming Crisis for Production Management: Technology and Organization', *International Journal of Production Research*, 9(1): 65–82.

Dobbins, T. and Gunnigle, P. (2009), 'Can Voluntary Workplace Partnership Deliver Sustainable Gains?', *British Journal of Industrial Relations*, 47(3): 546–570.

Donaghey, J., Cullinane, N., Dundon, T. and Dobbins, A. (2012), 'Non-Union Employee Representation, Union Avoidance and the Managerial Agenda', *Economic and Industrial Democracy*, 33(2): 163–183.

Dundon, T. (2002), 'Employer Opposition and Union Avoidance in the UK', *Industrial Relations Journal*, 33(3): 234–245.

Dundon, T., Curran, D., Ryan, P. and Maloney, M. (2006), 'Conceptualising the Dynamics of Employee Information and Consultation: Evidence from the Republic of Ireland', *Industrial Relations Journal*, 37(5): 492–512.

Geary, J. (2007), 'Employee Voice in the Irish Workplace: Status and Prospect' in R.B. Freeman, P. Boxall and P. Hayes (eds), *What Workers Say: Employee Voice in the Anglo-American World*, Ithaca, NY: Cornell University Press, 97–124.

Geary, J. and Roche, W.K. (2001), 'Multinationals and Human Resource Practices in Ireland: A Rejection of the 'New Conformance Thesis', *International Journal of Human Resource Management*, 12(1): 109–127.

Geoghegan, V. (1991), 'Ralahine: An Irish Owenite Community, 1831–1833', *International Review of Social History*, 36(3): 377–411.

Gunnigle, P. (1995), 'Collectivism and the Management of Industrial Relations in Greenfield Sites', *Human Resource Management Journal*, 5(3): 24–40.

Gunnigle, P., MacCurtain, S. and Morley, M.J. (2001), 'Dismantling Pluralism: Industrial Relations in Irish Greenfield Sites', *Personnel Review*, 30(3): 263–279.

Harvey, D. (2011), *The Enigma of Capital and the Crisis of Capitalism*, London: Profile Books.

Irish Business and Employers' Confederation (2003), 'New Approach Needed to Framing Employment Legislation', Press release, 11 July, Dublin: IBEC.

Marchington, M. and Wilkinson, A. (2005), 'Direct Participation and Involvement' in S. Bach (ed.), *Managing Human Resources: Personnel Management in Transition*, Oxford: Wiley-Blackwell, 398–423.

Marglin, S. (1974), 'What Do Bosses Do? The Origin and Functions of Hierarchy in Capitalist Production', *Review of Radical Political Economics*, 6(2): 60–112.

Millar, S. (2012), 'Sticking Together!', *Liberty*, 11(1): 9.

O'Connell, P.J., Russell, H., Watson, D. and Byrne, D. (2010), *The Changing Workplace: A Survey of Employees' Views and Experiences*, Dublin: National Centre for Partnership and Performance.

O'Sullivan, M. and Gunnigle, P. (2009), 'Bearing All the Hallmarks of Oppression: Union Avoidance in Europe's Largest Low-Cost Airline', *Labor Studies Journal*, 34(2): 252–270.

Pateman, C. (1970), *Participation and Democratic Theory*, Cambridge: Cambridge University Press.

Pollard, S. (1963), 'Factory Discipline in the Industrial Revolution', *Economic History Review*, 16(2): 254–271.

Rittau, Y. and Dundon, T. (2010), 'The Roles and Functions of Shop Stewards in Workplace Partnership: Evidence from the Republic of Ireland', *Employee Relations*, 32(1): 10–27.

Roche, W.K. and Geary, J. (1996), 'Multinational Companies in Ireland: Adapting to or Diverging from National Industrial Relations Practices and Traditions', *Irish Business and Administrative Review*, 17(1): 14–31.

Sorge, A. (1976), 'The Evolution of Industrial Democracy in the Countries of the European Community', *British Journal of Industrial Relations*, 14(3): 274–294.

Thompson, P. (2011), 'The Trouble with HRM', *Human Resource Management Journal*, 21(4): 355–367.

Turner, T., D'Art, D. and Gunnigle, P. (1997), 'Pluralism in Retreat: A Comparison of Irish and Multinational Manufacturing Companies', *International Journal of Human Resource Management*, 8(6): 825–840.

Wilkinson, A. and Dundon, T. (2010), 'Direct Participation' in A. Wilkinson, P.J. Gollan, M. Marchington and D. Lewin (eds), *The Oxford Handbook of Participation in Organizations*, Oxford: Oxford University Press, 167–185.

Williams, J., Blackwell, S., Gorby, S., O'Connell, P. and Russell, H. (2004), *The Changing Workplace: A Survey of Employers' Views and Experiences*, Dublin: National Centre for Partnership and Performance.

CHAPTER 5

Pay and Performance Management in Multinational Companies in Ireland

Patrick Gunnigle, Thomas Turner, Jonathan Lavelle and Anthony McDonnell[1]

Introduction

Pay and performance management represents a central tenet of organisational approaches to human resource management (HRM). Indeed, the idea that pay and performance management policy and practice strategically impact on organisational performance emerges as a major and often controversial theme in the strategic management and HRM literatures, particularly since the 1980s (Lawler, 2003; Armstrong, 2012). The normative proposition underpinning much of this work is that matching business strategy with pay and performance management policy improves organisational performance and competitiveness.

This chapter considers management practice with regard to pay and performance management in multinational companies (MNCs) in Ireland, focusing particularly on variation in the types of practices employed. Arguably, the strategic significance accorded to pay and performance management considerations is likely to be most evident among MNCs, many of whom compete in a highly competitive international business environment. The Irish economy is particularly reliant on its cohort of MNCs, many of which are US owned, and MNCs are often regarded as pay leaders in their respective industrial sectors (Central Statistics Office, 2008) and have traditionally been seen as innovators in human resource (HR) practice, notably in the use of performance-related pay (PRP) systems and performance appraisal (Mooney, 1989; Gunnigle et al., 1998). This chapter builds on previous Irish research in this area (Kelly and Monks, 1997; Heffernan et al., 2008; Roche, 1999).

We begin by reviewing some of the relevant literature. We then present and analyse empirical data on pay and performance management practices in MNCs in Ireland. Here we consider the main factors impacting on variation in reward systems across MNCs, especially differences related to ownership, sector and size. Finally, we summarily outline the main findings and implications of our work.

Pay and Performance Management: Theory and Practice

Organisational reward systems generally comprise two basic components, namely pay and benefits. Pay refers to the wage or salary that employees receive, and as Grace and Coughlan (1998: 205) observe, it '... remains the common currency of exchange at work'. Benefits encompass indirect financial rewards (e.g. pensions) and other types of rewards such as holiday entitlements and illness benefits. In the following analysis we concentrate on three specific theoretical debates, namely (i) strategic HRM and its implications for pay and performance management, (ii) contingent versus flat-rate pay systems and (iii) industrial relations dimensions of pay and performance, notably the influence of trade unions.

Strategic HRM and Pay and Performance Management

At the core of the concept of strategic HRM is the premise that organisations should better align HRM with overall business strategy as this will yield a premium in terms of enhanced organisational performance (Beer et al., 1984; Fombrun et al., 1984; Huselid, 1995; Guest, 1987). Since pay and performance management systems represent a central aspect of HRM, achieving greater 'fit' with business strategy is viewed as an important means through which organisations can more strategically manage compensation and realise a performance premium through, for example, higher levels of worker motivation or increased productivity (Milkovich et al., 2013). This strategic perspective is also based on the fact that organisations differ in their approach to pay and performance management, notably in the extent to which pay and benefits are used to attract and retain employees, and also to influence employee behaviour and performance 'on the job'. The so-called high commitment HR model (often labelled 'high performance work systems') places a strong emphasis on linking rewards to employee performance, while also focusing on providing various other rewards to employees, such as tenure commitments, share ownership and profit-sharing schemes, in return for high levels of job performance (Pfeffer, 1994; MacDuffie, 1995).

Performance management is normally seen as a strategic management process which seeks to ensure that employees focus on explicit goals or targets which are directly and explicitly linked to organisational goals (Sparrow and Hiltrop, 1994). It is a process which has evolved from Drucker's (1954) 'management by objectives' (MBO) and emphasises the need for workers to focus on achieving performance targets (results). It thus requires the establishment of explicit job targets which, in turn, are related to development objectives to ensure employees have the requisite knowledge and skills to achieve their targets. Normative models of performance management generally outline a step-by-step approach premised on the idea that performance targets for employees are directed and driven by corporate objectives (McDonnell and Gunnigle, 2009) which are in turn translated into team/sectional targets and ultimately to individual job targets (see Figure 5.1).

As Figure 5.1 indicates, setting targets and evaluating employee performance are viewed as integral components of a performance management system. Performance appraisal is seen as a central pillar in the evaluation process, representing a formal systematic process for evaluating employee performance which, in turn, informs decisions on pay, promotion, training and development. It normally involves a formal annual review of individual employee performance conducted by line managers. However, considerable variation can occur in both the frequency of appraisals and in those responsible for the conduct of appraisal (e.g. other higher-level managers may be involved, while 360 degree appraisals, possibly involving peers or 'customers', may also be used).

Figure 5.1: The Performance Management Loop

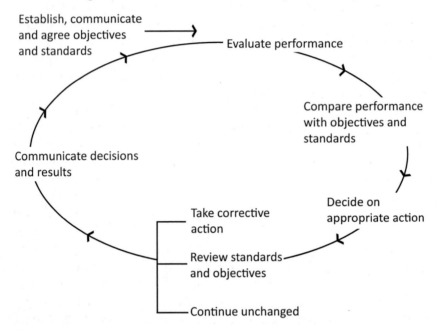

Source: Gunnigle, Heraty and Morley, *Human Resources in Ireland* (Dublin: Gill & Macmillan, 2011), p. 190. Reproduced with permission.

Related and important aspects of pay and performance management are external competitiveness and the need for external pay equity. External competitiveness, or the pay levels offered relative to those of competitors, is an important influence on the organisation's capacity to attract and retain labour. Firms normally seek to maintain pay competiveness through establishing intelligence on pay norms and movement (e.g. pay surveys), the economic climate, state of the labour market (e.g. over or under supply of labour) and pressure from trade unions.

Contingent/Performance-Related Pay

Organisations are also concerned about the need to establish and maintain internal pay equity. This involves two dimensions. First is the creation of differential pay rates for various jobs within the firm to reflect variation in job demands and content. This goal is commonly pursued through analyses of job content and generally leads to the creation of some form of grade hierarchy (see Armstrong and

Stephens, 2005; Gunnigle et al., 2011; Armstrong, 2012). The second dimension relates to the choice of payment system. Clearly the range of options here is substantial yet ultimately a fundamental factor is whether the level of pay received by employees is contingent upon, or independent of, employee performance (Lawler, 2003; Armstrong and Stephens, 2005). The amount of pay employees receive may be based on a 'flat rate' (e.g. a fixed hourly, weekly or annual rate) and is therefore independent of job performance, meaning that all workers in a particular grade or category receive similar pay regardless of variations in the levels of individual performance. Alternatively, many organisations use contingent pay, where the payment varies based on some measure of employee performance.

Performance-related pay (PRP) broadly describes systems which aim to pay more for high levels of job performance than for average performance (cf. McBeath and Rands, 1989). Though generally viewed as an integral element in strategic HRM, PRP has numerous critics (McDonnell and Gunnigle, 2009). For example, Kessler and Purcell (1992) argue that the deployment of PRP involves a fundamental restructuring of the employment relationship, which often results in greater managerial control over workers and work systems. However, support for PRP is predicated on the idea that it is fair and logical to reward employees differentially, based on some measure, or combination of measures, of performance (Armstrong and Stephens, 2005: 233). For example, Bowey and Thorpe (1986) point to the correlation between individual performance and incentive payments leading to improvement in costs and quality, while also noting its potentially adverse effects on attitudes to work and industrial relations. Indeed, the major source of concerns about PRP lies not in the principle but rather in its operationalization. These problems include the limited criteria used to measure performance (e.g. work-study), inconsistencies in performance measurement techniques (e.g. performance appraisal), and bias and inequity in evaluating employee performance. This means contingent pay systems may not necessarily deliver higher levels of motivation and performance.

Despite these reservations, merit/incentive pay systems often comprise part of the remuneration packages in the private sector in Ireland (Watson et al., 2010). Previous Irish-based research identifies increased utilisation of PRP systems through the 1990s, particularly among US-owned MNCs (Morley and Gunnigle, 1997). However, pay and performance management has been identified as a domain where Irish organisations have fared rather poorly in regard to the implementation of sophisticated practices (Roche, 1999; Heffernan et al., 2008). Traditionally, PRP systems have been more commonly used among managerial and professional categories (cf. Heffernan et al., 2008).

A related but important issue is the industrial relations problems that may arise from employee resentment towards the exercise of managerial control via more intense performance measurement and more generally to the greater individualisation of the employment relationship as a result of unilateral determination of pay increases by management (Ferner and Almond, 2013).

Industrial Relations Considerations

Collective bargaining has traditionally been the primary means of determining pay increases in Ireland (Wallace et al., 2013). Despite growing union avoidance, especially in the MNC sector, it remains a key institution with regard to the determination of pay and working conditions. Negotiations between worker and employer representatives over pay and conditions of employment tend to be 'distributive' in nature, characterised by a sequence of claims, offers, bluff, threats, compromise, movement, agreement or conflict where invariably a favourable settlement for one party means an element of loss for the other (Walton and McKersie, 1965; Gunnigle et al., 2011). While this adversarial approach has its critics, a crucial benefit is that it allows workers, through trade unions, the opportunity to actively engage with employers on pay and related matters, while also redressing the disparity in bargaining power that generally exists between employers and individual employees. It also means that decisions on pay increases achieved through collective bargaining generally apply 'across the board' to all relevant employee categories.

In contrast, many forms of PRP decisions, especially those based on reviews (appraisals) of individual employee performance conducted by higher-level managers (only), mean that worker input into pay decisions is greatly reduced and collective voice often absent (Gunnigle et al., 1998). Moreover, the pay received will vary between individual employees as opposed to collective bargaining where a standard increase applies equally to all relevant employee categories. Yet PRP systems may also be subject to joint regulation through collective bargaining (Heery, 1997; Roche and Turner, 1994). Indeed, traditional forms of PRP (e.g. measured day work – see Kessler, 1998) were based on quantitative evaluations of employee performance and normally the subject of collective bargaining. However evidence to date suggests that PRP systems linked to appraisals of individual employee performance are much more common in non-union firms, with unionised firms far less likely to use PRP based on appraisals (Gunnigle et al., 1998). The influence of MNCs, particularly US-owned MNCs, represents an important factor in accounting for the increased incidence of PRP. The available evidence points to variation in the application of PRP between employee categories and also according to ownership and trade union presence (cf. Almond, 2006; Heery, 1997). With regard to the former, it seems that PRP linked to performance appraisal is more common among managerial and other higher-level employees (Lepak and Snell, 1999). The reasons here seem fairly straightforward. First, there are smaller numbers so the process of conducting appraisals is confined in terms of scale. Second, the impact of senior-level employees on organisation performance is arguably greater and therefore it makes logical sense to more closely monitor their performance and to reward better performers differentially. Finally, managerial and related categories are less likely to be unionised and thus opposition, if any, to PRP regimes will be more muted. In contrast, we find a lower incidence of PRP-based formal performance appraisals of individual employee performance among non-managerial/professional/related categories. The reasons here may relate to scale since undertaking individual performance reviews among the largest occupational groups in an organisation represents a major logistical undertaking requiring extensive managerial resources. As these categories are also more likely to be unionised the introduction of PRP systems based on performance appraisals of individual workers may well encounter trade union opposition.

HRM Practices in MNCs: Research Challenges

This section examines pay and performance management practices using data from a highly representative large-scale survey of MNCs in Ireland (for details see McDonnell et al., 2007; Lavelle et al., 2009).[2] The fieldwork involved the completion of structured face-to-face interviews with the most senior HR director or manager able to answer for all of the Irish operations. A total of 260 interviews were completed, giving a response rate of 63 per cent. The survey sought information on HR practice as it related to three specific groups of employees, namely the 'largest occupational group' (LOG) among the employees in the 'headcount' in Ireland', 'managers' and the 'key group', i.e. employees identified as critical to a firm's organisational learning and core competence.

Pay Levels Relative to Market Comparators

We first address company strategy with respect to basic pay levels, specifically whether MNCs in Ireland sought to pay above, at or below the market average for their sector. As Table 5.1 indicates, responses were categorised into positioning pay levels in either the top quartile, second quartile, at the median/midpoint or below the median/midpoint, for the three groups of employees outlined above.

Table 5.1: Pay Levels Relative to Market Comparators

	Largest Occupational Group (LOG)	Managers	Key Group
Top quartile	18% (45)	23% (56)	31% (39)
Second quartile	21% (51)	29% (71)	29% (37)
Median/midpoint	60% (146)	48% (119)	40% (51)
Below the median/midpoint	1% (3)	0%	0%

The majority of MNCs (60 per cent) aim to set pay levels for the LOG at the average for the sector, though pay levels above the average were evident among a substantial proportion of MNCs in Ireland (39 per cent). However, managers and the key group were far more likely to be paid above the market average when compared to the LOG. Almost one-third of MNCs that recognised a key group of employees aimed to set their pay levels in the top quartile. Arguably, this reflects a managerial perspective which sees such key groups as playing a more important role in contributing to organisational performance when compared to the LOG. It may equally reflect greater labour market difficulties in recruiting employees in this category and the consequent need to offer higher levels of pay. A similar trend is evident for managers. Just over half of the MNCs (52 per cent) aimed to set managerial pay above the market average.

Turning to factors impacting on the setting of pay levels, we initially find evidence of differences between foreign- and Irish-owned MNCs. In regard to the LOG, a greater proportion of Irish-owned MNCs (68 per cent) aim to set pay levels at the market average (median/midpoint). Consequently, a smaller proportion of Irish MNCs (32 per cent) aimed to set pay levels for the LOG above the median/midpoint. However, this pattern changes when we look at pay levels for managers and the key group. Some 55 per cent of Irish MNCs aimed for pay levels above the market average for managers compared to 50 per cent of foreign-owned MNCs. For the key group of employees, 65 per cent of Irish MNCs aimed to set pay levels above the median/midpoint whereas the equivalent figure among foreign-owned MNCs was 59 per cent. Overall, we find that very few MNCs aimed for pay levels below the market average across all three employment categories (see Table 5.2)

Table 5.2: Pay Levels in MNCs by Country of Ownership

Employment Category	Country of Ownership				
	UK	US	Rest of Europe	Ireland	Rest of World
Pay above the midpoint for LOG	56%	37%	44%	32%	14%
Pay above the midpoint for managers	65%	43%	59%	55%	36%
Pay above the midpoint for key group	75%	52%	61%	65%	57%

Finally we considered the impact of sector on pay levels (see Table 5.3). Here we find a pattern whereby MNCs in the services sector were more likely to aim for pay levels above the market average across all three employment categories.

Table 5.3: Pay Levels in MNCs by Industry/Sector

Employment Category	Manufacturing	Services	Multi-Sector
Pay above the midpoint for LOG	35%	43%	30%
Pay above the midpoint for managers	45%	59%	35%
Pay above the midpoint for key group	59%	64%	36%

Contingent Pay

As noted earlier, the extent to which pay is contingent upon, or independent of, employee performance varies considerably between organisations. Our findings demonstrate that PRP enjoys a high level of utilisation among all employee categories in MNCs but is most prominent among managers and the 'key group'. Coverage levels among managers were particularly high, averaging over 90 per cent. The take up of PRP was greatest in US-owned MNCs, although utilisation levels were quite high across MNCs of varying national origin as shown in Table 5.4. We found no great differences in the use of PRP by sector.

Table 5.4: PRP Coverage by Country of Origin

Employment Category	Country of Ownership				
	UK	*US*	*Rest of Europe*	*Ireland*	*Rest of World*
LOG	63%	70%	67%	60%	79%
Managers	91%	91%	92%	87%	100%
Key group	71%	88%	89%	83%	100%

Performance Management and Performance Appraisal

The incidence of formal periodic performance appraisals among two categories of staff (LOG and managers) in MNCs in Ireland by country of origin is outlined in Table 5.5. As expected, utilisation levels are much higher for managerial groupings than for the LOG. This is related to a number of factors, particularly the 'weight of numbers', as noted earlier. Generally speaking, firms will employ far smaller numbers of managers than most other categories of employees and therefore the burden of conducting regular formal appraisals among a comparatively small group of managers is less onerous. In addition, trade union membership tends to be much higher among lower occupational groupings and unions have traditionally harboured concerns about performance appraisals (especially linked to variable pay decisions). We also find a lower take-up of formal performance appraisal among Irish than among foreign MNCs, particularly for the LOG. This may in part be explained by the higher levels of union recognition among Irish MNCs. US-owned MNCs report the highest level of utilisation of formal appraisals. Overall, our data show a high level of utilisation of formal appraisal schemes: 94 per cent of foreign-owned MNCs report the use of formal appraisal among managerial staff and 75 per cent among the LOG. This compares to a level of 87 per cent of managers and 60 per cent of the LOG in Irish-owned companies.

Table 5.5: Performance Appraisal Coverage by Country of Origin

Employment Category	Country of Ownership				
	UK	US	Rest of Europe	Ireland	Rest of World
LOG	71%	82%	65%	60%	79%
Managers	91%	97%	90%	87%	93%

Conventional performance appraisals normally involve line managers reviewing the performance and development needs of subordinates. Table 5.6 reports the use of two differentiated schemes of performance appraisal, namely 'forced distribution' and '360 degree/peer appraisal'. A forced distribution scheme requires appraisers to place a fixed proportion of appraisees in different performance categories or grades in order to avoid 'bunching' into 'average' or higher-performance categories (see McDonnell and Gunnigle, 2009). In 360 degree or multi-rater appraisal schemes feedback on employee performance is gathered through collating perceptions of employee performance from sources such as sub-ordinates/direct reports, peers/colleagues and supervisors. Thus 360 degree (or peer appraisal) is novel in so far as it utilises the perspectives of numerous stakeholders (Nowack, 1993; Toegel and Conger, 2003; Latham et al., 2005) rather than relying solely on line managers. Table 5.6 summarises the diffusion of both forced dis-tribution and 360 degree appraisal in MNCs in Ireland. We find substantial variation between foreign and Irish MNCs, with both these formats of appraisal more common among foreign MNCs. In foreign-owned MNCs, 28 per cent used forced distribution for the LOG and 25 per cent used 360 degree appraisal for this group. In contrast, just 8 per cent of Irish MNCs used forced distribution and 23 per cent used 360 degree appraisal for the LOG. With regard to managerial categories we find a broadly similar picture with foreign MNCs using both methods far more extensively than their Irish-owned counterparts. Forced distribution and 360 degree appraisal are more commonly used by US-owned MNCs than those of other national origin.

Table 5.6: Methods of Performance Appraisal by Country of Origin

Performance Appraisal Method	Country of Ownership				
	UK	US	Rest of Europe	Ireland	Rest of World
LOG – forced distribution	9%	41%	15%	8%	27%
LOG – 360 degree appraisal	20%	28%	16%	23%	60%
Managers– forced distribution	16%	44%	14%	13%	33%
Managers – 360 degree appraisal	53%	61%	40%	8%	42%

Profit Sharing and Employee Share Options

'Profit sharing' is a generic term embracing systems through which a portion of company profits are distributed to employees via an additional variable payment linked to profitability or some other measure of company performance. Profit sharing can take a variety of forms and can be paid in cash, shares or via designated employee funds (Poutsma, 2001; Lavelle et al., 2012). Share option schemes represent a particular form of profit sharing whereby employees have an option to buy company shares under favourable terms. Since the early 1980s, profit sharing in general and employee share ownership schemes in particular have become more common-place in Ireland, with particularly strong growth in the incidence of such schemes during the 1990s (D'Art and Turner, 2006). This was largely driven by legislative provision (notably the Finance Acts 1982, 1984, 1986), which incentivised the use of such schemes via the taxation system, though more recent legislative changes combined with the severe economic downturn is likely to have severely dampened the appetites of both employers and workers for such schemes.

The overall incidence of profit sharing and share ownership in Ireland remains low. In 1996 the Employee Direct Participation in Organisational Change survey found that just 8 per cent and 4 per cent of Irish workplaces reported the presence of profit sharing and share ownership respectively (Sisson, 1996). The more recent European Company Survey conducted in 2009 reported that 11 per cent of private sector Irish companies had a profit-sharing scheme, a figure slightly below the European average of 14 per cent, though the incidence of such schemes rose in line with company size (European Foundation for the Improvement of Living and Working Conditions, 2010). Generally speaking, the specific tax legislation and related regulations in place at any point in time strongly influence the incidence of employee share options.

Our survey examined the incidence of three specific types of schemes in MNCs operating in Ireland:

- Approved employee share ownership schemes (whereby the organisation establishes a trust which acquires shares on behalf of employees)
- Profit sharing
- Share options

As outlined in Table 5.7, our overall findings indicate that approximately one-third of MNCs use share ownership and profit sharing, while the use of share options is higher among the key group and managers.

Table 5.7: Share Ownership, Profit Sharing and Share Options in MNCs in Ireland

	Employee Share Ownership	Profit Sharing	Share Options
LOG	30%	27%	24%
Managers	32%	34%	49%
Key group	35%	35%	40%

The incidence of these various schemes by ownership is outlined in Table 5.8. This shows that such schemes are most commonly found among US MNCs, particularly when it comes to employee share ownership, a finding which finds resonance in previous Irish and international research (Morley and Gunnigle, 1997; Björkman and Furu, 2000). It seems that MNCs, particularly US MNCs, have traditionally sought to apply a form of so-called 'shareholder capitalism' to increase employee identity and commitment to the firm through profit sharing and share ownership schemes (Dore et al., 1999). At a broader level, deregulation of financial and capital markets from the 1980s and the increased credence attributed to the concept of 'shareholder value' further boosted the deployment of profit sharing and share options as a means of linking the rewards of managers in particular to company fortunes (O'Sullivan, 2000). The onset of the current global financial crisis and particularly the banking crisis has now severely curbed this tendency and forced a review of the structures and characteristics of executive remuneration practices, involving greater analysis of the extent to which executive pay is correlated to performance (Bebchuk and Fried, 2006).

Table 5.8: Financial Schemes for Employees by Country of Origin

	Country of Origin				
	UK	US	Rest of Europe	Ireland	Rest of World
LOG					
Employee share ownership scheme	29%	40%	17%	30%	7%
Profit sharing	33%	31%	21%	26%	8%
Share options	25%	27%	23%	14%	33%
Key group					
Employee share ownership scheme	25%	50%	22%	33%	17%
Profit sharing	31%	42%	26%	41%	14%
Share options	31%	45%	35%	35%	67%
Managers					
Employee share ownership scheme	32%	44%	16%	35%	8%
Profit sharing	50%	34%	28%	34%	25%
Share options	36%	66%	29%	44%	64%

Table 5.9: Determinants of Pay and Performance Management Practices in MNCs

	Variable Pay for LOG	Variable Pay for Managers	Appraisal for LOG	Appraisal for Managers	Pay Policy for LOG	Pay Policy for Managers	Forced Distribution for LOG	Forced Distribution for Managers	Peer/360 for LOG	Peer/360 for Managers
Manufacturing										
Services	1.049	2.247	4.372***	-0.940	1.759*	2.076**	2.496**	1.472	2.310*	1.540
USA										
UK	-0.977	-0.751	-0.436	-0.308	1.503	1.642	-0.105***	-0.201***	-0.705	-0.641
Rest of Europe	1.122	1.164	-0.473*	-0.326	1.158	1.660	-0.216***	-0.206***	-0.498	-0.436**
Ireland	-0.812	-0.440	-0.232***	-0.139**	-0.497	1.050	-0.088***	-0.164***	-0.869	-0.313***
100–499										
500–999	1.069	1.033	1.787	5.213	1.110	1.249	2.065	1.845	-0.662	1.432
1,000+	1.275	2.058	1.810	2.964	1.579	1.310	1.096	1.079	-0.791	1.727
Unionised	-0.412**	1.064	-0.267***	-0.997	1.681	1.773*	-0.942	1.030	-0.618	-0.909
Chi Square	10.058	5.543	55.381***	10.905	12.635*	15.280**	28.698***	28.105***	10.117	14.955**

Levels of significance: * = 10% level, ** = 5% level, *** = 1% level; All independent variables are categorical variables; the reference categories are in italics.

Determinants of Pay Reward and Performance Schemes in MNCs

In Table 5.9 multivariate analysis is used to determine the factors that influence the presence and nature of certain pay and performance management practices and policies in MNCs (see Lavelle et al., 2012 for a more detailed review). Each of the different pay and performance management variables were treated as a dependent variable (e.g. use of performance appraisal among the LOG), while country of origin, sector, size and unionisation were used as the independent (predictor) variables. For each of the regression analyses a number of statistical tests were run to ensure this type of analysis was suitable.[3]

The results from Table 5.9 generally support the previous descriptive analysis. Looking first at the impact of sector it appears that several important pay and performance practices are more likely to be present in MNCs operating in the service sector as opposed to manufacturing. This is especially the case in regard to the use of formal performance appraisal, forced distribution and peer/360 degree appraisal for the LOG. On the influence of ownership we find that British, European and Irish MNCs differ significantly from their US counterparts with regard to several pay and performance practices, most notably in their lower levels of utilisation of formal performance appraisals among managers and (especially) the LOG, forced distribution and peer/360 degree appraisal, especially among managers. The size of the MNC (in terms of numbers employed) did not emerge as significant in determining the use of pay and performance schemes. This may be related to the fact that we used a minimum size threshold and thus excluded smaller MNCs, thereby ensuring that all of the MNCs we surveyed employed a relatively large number of employees. Finally, we find that while trade union presence negatively and significantly impacted on the use of variable pay and performance appraisal among the LOG, its impact was quite limited in regard to most other pay and performance practices.

Conclusion

Pay and performance management represents a key strategic aspect of organisational management. The average wage for workers employed in foreign firms compared to domestic firms has increased substantially in recent years (Central Statistics Office, 2008). This is confirmed by our data which indicate that the vast majority of MNCs aim to have pay levels at or above the median/midpoint for all employees. Given the centrality of MNCs in Irish industry, the use of various reward schemes may have an influence or spill-over effect on domestic Irish firms. With regard to the incidence of formal performance appraisal, this now appears to be in common usage in MNCs, though the traditional gap in utilisation between managerial and lower level occupational categories remain with particularly high levels of utilisation of formal performance appraisal among managerial categories. We also found a lower, though sizeable, proportion of MNCs using more 'advanced' forms of performance evaluation (forced distribution and peer appraisal) which would seem to indicate increasingly sophisticated performance management in MNCs at least. A largely similar picture emerges with regard to the incidence of PRP schemes whereby the overall level of utilisation in MNCs was quite high but again the uptake was greatest among managers. Overall, the use of profit sharing and share ownership schemes in MNCs was above the average for Irish organisations (cf. European Foundation for the Improvement of Living and Working Conditions, 2010). This arguably points to increased sophistication with regard to pay and performance management. This might also be interpreted as part of a process signalling the greater individualisation of the employment relationship in the MNC sector. However, it is also likely that such incentive schemes exist in parallel with established standard pay systems, at least for routine employees.

In looking at potential explanatory factors, while there are some differences due to sectoral location (manufacturing or services), country of ownership has a more substantial impact. US MNCs are more likely than other MNCs to use regular performance appraisal and the various other reward mechanisms that we investigated. Overall our findings point to a comparatively high take-up of what might be viewed as more modern pay and performance management practices in MNCs, though predictably we find variation, particularly with regard to occupational category and also related to the characteristics of the MNC itself (notably ownership). We should note that survey data of this nature cannot accurately capture information on the operation of pay and performance management systems (i.e. process issues) nor indeed can it provide insights into how managers and employees experience the operation of such systems. With regard to future research, it would clearly be beneficial to compare our work in MNCs with other Irish research on different sectors of the economy, such as the small and medium enterprise (SME) sector or indeed the public sector (McCarthy et al., 2011), which has been the subject of much recent focus in terms of securing enhanced levels of performance and productivity, or 'getting more from less' in modern parlance.

Notes

[1] The authors wish to acknowledge financial support provided by the Labour Relations Commission, the Irish Research Council for the Humanities and Social Sciences, the University of Limerick Research Office and the European Commission's International Research Staff Exchange Scheme (FP7 IRSES-GA-2008-230854 - INTREPID). Additional and more in-depth information on this topic is available in a recent paper by Lavelle et al. (2012) in the *International Journal of Human Resource Management*, while the overall survey findings are reported in *Human Resource Practices in Multinational Companies in Ireland: A Contemporary Analysis* by Lavelle et al. (2009) – full citations are provided in the list of references.

[2] In so doing we distinguished between foreign- and domestic-owned MNCs and established a size threshold as follows: (i) Foreign-owned MNCs were defined as wholly or majority foreign-owned organisations with 500 or more employees worldwide and 100 or more employed in Ireland; (ii) Domestic-owned MNCs were defined as wholly or majority Irish-owned organisations with 500 or more employees worldwide and at least 100 employed abroad.

[3] For example, all of the independent variables used were tested for multicollinearity, whilst the Hosmer and Lemeshow Goodness-of-Fit Test, a robust test for overall fit in a logistic regression model, was also employed. Each of the tests showed up as satisfactory.

References

Almond, P. (2006), 'Pay and Performance' in P. Almond and A. Ferner (eds), *American Multinationals in Europe: Managing Employment Relations Across National Borders*, Oxford: Oxford University Press, 119–145.

Armstrong, M. (2012), *Handbook of Human Resource Management*, twelfth edition, London: Kogan Page.

Armstrong, M. and Stephens, T. (2005), *A Handbook of Employee Reward Management and Practice*, London: Kogan Page.

Bebchuk, L. and Fried, J. (2006), 'Pay Without Performance: Overview of the Issues', *Academy of Management Perspectives*, 20(1): 5–24.

Beer, M., Spector, B., Lawrence, P.R., Quinn-Mills, D. and Walton, R.E. (1984), *Managing Human Assets*, New York, NY: The Free Press.

Björkman, I. and Furu, P. (2000), 'Determinants of Variable Pay for General Managers of Foreign-Owned Subsidiaries in Finland', *International Journal of Human Resource Management*, 11(4): 698–713.

Bowey, A. and Thorpe, R. (1986), *Payment Systems and Productivity*, London: Macmillan.

Central Statistics Office (2008), *Census of Industrial Production: Annual Services Inquiry*, Dublin: CSO.

D'Art, D. and Turner, T. (2006), 'Profit Sharing and Employee Share Ownership in Ireland: A New Departure?', *Economic and Industrial Democracy*, 27(4): 543–564.

Dore, R., Lazonick, W. and O'Sullivan, M. (1999), 'Varieties of Capitalism in the Twentieth Century', *Oxford Review of Economic Policy*, 15(4): 102–120.

Drucker, P.F. (1954), *The Practice of Management*, New York, NY: Harper.

European Foundation for the Improvement of Living and Working Conditions (2010), *European Company Survey 2009*, Luxembourg: Office for Official Publications of the European Communities.

Ferner, A. and Almond, P. (2013), 'Performance and Reward Practices in Foreign Multinationals in the UK', *Human Resource Management Journal*, 23(3): 241–261.

Fombrun, C., Tichy, N. and Devanna, M. (1984), *Strategic Human Resource Management*, New York, NY: Wiley.

Grace, P. and Coughlan, A. (1998), 'Reward Systems and Reward Strategies' in W.K. Roche, K. Monks and J. Walsh (eds), *Human Resource Strategies: Policy and Practice in Ireland*, Dublin: Oak Tree Press, 205–246.

Guest, D. (1987), 'Human Resource Management and Industrial Relations', *Journal of Management Studies*, 24(5): 503–521.

Gunnigle, P., Heraty, N. and Morley, M. (2011), *Human Resource Management in Ireland*, fourth edition, Dublin: Gill & Macmillan.

Gunnigle, P., Turner, T. and D'Art, D. (1998), 'Counterpoising Collectivism: Performance-Related Pay and Industrial Relations in Greenfield Sites', *British Journal of Industrial Relations*, 36(4): 565–579.

Heery, E. (1997), 'Performance-Related Pay and Trade Union Membership', *Employee Relations*, 19(5): 430–442.

Heffernan, M., Harney, B., Cafferkey, K. and Dundon, T. (2008), 'People Management and Innovation in Ireland', *CISC Working Paper*, 27(1): 1–26.

Huselid, M.A. (1995), 'The Impact of Human Resource Management Practices on Turnover, Productivity, and Corporate Financial Performance', *Academy of Management Journal*, 38(3): 635–672.

Kelly, A. and Monks, K. (1997), 'View from the Bridge and Life on Deck: Contrasts and Contradictions in Performance-Related Pay' in T. Clark, C. Mabey and D. Skinner (eds), *Experiencing Human Resource Management*, London: Sage, 113–128.

Kessler, I. (1998), 'Financial Incentives' in M. Poole and M. Warner (eds), *The Handbook of Human Resource Management*, London: International Thomson Business Press, 124–149.

Kessler, I. and Purcell, J. (1992), 'Performance Related Pay: Objectives and Application', *Human Resource Management Journal*, 2(3): 16–33.

Latham, G., Almost, J., Mann, S. and Moore, C. (2005), 'New Developments in Performance Management', *Organizational Dynamics*, 34(1): 77–87.

Lavelle, J., McDonnell, A. and Gunnigle, P. (2009), *Human Resource Practices in Multinational Companies in Ireland: A Contemporary Analysis*, Dublin: The Stationery Office.

Lavelle, J., Turner, T., Gunnigle, P. and McDonnell, A. (2012), 'The Determinants of Financial Participation Schemes within Multinational Companies in Ireland', *International Journal of Human Resource Management*, 23(8): 1590–1610.

Lawler, E.E. (2003), 'Reward Practices and Performance Management System Effectiveness', *Organizational Dynamics*, 32(4): 396–404.

Lepak, D.P. and Snell, S. (1999), 'The Human Resource Architecture: Toward a Theory of Human Capital Allocation and Development', *Academy of Management Review*, 24(1): 31–48.

MacDuffie, J. (1995), 'Human Resource Bundles and Manufacturing Performance: Organisational Logic and Flexible Production Systems in the World Auto Industry', *Industrial and Labor Relations Review*, 48(2): 197–221.

McBeath, G. and Rands, D. N. (1989), *Salary Administration*, London: Gower.

McCarthy, A., Grady, G. and Dooley, G. (2011), 'Leadership in the Irish Civil Service: A 360° Review of Senior Management Capability', Centre for Innovation and Structural Change, NUI Galway, available from: <http://www.nuigalway.ie/cisc/documents/leadership_in_the_irish_civil_service.pdf>.

McDonnell, A. and Gunnigle, P. (2009), 'Performance Management' in D. Collings and G. Wood (eds), *Human Resource Management: A Critical Approach*, Milton Park: Routledge, 189–207.

McDonnell, A., Lavelle, J., Collings, D.G. and Gunnigle, P. (2007), 'Management Research on Multinational Corporations: A Methodological Critique', *Economic and Social Review*, 38(2): 235–258.

Milkovich, G., Newman, J. and Gerhart, B. (2013), *Compensation*, eleventh edition, New York, NY: McGraw-Hill.

Mooney, P. (1989), 'The Growth of the Non-Union Sector and Union Counter Strategies in Ireland', Unpublished PhD thesis, Trinity College Dublin.

Morley, M. and Gunnigle, P. (1997), 'Compensation and Benefits' in P. Gunnigle, M. Morley, N. Clifford and T. Turner (eds), *Human Resource Management in Irish Organisations: Practice in Perspective*, Dublin: Oak Tree Press.

Nowack, K. (1993), '360 Degree Feedback: The Whole Story', *Training and Development*, 47(1): 69–73.

O'Sullivan, M. (2000), *Contests for Corporate Control: Corporate Governance and Economic Performance in the United States and Germany*, Oxford: Oxford University Press.

Pfeffer, J. (1994), *Competitive Advantage through People*, Boston, MA: Harvard Business School Press.

Poutsma, E. (2001), *Recent Trends in Employee Financial Participation in the European Union*, Dublin: European Foundation for the Improvement of Living and Working Conditions.

Roche, W.K. (1999), 'In Search of Commitment-Orientated Human Resource Management Practices and the Conditions that Sustain Them', *Journal of Management Studies*, 36(5): 653–678.

Roche, W.K. and Turner, T. (1994), 'Testing Alternative Models of Human Resource Policy Effects on Trade Union Recognition in the Republic of Ireland', *International Journal of Human Resource Management*, 5(3): 721–753.

Sisson, K. (1996), *Closing the Gap: Ideas and Practice in Organisational Change*, EF/96/15/EN, Luxembourg: Office for the Official Publication of the European Communities.

Sparrow, P. and Hiltrop, J.-M. (1994), *European Human Resource Management in Transition*, Hemel Hempstead: Prentice Hall.

Toegel, G. and Conger, J. (2003), '360-Degree Assessment: Time for Reinvention', *Academy of Management, Learning and Education*, 2(3): 297–311.

Wallace, J., Gunnigle, P., McMahon, G. and O'Sullivan, M. (2013), *Industrial Relations in Ireland*, fourth edition, Dublin: Gill & Macmillan.

Walton, R.E. and McKersie, R.B. (1965), *A Behavioral Theory of Labor Negotiations*, New York, NY: McGraw-Hill.

Watson, D., Galway, J., O'Connell, P. and Russell, H. (2010), *The Changing Workplace: A Survey of Employers' Views and Experiences*, Dublin: National Centre for Partnership and Performance.

CHAPTER 6

Learning and Knowledge[1]

Claire Gubbins and Jennifer Kennedy

Introduction

The organisational learning (OL) and organisational knowledge (OK) literatures have long recognised the strategic importance of learning and knowledge for providing sustainable competitive advantage (Crossan et al., 1995; Anand et al., 2010). While these literatures exist within two oftentimes academically and commercially competing domains, the underpinning concepts are similar and there is evidence of gradual convergence (Vera and Crossan, 2005). This convergence is grounded in the basic recognition that learning occurs first and foremost at the individual level and that it is the process of learning that develops current or new knowledge for both individuals and organisations.

In this chapter we begin by conceptualising learning and orientations of the learning process. We illustrate, using empirical evidence from an Irish context, how theory informs practice in the design of individual and organisational learning initiatives. We then explore the concept of knowledge, which is both an input into, and a product of, learning. Then we elucidate the relationship between learning and knowledge and outline the debates surrounding the processes through which individual learning relates to organisational learning. The chapter concludes with a review and critique of the most notable frameworks on OL and knowledge creation and presents some evidence from the Irish context which illustrates components of these frameworks.

Learning

Definitions of learning are numerous and vary based on the discipline of study (see Sadler-Smith, 2006). Smith (1982) argues that the difficulty in defining learning is due to its multiple uses: learning refers to the acquisition and mastery of what is already known, the extension and clarification of meaning from one's experience or an organised, intentional process of testing ideas relevant to problems. Essentially it is at the same time a product, a process and a function. While learning is often defined simply as a change in behaviour, such a view is critiqued for failing to capture all the complexities involved in learning (Hill, 2002). Yet the notion of change or potential to change still underlies most definitions (Merriam et al., 2007). A definition which synthesises several views is that learning is a process that brings together cognitive, emotional and environmental influences and experiences for acquiring, enhancing or making changes in one's knowledge, skills, values and worldviews (Illeris, 2000).

Learning, when viewed as a process rather than a product, relates to what happens when learning takes place. There are a plethora of theories concerned with elucidating this process and Marquardt and Waddill (2004) have categorised these into five orientations of learning: behaviourist, humanist, cognitivist, social cognitivist and constructivist.

Behaviourist

The behaviourist orientation of the learning process is grounded in the work of Thorndike (1913), Pavlov (1927) and Skinner (1974). It holds three assumptions: the focus is on observable behaviour rather than internal thought processes; what one learns is influenced by elements in the environment rather than the individual; and repeated stimulus and response events are central to the learning process. These assumptions inform the design of learning initiatives by emphasising a focus on measurable changes in behaviour that are to be exhibited by a learner and can be tied to the intervention, and rewards, reinforcement and altering the environmental stimuli should be used to encourage learning. There is evidence from the Irish context to illustrate how these assumptions operate in practice. A Chartered Institute of Personnel and Development (CIPD) study (Garavan et al., 2008) found that 74.3 per cent of organisations evaluated their human resource development (HRD) activities but the process was largely informal. It concluded that the use of more structured and valid evaluation criteria that quantifiably measure learning and learning transfer was negligible or *ad hoc*. Similarly, O'Connor et al. (2006) concluded that though Kirkpatrick's (1976) model suggests evaluating HRD initiatives in terms of reaction, learning, change in behaviour and results for the business, in practice only some Irish organisations evaluated management development initiatives in relation to job performance and impact on the business. The more likely scenario was where organisations conducted evaluations of reactions or learning. Gubbins et al. (2006) investigated various dimensions of the strategic integration of HRD as perceived by management and non-management personnel including technical, administrative and nursing staff in an Irish health services organisation. They concluded that managers play a relatively limited role in making systematic evaluations of employee performance post-training and the majority of evaluations conducted were informal.

Humanist

The humanist orientation rejects the behaviourists' view of human nature as controlled by the environment or the subconscious. It argues that human beings can control their own destiny and that people possess unlimited potential for growth and development (Rogers, 1983; Maslow, 1970). Two assumptions underlying this orientation are (i) the value of experience and that perceptions are centred in experience, and (ii) that people possess freedom and responsibility to become what they are capable of becoming and thus learning is self-directed (Merriam et al., 2007). This orientation illustrates that in the design of learning initiatives the primary responsibility for learning is with the learner and initiatives must focus on learner-identified learning needs and learner motivations to learn.

In relation to learning needs, Reinl and Kelliher (2010) investigated an Irish Tourism Learning Network (TLN) development programme and reported that participants did not see the value of completing a learning needs analysis before the start of the programme. A possible means of helping learners more clearly see the value of needs analysis before partaking in learning programmes may be located in McCarthy and Garavan's (1999) study of participants from an Irish financial institution. Participants evaluated the value of the Myers Briggs Type Inventory and 360 degree feedback for increasing self-awareness. They concluded that both instruments were effective in enhancing self-awareness and that subsequently participants were more aware of their developmental needs. Participants also found the 360 degree feedback helpful in identifying development needs and making plans for development.

With regard to learner motivation to learn, a CIPD survey (Garavan and Carbery, 2003) of 750 employees working in 250 Irish organisations who had undertaken training in the twelve months prior to the survey concluded that participants were in general motivated to engage in learning initiatives and that there was evidence to indicate that individuals who were motivated to learn took a more active part in voluntary training and development activities. The factors identified as driving learning included a desire to learn as much as possible, to improve skills, to develop skills for their current jobs and a belief that learners could learn.

Cognitivist

The cognitivist or information processing orientation argues that, contrary to the behaviourist orientation, the human mind does not simply receive stimuli and send out the appropriate response but engages in thinking to interpret sensations and give meaning to events that impinge upon its consciousness (Grippin and Peters, 1984). Two assumptions underpinning this orientation are that the memory system is an active organised processor of information and that prior knowledge plays an important role in learning (Gredler, 1997). A difference between cognitivists and behaviourists is in their views about the locus of control for learning; cognitivists believe it lies with the individual learner whereas behaviourists position it in the environment. This orientation is concerned with the organisation of the information to be learned, the learner's prior knowledge, the processes involved in perceiving, comprehending and storing information (Gredler, 1997), the nature of schemata, memory systems, the development of cognitive skills, and ways of aiding understanding and learning (Di Vesta, 1987).

Social Cognitivist

The social cognitive orientation combines elements of both the behaviourist and cognitivist orientation and is based on the assumption that people learn from observing others in social settings (Lefrancois, 1999). Miller and Dollard (1941) drew on the behaviourist stimulus–response and reinforcement theory and argued that, for learning, behaviour must be imitated and reinforced. Bandura (1986) drew on the cognitive orientation and argued, conversely, that one could learn without imitation, observation, modelling others, mentoring or shadowing.

This orientation advises that learning initiatives simulate the context where individuals must apply their learning, or the knowledge already possessed by the learner. For example, through on-the-job or workplace-based learning initiatives. A 1995 study of HRD methods in use in Irish organisations (Heraty and Morley, 2000) revealed that the least popular mechanisms were those of mentoring and coaching. However, evidence from the CIPD surveys of training and development in Ireland (Garavan et al., 2003, 2008) concluded that there was considerable consistency in the learning methods in use over this timespan (Garavan et al., 2008). The most frequently used, and also cited as the most effective, methods included face-to-face training, on-the-job training, formal education programmes, and coaching and mentoring. Another practice cited as effective, though used less frequently, was shadowing.

Constructivist

The constructivist orientation maintains that learning is a process of constructing meaning; it is about how people make sense of their experiences. Beyond this basic assumption, constructivists adopting the individual view of learning argue that experiences must encourage learners to question their knowledge schemes and develop new ones based on their experiences (Driver et al., 1994: 6). Conversely, the social constructivist view argues that when individuals engage socially and talk about shared problems and tasks they learn about culturally shared ways of understanding and talking about the world (Vygotsky, 1978). This orientation emphasises dialogue, collaboration, cooperation, inquiry, self-direction, reflection and experiences as evidenced in approaches such as reflective practice and communities of practice (Merriam et al., 2007).

For example, Reinl and Kelliher (2010), in investigating the TLN initiative, used Kolb's (1984) learning cycle, a constructivist theory, to explore the initiative's impact on participants' learning processes. Observations related to the Kolb cycle stage of active experience included participants' preferences for drawing on previous experience and knowledge. However, the quality and accuracy of the group's own information and experience were not always conducive to effective learning and needed to be managed. The conceptualisation stage was enabled through cooperative learning strategies such as peer discussion and cooperative reflection. Finally, during the action stage, participants had the opportunity to relate learning to action-focused goals and gain valuable outside perspectives from other participants. However, their reflections did not necessarily lead to action, thus suggesting a need for further supports to enable action.

Research on action learning can illustrate all five learning orientations in tandem. Marquardt and Waddill (2004) devised an approach to action learning composed of:

- A problem of importance to the group
- A process that emphasises questions and reflection
- The power to take action on strategies developed
- A commitment to learning
- A coach who focuses the intervention

An action learning intervention in the Irish context is outlined in Box 6.1 and is illustrative of the benefits obtainable from this type of initiative (see also O'Hara et al., 2001 for an action learning study in the North Western Health Board in Ireland).

Box 6.1: Action Learning at CMW

Coghlan and Coghlan (2003) investigated the practice, learning and changes accruing to CMW, an Irish headquartered company that designs and manufactures electrical systems, as a result of participating in an inter-organisational action learning programme from 1998 to 2000. CMW management realised that maintaining existing levels of practice and

---

performance did not sustain competitiveness. They saw action learning as a vehicle for change. The action learning initiative applied the steps of self-assessment, analysis of the issues, taking action and reflecting on the actions taken. The management reported improvements in performance indicators such as external customer focus and satisfaction, vendor appraisal system, staff turnover and quality of working life. These improvements came about through changes in operational practices such as product design, processes and external supplier management. Coghlan and Coghlan (2003) concluded that though CMW may have worked to address these issues independently, participation in the action learning initiative provided rigour, discipline, access to others and conceptual material for ideas. It also developed ownership in the organisation and made completion of tasks or the cessation of ineffective tasks more likely.

The Product of Learning: Knowledge

The definitions of learning illuminate the products of learning as knowledge, skills, values and worldviews. The literature from the fields of OL and OK have traditionally failed to acknowledge each other's domains, with those in the OL field neglecting to mention 'knowledge' and those in the OK field neglecting to mention 'learning', though efforts to integrate the domains is emerging (Vera and Crossan, 2005).

The definition of knowledge is much debated in the knowledge management (KM) literature, traditionally with an emphasis on differentiating knowledge from data and information (Zack, 1999). 'Data' represents observations or facts out of context and 'information' places data in some meaningful context. The construct of knowledge is further deconstructed. Zack (1999) identifies three forms of knowledge: declarative, procedural and causal. These forms of knowledge have also been described as tacit and explicit knowledge (Davenport and Prusak, 1998; Nonaka and Takeuchi, 1995). In essence, knowledge 'about' something is defined as declarative or explicit. 'Explicit', 'articulated' (Saint-Onge, 1996), 'objective', 'articulable', 'verbal' and 'declarative' are all terms utilised to refer to the same form of knowledge (Ambrosini and Bowman, 2002). 'How to' knowledge can be described as procedural or tacit. Tacit knowledge is difficult to express, comes from experience, is often unconscious, is tied to senses, intuition and unarticulated mental models (Polanyi, 1966; Nonaka and von Krogh, 2009), and is practical knowledge demonstrated in 'know how', action, procedures and routines. The concept of 'tacit knowledge' is a cornerstone of OK theories as it overcame mainstream theory's tendency to equate knowledge with information (Nonaka and von Krogh, 2009), and it constitutes a unique organisational competitive advantage.

Making the link between information, knowledge and learning, Davenport and Prusak (1998) define knowledge as information acquired through implicit or explicit learning means and in the process combined with experience, context, interpretation and reflection. Similarly, Sadler-Smith (2006:183) states that 'the root of knowledge creation is learning'.

Organisational Learning and Organisational Knowledge

While the learning orientations are informative in exploring the processes behind the learning–knowledge link at the individual level, extensive literatures from the OK and OL fields focus on translating this to the organisational level. There are various definitions of OL mirroring the learning orientations. Some adopt the cognitive orientation and argue that only individuals can learn and therefore OL refers to individual learning in the context of the organisation (e.g. March and Olsen, 1976; Simon, 1991). Conversely, others argue that an organisation is an entity capable of learning on a collective basis (e.g. Cook and Yanow, 1993). Shared learning outcomes are realised when change takes place for two or more people (Sadler-Smith, 2006) and the results are explicit. For example, where a group solves a problem and develops new insights that affect the group's working process (Mittendorf et al., 2006), leading to outcomes that are embedded in the organisation's structure and culture (Snyder and Cummings, 1998). While both the OL and OK fields recognise these multiple levels of learning and knowledge, they vary with respect to what their models emphasise as fundamental to the learning and knowledge creation process.

Nonaka (1994), coming from the OK perspective, developed a theory of organisational knowledge creation to build a model of how organisations learn. This model focuses on the content of learning more so than the learning process and as such is focused on forms of knowledge and knowledge conversion. This socialisation, externalisation, combination and internalisation (SECI) model of knowledge creation argues that 'knowledge is created through the interaction between tacit and explicit knowledge' (Nonaka and Takeuchi, 1995: 62). Despite criticisms of the model (Freyens and Martin, 2007; Gourlay, 2006), it is widely cited in research and acknowledged in practice.

Socialisation refers to the conversion of tacit knowledge to new tacit knowledge through the informal sharing of feelings, emotions, experiences and mental models through communication (Nonaka and Takeuchi, 1995). *Externalisation* is the process of converting tacit knowledge into explicit knowledge through reflective dialogue and writing. This is seen as a vital step in knowledge creation (Nonaka and Takeuchi, 1995) but it rests on the assumption that tacit knowledge can be codified or articulated. There are divergent arguments as to whether tacit knowledge can be codified. Nonaka and von Krogh (2009) discuss explicit and tacit knowledge as existing along a continuum of knowledge and argue that some tacit knowledge must be the basis for explicit knowledge. Similarly, Ambrosini and Bowman (2002) discuss the possibility of tacit knowledge codification through high to low degrees of tacitness. However, authors within the OL field differ and argue that explicit and tacit knowledge are complementary (Subashini, 2010). Tsoukas (2003) claims that the capability to know is possessed by people and always stays with the subject and so tacit knowledge cannot be converted into explicit knowledge and 'managed'.

Combination is the process of creating explicit knowledge by combining existing explicit knowledge to form a new basis of knowledge. This can be achieved through conversations, meetings or memos, and can be sorted and categorised (Nonaka and Takeuchi, 1995). *Internalisation* is the process of converting explicit knowledge into tacit knowledge. It is learning 'by doing' and involves individuals internalising their experiences and changing their perceptions, beliefs and activities through practising new approaches. While the SECI framework only implies that individual knowledge is transformed into OK, this claim is made explicit in Nonaka's (1994: 20) spiral of organisational knowledge creation.

The prescriptive or practice implications of the SECI model refer to KM. A survey of KM practices in a sample of Irish public and private sector organisations involved in ongoing business improvement through the use of a business excellence model investigated knowledge embodiment and dissemination (McAdam and Reid, 2000). The data analysis of 97 questionnaires revealed that knowledge was systematically captured at senior management level and to a lesser degree at all other levels. The capture of tacit elements such as individuals' daily experiences, benchmarking data and competitor findings were all low. Tacit knowledge was captured mainly through informal discussions and also, particularly for the public sector, formal discussion. Overall, the study found a lack of systematic knowledge capture and assigned responsibility, indicating that KM was an emergent rather than an established system. In terms of knowledge embodiment, the majority of respondents agreed that their organisations facilitated dialogue and that employees took responsibility for their learning. In relation to dissemination, the key methods for knowledge sharing included discussion forums, workshops and training needs analysis. However, these methods were not used systematically, again reflecting the lack of maturity in KM.

Irish evidence of KM practices is also identifiable from studies which focus on methodologies that enable socialisation, externalisation, combination or internalisation. Such studies, for example those on action learning outlined in Box 6.1, were discussed previously. Additionally, Basri and O'Connor (2011), in a study of Irish small and medium enterprises, examined the practices of communicating, learning and documentating past knowledge/experience. These concepts can be related to the processes of socialisation, externalisation and combination as outlined in Nonaka's (1994) SECI model. Of note here are the results that revealed that, in terms of communication, the organisations had clear communication processes and channels but had no regular formal meetings. Instead, communication was informal in the form of face-to-face, informal discussion, online communication, informal internal feedback or 'on-the-job' training processes. Equally, the learning and sharing activities were informal in the form of self-learning or informal sharing among the team. The documentation process was formal when related to business and technical processes but individual knowledge, experience, lessons learnt and activities were not properly documented or were documented informally at a personal level.

There is also evidence of some emerging Irish research in this area. The Leadership, Innovation and Knowledge (LInK^2) Research Centre, based in Dublin City University, is involved in two research projects of note. First, a project on knowledge-intensive firms in Ireland and the UK examined HRM practices and outcomes such as knowledge sharing and skill levels (see **Chapter 9**). Second, a project on the dynamics of knowledge creation and diffusion in university research centres focused on the ways in which team processes facilitate the successful sharing of knowledge (Buckley and Chughtai, 2013). Third, the Irish Centre for Manufacturing Research (ICMR[3]) a university–industry collaboration, also connected to LInK, is implementing a project on tacit knowledge learning. This project is directly concerned with processes outlined in the SECI and 4I models, the resultant outcomes for knowledge processes and the tacit-to-explicit conversion process as discussed by Nonaka (1994) and outlined in Box 6.2 (Gubbins et al., 2012). The Centre for Research in Innovation, Knowledge, Organisation and Networks (RIKON[4]) in Waterford Institute of Technology has a number of in-house publications on its website addressing learning and knowledge sharing from a socialisation perspective in terms of networks and interpersonal relationships.

Box 6.2: Tacit Knowledge Sharing and Conversion Initiative

A division of a large multinational manufacturing organisation in Ireland employed engineers with tacit 'know-how' about their jobs. Management, concerned about the loss of this tacit know-how should the engineers leave the organisation, were interested in initiatives to enable tacit knowledge sharing and its conversion to explicit forms. The study implemented an experimental procedure which first required experienced engineers to attempt to 'capture' their tacit know-how in words and images in a document. Secondly, the inexperienced engineers attempted to conduct the task with the aid of the document and no other knowledge source.

The experiment found that some know-how was converted from being tacitly held (Ambrosini and Bowman, 2002) by experienced engineers to being codified, shared and transferred to inexperienced engineers so they could conduct the task. However, challenges also emerged with the tacit-to-explicit knowledge conversion process. These included:

- Differences in how 'codes in use' in the documents of experienced engineers were interpreted and meaning attributed by the less experienced engineers. The inexperienced engineers made incorrect inferences about the information presented in the document based on their prior knowledge.
- The experienced engineers could not codify some elements of the task in words or images, such as how much force to exert on a machine part – a psychomotor component of tacit knowledge – as it

---

> required physical illustration. They resorted to the use of metaphors such as 'wiggle', which can facilitate articulation but can also add new meaning if taken too literally (Goatly, 1997).
>
> - The experienced engineers' attempts to 'capture' their know-how required that they recall what was relevant for an inexperienced engineer. However the experienced engineers 'forgot' to share some knowledge because they were no longer consciously aware of its use.
>
> *Source:* Gubbins et al. (2012)

From the OL perspective, which focuses on the process of learning rather than the content, Crossan et al. (1999) proposed the 4I framework of organisational learning. It consists of four related (sub) processes – intuiting, interpreting, integrating and institutionalising – that occur at individual, group and organisational levels. *Intuiting* is the preconscious recognition of the pattern and/or possibilities inherent in a personal stream of experience (Weick, 1995: 25; see also Sadler-Smith, 2010). *Interpreting* is explaining, through words and/or actions, an insight or an idea to oneself or others. *Integrating* is the process of developing shared understanding among individuals and taking coordinated action through mutual adjustment. *Institutionalising* is the process of embedding individual and group learning into the organisation's systems, structures, procedures and strategy (Crossan et al., 1999: 525). The framework recognises that overlap within these levels can occur at the individual, group or organisational level.

In terms of prescription, this framework emphasises the creation of a learning organisation. With respect to Irish sites implementing practices to enable the development of a learning organisation, a 1999 study conducted on 126 multinational organisations (O'Keeffe and Harrington, 2001) concluded that 56 per cent of them had undertaken, were implementing or had plans in the near future to implement a learning programme to enable a learning organisation. McDonnell et al. (2010), in their study of multinational corporations (MNCs) based in Ireland, reported that approximately half of all MNCs have a formal OL policy.

More specific to the process of learning as outlined in the 4I framework, a study by Buckley and Monks (2008) showed how learning theory can inform and shape the design of an executive education programme to result in multi-level learning. For example, residential weekends, team projects, orienteering, drama workshops and action learning were used to encourage group learning and all participants reported acquiring a new language, concepts and ideas from the academic content of the programme. At an organisational level, action learning sets were used to resolve a work-based change management problem. In addition, non-participants, when working with participants who completed the programme, referred to the new language, new behaviours and new ways of thinking participants brought back from the programme. Roche's (2002) study illustrates multiple learning processes in action in an Irish manufacturing company, through implementation of a 'business excellence model' and continuous improvement initiatives. These included a variety of learning perspectives in action: the psychological perspective was evident from individual and team learning; the management science perspective was evident where individuals and teams engaged in a process of knowledge acquisition, information distribution and interpretation; the organisation perspective was evident as structures, procedures and processes were modified; and the cultural perspective was evident as efforts were made to create a culture embracing learning. This study is illustrative of the methods that may enable the processes of integrating and institutionalising outlined in the 4I framework.

Conclusion

The strategic importance of individual and organisational learning and knowledge for providing sustainable competitive advantage to organisations is well established. The importance of knowledge embedded in people alongside a focus on how this knowledge is shared and retained in organisational memory is emphasised as a national priority for Ireland's future economic development (Department of Enterprise, Trade and Employment, 2008). Furthermore, the management of knowledge and 'know-how' are perceived as necessary to ensure the continued contribution and market position of the Irish manufacturing industry (Expert Group on Future Skills Needs, 2007).

This review illuminates some important implications for practices and future research to enhance learning and knowledge management in Irish organisations. First, the most frequently implemented learning practices in Ireland are more traditional in nature, such as face-to-face training (Garavan et al., 2008), despite recognition in both learning theory and Nonaka's (1994) SECI model that non-traditional practices such as mentoring, socialisation and action learning may be more effective. Second, research also suggests that it is difficult to decipher the true levels of effectiveness of any intervention in enabling learning and knowledge creation as evaluation in Irish organisations is lacking (O'Connor et al., 2006). Third, it seems that additional organisational supports such as facilitators of learning needs analyses (Reinl and Kelliher, 2010) and action learning sets (O'Hara et al., 2001) are required to motivate learning in participants. Fourth, though there was evidence of practices in Irish organisations conducive to effective knowledge management, these were informal and not used systematically and thus it may be concluded that there is a general lack of maturity in KM (McAdam and Reid, 2000). Thus, more in-depth research (see Gubbins et al., 2012; Basri and O'Connor, 2011; Reinl and Kelliher, 2010; Buckley and Monks, 2008; Roche, 2002) is required to investigate the more complex processes proposed in the SECI and 4I frameworks rather than simply auditing and describing the practices in use. For example, when studies refer to learning methods, OL policies and KM, the more important questions are:

- What practices are contained within these that illustrate the SECI or 4I components in action?
- To what extent and level of effectiveness are Irish organisations engaged in practices that facilitate socialisation, externalisation, combination, or intuiting, integrating and institutionalising?
- What are these practices?
- How do they work?

Without such research, Irish organisations will be unable to determine how best to facilitate learning and knowledge creation processes for the competitive advantages that are obtainable.

Notes

[1]   Jennifer Kennedy acknowledges PhD scholarship funding provided by the Higher Education Authority (HEA) under the Programme for

Research in Third Level Institutions (PRTLI) Cycle 4 as part of the Irish Social Sciences Platform (ISSP) stream on Knowledge, Economy and Society.

[2]   LInK – see http://link.dcu.ie/?page_id=136.

[3]   ICMR – see http://www.icmr.ie/current-research/tacit-knowledge-management.html.

[4]   RIKON – see http://www.rikon.ie/academic_projects.

References

Ambrosini, V. and Bowman, C. (2002), 'Tacit Knowledge: Some Suggestions for Operationalization', *Journal of Management Studies*, 38(6): 811–829.

Anand, G., Ward, P.T. and Tatikonda, M.V. (2010), 'Role of Explicit and Tacit Knowledge in Six Sigma Projects: An Empirical Examination of Differential Project Success', *Journal of Operations Management*, 28(4): 303–315.

Bandura, A. (1986), *Social Foundations of Thought and Action: A Social Cognitive Theory*, Englewood Cliffs, NJ: Prentice Hall.

Basri, S. and O'Connor, R.V. (2011), 'A Study of Software Development Team Dynamics in SPI', *Proceedings of the 18th European Conference EuroSP1 Systems, Software and Services Process Improvement*, Roskilde, Denmark, 27–29 June, 143–154.

Buckley, F. and Chughtai, A. (2013), 'Exploring the Impact of Trust on Research Scientists' Work Engagement: Evidence from Irish Science Research Centres', *Personnel Review*, 44(4): 1–25.

Buckley, F. and Monks, K. (2008), 'Responding to Managers' Learning Needs in an Edge-of-Chaos Environment: Insights from Ireland', *Journal of Management Education*, 32(2): 146–163.

Coghlan, D. and Coughlan, P. (2003), 'Acquiring the Capacity for Operational Improvement: An Action Research Opportunity', *Human Resource Planning*, 26(2): 30–38.

Cook, S.D. and Yanow, D. (1993), 'Culture and Organizational Learning', *Journal of Management Inquiry*, 2(4): 373–390.

Crossan, M., Lane, H. and White, R. (1999), 'An Organizational Learning Framework: From Intuition to Institution', *Academy of Management Review*, 24(3): 522–537.

Crossan, M.M., Lane, H.W., White, R.E. and Djurfeldt, L. (1995), 'Organizational Learning: Dimensions for a Theory', *International Journal of Organizational Analysis*, 3(4): 337–360.

Davenport, T. and Prusak, L. (1998), *Working Knowledge: How Organizations Manage What They Know*, Cambridge, MA: Harvard Business School Press.

Department of Enterprise, Trade and Employment (2008), *Report of the High Level Group on Manufacturing: Towards 2016*, Dublin: Department of Enterprise, Trade and Employment.

Di Vesta, F.J. (1987), 'The Cognitive Movement in Education' in J. Glover and R. Ronning (eds), *Historical Foundations of Education*, New York, NY: Plenum, 203–233.

Driver, R., Asoko, H., Leach, J., Scott, P. and Mortimer, E. (1994), 'Constructing Scientific Knowledge in the Classroom', *Educational Researcher*, 23(7): 5–12.

Expert Group on Future Skills Needs (2007), *Tomorrow's Skills: Toward a National Skills Strategy*, Report of the Expert Group on Future Skills Needs, Dublin: Department of Enterprise, Trade and Employment.

Freyens, B. and Martin, M. (2007), 'Multidisciplinary Knowledge Transfer in Training Multimedia Projects', *Journal of European Industrial Training*, 31(9): 680–705.

Garavan, T.N. and Carbery, R. (2003), *Who Learns At Work – A Study of Learners in the Republic of Ireland*, Dublin: Chartered Institute of Personnel Development.

Garavan, T., Carbery, R. and Shanahan, V. (2008), *2007 Training and Development National Employer Survey of Benchmarks*, Dublin: Chartered Institute of Personnel Development.

Garavan, T., Collins, E. and Brady, S. (2003), *Results of the 2003 National Survey of Benchmarks: Training and Development in Ireland*, Dublin: Chartered Institute of Personnel and Development.

Goatly, A. (1997), *The Language of Metaphors*, London and New York, NY: Routledge.

Gourlay, S. (2006), 'Conceptualizing Knowledge Creation: A Critique of Nonaka's Theory', *Journal of Management Studies*, 43(7): 1415–1436.

Gredler, M.E. (1997), *Learning and Instruction: Theory into Practice*, third edition, Englewood Cliffs, NJ: Prentice Hall.

Grippin, P. and Peters, S. (1984), *Learning Theory and Learning Outcomes: The Connection*, Lanham, MD: University Press of America.

Gubbins, C., Corrigan, S., Garavan, T.N., O'Connor, C., Leahy, D., Long, D. and Murphy, E. (2012), 'Evaluating a Tacit Knowledge Management Initiative: Its Business Value, ROI and Challenges', *European Journal of Training and Development*, 36(8): 827–847.

Gubbins, C., Garavan, T.N., Hogan, C. and Woodlock, M. (2006), 'Enhancing the Role of the HRD Function: The Case of a Health Services Organisation', *Irish Journal of Management*, 27(1): 171–206.

Heraty, N. and Morley, M.J. (2000), 'Human Resource Development in Ireland: Organizational Level Evidence', *Journal of European Industrial Training*, 24(1): 21–33.

Hill, W.F. (2002), *Learning: A Survey of Psychological Interpretations*, seventh edition, Needham Heights, MA: Allen and Bacon.

Illeris, K. (2000), *Three Dimensions of Learning*, Roskilde: Roskilde University Press/Leicester: National Institute of Adult Continuing Education.

Kirkpatrick, D.L. (1976), *Evaluating Training Programs*, New York, NY: McGraw-Hill.

Kolb, D.A. (1984), *Experiential Learning: Experience as the Source of Learning and Development*, Englewood Cliffs, NJ: Prentice Hall.

Lefrancois, G.R. (1999), *The Lifespan*, sixth edition, Belmont, CA: Wadsworth.

March, J.G. and Olsen, J.P. (1976), 'Organizational Learning and the Ambiguity of the Past' in J.G. March and J.P. Olsen (eds), *Ambiguity and Choice in Organizations*, Bergen: Universitetsforlaget, 54–68.

Marquardt, M. and Waddill, D. (2004), 'The Power of Learning in Action Learning: A Conceptual Analysis of How the Five Schools of Adult Learning Theories Are Incorporated within the Practice of Action Learning', *Action Learning: Research and Practice*, 1(2): 185–202.

Maslow, A.H. (1970), *Motivation and Personality*, second edition, New York, NY: HarperCollins.

McAdam, R. and Reid, R. (2000), 'A Comparison of Public and Private Sector Perceptions and Use of Knowledge Management', *Journal of European Industrial Training*, 24(6): 317–329.

McCarthy, A.M. and Garavan, T.M (1999), 'Developing Self-Awareness in the Managerial Career Development Process: The Value of 360-Degree Feedback and the MBTI', *Journal of European Industrial Training*, 23(9): 437–445.

McDonnell, A., Gunnigle, P. and Lavelle, J. (2010), 'Learning Transfer in Multinational Companies: Explaining Inter-Organisation Variation', *Human Resource Management Journal*, 20(1): 23–43.

Merriam, S.B., Caffarella, R.S. and Baumgartner, L.M. (2007), *Learning in Adulthood: A Comprehensive Guide*, San Francisco, CA: Jossey-Bass.

Miller, N. and Dollard, J. (1941), *Social Learning and Imitation*, New Haven, CT: Yale University Press.

Mittendorf, K., Evjset, F., Hoeve, A., deLaat, M. and Nieuwenhius, L. (2006), 'Communities of Practice as Stimulating Forces for Collective Learning', *Journal of Workplace Learning*, 18(5): 298–312.

Nonaka, I. (1994), 'A Dynamic Theory of Organizational Knowledge Creation', *Organization Science*, 5(1): 14–37.

Nonaka, I. and Takeuchi, H. (1995), *The Knowledge-Creating Company: How Japanese Companies Create the Dynamics of Innovation*, New York, NY: Oxford University Press.

Nonaka, I. and von Krogh, G. (2009), 'Tacit Knowledge and Knowledge Conversion: Controversy and Advancement in Organizational Knowledge Creation Theory', *Organization Science*, 20(3): 635–652.

O'Connor, M., Mangan, J. and Cullen, J. (2006), 'Management Development in Ireland: Justifying the Investment', *Journal of Management Development*, 25(4): 325–349.

O'Hara, S., Webber, T. and Murphy, W. (2001), 'The Joy of Sets', *People Management*, 7(3): 30–34.

O'Keeffe, T. and Harrington, D. (2001), 'Learning to Learn: An Examination of Organisational Learning in Selected Irish Multinationals', *Journal of European Industrial Training*, 25(2/3/4): 137–147.

Pavlov, I.P. (1927), *Conditioned Reflexes*, translated by G.V. Anrep, London: Oxford University Press.

Polanyi, M. (1966), *The Tacit Dimension*, London: Routledge.

Reinl, L. and Kelliher, F. (2010), 'Cooperative Micro-Firm Strategies: Leveraging Resources through Learning Networks', *International Journal of Entrepreneurship and Innovation*, 11(2): 141–150.

Roche, E. (2002), 'The Implementation of Quality Management Initiatives in the Context of Organisational Learning', *Journal of European Industrial Training*, 26(2/3/4): 142–153.

Rogers, C.R. (1983), *Freedom to Learn for the 80s*, Columbus, OH: Merrill.

Sadler-Smith, E. (2006), *Learning and Development for Managers: Perspectives from Research and Practice*, Oxford: Blackwell Publishing.

Sadler-Smith, E. (2010), *The Intuitive Mind: Profiting from the Power of Your Sixth Sense*, Hoboken, NJ: Wiley.

Saint-Onge, H. (1996), 'Tacit Knowledge: The Key to the Strategic Alignment of Intellectual Capital', *Strategy and Leadership*, 24(2): 10–14.

Simon, H.A. (1991), 'Bounded Rationality and Organizational Learning', *Organization Science*, 2(1): 125–134.

Skinner, B.F. (1974), *About Behaviourism*, New York, NY: Knopf.

Smith, R.M. (1982), *Learning How to Learn: Applied Learning Theory for Adults*, Chicago, IL: Follett.

Snyder, W.M. and Cummings, T.G. (1998), 'Organization Learning Disorders: Conceptual Model and Intervention Hypotheses', *Human Relations*, 51(7): 873–895.

Subashini, R. (2010), 'Tacit Knowledge – The Ultimate Essence of an Organization', *Advances in Management*, 3(8): 36–40.

Thorndike, E.L. (1913), *Educational Psychology*, The Psychology of Learning, Vol. 2, New York, NY: Columbia Teachers' College.

Tsoukas, H. (2003), 'Do We really Understand Tacit Knowledge?' in M. Easterby-Smith and M.A. Lyles (eds), *The Blackwell Handbook of Organizational Learning and Knowledge Management*, Oxford: Blackwell Publishing, 410–427.

Vera, D. and Crossan, M. (2005), 'Organizational Learning and Knowledge Management: Toward an Integrative Framework' in M. Easterby-Smith and M. Lyles (eds), *The Blackwell Handbook of Organizational*

Learning and Knowledge Management, Oxford: Blackwell Publishing, 122–142.

Vygotsky, L.S (1978), *Mind in Society: The Development of Higher Psychological Processes*, Cambridge, MA: Harvard University Press.

Weick, K.E. (1995), *Sensemaking in Organizations*, Thousand Oaks, CA; London and New Delhi: Sage Publications.

Zack, M. (1999), 'Managing Codified Knowledge', *Sloan Management Review*, 40(4): 45–58.

Section 3

Context

CHAPTER 7

International Human Resource Management

Jonathan Lavelle, Anthony McDonnell and
Patrick Gunnigle

Introduction

International human resource management (IHRM) is a relatively
new field, emerging largely due to the pressures of globalisation
and growth of companies operating internationally. A commonly
used definition defines IHRM as 'the HRM issues and problems
arising from the internationalisation of business and the HRM
strategies, policies and practices which firms pursue in response to
the internationalisation process' (Scullion, 1995: 352). This chapter
focuses on how multinational companies (MNCs) manage human
resource management (HRM) in Ireland. The chapter commences
by reviewing international evidence concerning the role and significance of MNCs. It then explores some key theoretical debates,
namely the debate between country of origin and host country
effects. The chapter explores how this debate has been played out in
an Irish context before considering more recent empirical evidence
relating to the role of MNCs in Ireland. The chapter concludes by
discussing key implications.

The Significance and Role of MNCs

The issue of how MNCs manage their foreign operations has been a long-standing area of academic debate and research (Collings, 2008). The rapid growth in globalisation and the role of MNCs in the process drives much of this interest (Ferner and Quintanilla, 1998). In its *World Investment Report* (2009), the United Nations Conference on Trade and Development (UNCTAD) identifies approximately 82,000 MNCs worldwide that, in turn, operate some 810,000 affiliates, employing 77 million people (UNCTAD, 2009). The scale of MNC activity is illustrated by the fact that of the world's largest 150 economic entities, 76 (51 per cent) are MNCs (Butler, 2006). The significance of MNCs within a host country is nowhere more evident than in Ireland. Inward foreign direct investment (FDI) stocks as a percentage of gross domestic product (GDP) in Ireland were estimated at 73.6 per cent in 2007, compared to a 27.9 per cent world average (UNCTAD, 2008). The proportion of employment in foreign-owned companies, as a percentage of total international trade related employment in Ireland, is the highest in the world (UNCTAD, 2007). A more recent and equally significant development in the Irish economy has been the surge in outward FDI (UNCTAD, 2006, 2007, 2008). Over the last number of years outward FDI has more than rivalled inward FDI, with FDI outflows exceeding inflows in 2004, 2005 and 2006 (UNCTAD, 2007).

Given their scale and significance, it is unsurprising that foreign-owned MNCs have long been a focus of investigation for HRM researchers (Gennard and Steuer, 1971; Rosenzweig and Nohria, 1994; Fenton-O'Creevy et al., 2008; Edwards and Ferner, 2002; Ferner and Quintanilla, 2002; Almond and Ferner, 2006; Pudelko and Harzing, 2007; Brewster et al., 2008). Gennard and Steuer (1971) noted that it is the 'foreignness'of these MNCs that matters to employee relations. Indeed, Ferner and Quintanilla (2002: 245) argue that foreign-owned MNCs 'act as agents of change by introducing innovations into their subsidiaries and thence into the host business system'. It is this 'foreignness' and ability to innovate and ultimately impact on the host HRM system that drives much of the HRM research on MNCs. A key debate within the Irish literature, and similarly in the broader IHRM literature, is the question of whether foreign-owned MNCs adopt their own HRM policies and practices in host countries, or do they adopt those of the host country?

International HRM: Country of Origin and Host Country Effects

The country of origin effect is well exploited in the literature as an important source of potential variation in HRM policy and practice. It is claimed that the country in which the MNC originates exerts a distinctive effect on the way labour is managed (Ferner, 1997). A range of sources indicate that even the largest MNCs retain strong roots in their home country. For example, the majority of sales, assets, employment, financial resources, and research and development activity are likely to be located within the country of origin (cf. Rees and Edwards, 2011). Furthermore, individuals from the country of origin are likely to hold the most senior managerial positions within the company. These strong roots in the home country mean that senior managers at the company headquarters (HQ) may seek to transfer HRM practices to their foreign subsidiaries. The result of such a transfer of HRM practices mean that foreign subsidiaries' HRM practices resemble those of their parent company. There is strong evidence in the literature that the country of origin influences management practice within foreign subsidiaries (Ferner, 1997; Almond and Ferner, 2006; Edwards et al., 2007; Lavelle et al., 2009).

The host country, the country in which the foreign subsidiary operates, can have a significant influence on the transfer of HRM practices. Indeed, the host country context may provide constraints and/or opportunities for the transfer of HRM practices. For example, there are a number of aspects of the host country's national business system which can limit the scope of MNCs' transference of HRM practices. These include employment legislation, labour market institutions (such as trade unions and works councils), cultural barriers and lack of specific skills or aptitudes. It is important to note the strength of these host country effects as in some cases the limitations provided by the national business system may only be partial. For example, it may be a case that HRM practices are tweaked or adapted so that they can be successfully implemented as they may be malleable to the influence of large MNCs, particularly MNCs from dominant economies. MNCs operating in highly regulated business systems such as Germany may find it more difficult to transfer home country HRM policies and practices than they do in countries such as the UK (Almond and Ferner, 2006).

The Irish Evidence

With Ireland being described as one of the world's most MNC-dependent economies (Gunnigle et al., 2005), it is of no surprise that there is a plethora of literature investigating HRM issues within MNCs operating in Ireland (Kelly and Brannick, 1985; Turner et al., 1997a, 1997b; Geary and Roche, 2001; Gunnigle et al., 2005; Collings et al., 2008). Edwards and Rees (2006) suggest that Ireland represents the best illustration of where the debate around country of origin and host country effects has been pursued. It is possible to identify two contrasting perspectives within this literature. First, an early body of literature on HRM in MNCs laid the foundations for the so-called 'conformance thesis' (Kelly and Brannick, 1985; Enderwick, 1986). Proponents of this argument suggested that HRM practices of foreign-owned MNCs operating in Ireland conformed to the prevailing traditions of larger Irish companies, notably in conceding trade union recognition and in relying on adversarial collective bargaining as the primary means of handling employment relations matters. For instance, Kelly and Brannick (1985: 109) found that 'in general, MNCs are regarded as no different as Irish firms and the trend seems to be one of conformity with the host country's institutions, values and practices.' Enderwick (1986), in reviewing the impact of MNCs on HRM in Ireland, identified a number of theoretical propositions as to why foreign-owned MNC subsidiaries might utilise different HRM practices to those prevailing in indigenous organisations. However, his empirical appraisal found no supporting evidence (see also Roche and Geary, 1996). Consequently, this early body of research pointed towards a dominance of host country effects whereby foreign-owned companies largely conformed to the HRM model prevailing among indigenous companies.

However, a countervailing perspective has since emerged which argues that a 'new orthodoxy' now characterises Irish HRM. The argument put forward under this perspective is that foreign-owned MNCs no longer conform to prevailing local HRM practices, pointing towards a 'country of origin effect' (Roche and Geary, 1996; Turner et al., 1997a, 1997b; Geary and Roche, 2001; Collings et al., 2008). Though there is some debate around the reasons, this literature broadly posits that foreign-owned MNC operations have increasingly adopted HRM approaches more reflective of their own (home country) policies and practices. This evidence is most pronounced in the union avoidance strategies of United States (US) MNCs in Ireland, particularly those that have established operations since the 1980s. Indeed, US companies operating in Ireland appear much more likely to adopt HRM practices that are different to those of indigenous companies (Gunnigle, 1995; Gunnigle et al., 1997; Geary and Roche, 2001; Collings et al., 2008). Whilst acknowledging differences between foreign MNCs and Irish companies, Geary and Roche (2001) suggest that we may witness a spill-over effect from foreign MNCs, predicting that the convergence of HRM is more likely to be from indigenous companies towards foreign MNCs' HRM practice.

However, whilst the intense focus on MNCs as the unit of analysis in the Irish literature is unsurprising, the ability of this research to provide a representative picture of what is happening within these organisations is quite alarming (McDonnell et al., 2007). A cursory review of the existing MNC literature in Ireland identifies this lack of representativeness. For example, existing empirical research has generally either relied upon small-scale surveys of MNCs (cf. Kelly and Brannick, 1985), extracting findings on MNCs from larger surveys or consultancy reports (cf. Gunnigle et al., 1994, 1997; Geary and Roche, 2001; National Centre for Partnership and Performance, 2004); or case study based research (cf. Dundon et al., 2004, 2006; Gunnigle et al., 2005). This gap in the literature is not just confined to the Irish context but to the management literature more generally (cf. Collinson and Rugman, 2010; Edwards et al., 2007).

Two key issues emerge from the extant literature on MNCs operating in Ireland. First, much of this research relies on small sample numbers and indeed some do not set out to look specifically at MNCs. Second, this empirical research has generally excluded two key categories of MNCs: (i) foreign-owned MNCs that are not assisted or aided by the main industrial promotions agencies, and (ii) Irish-owned MNCs. These omissions are likely to bias findings on key aspects of the practice and behaviour of MNCs. For example, Whitley (1999: 128) argues that 'the more dependent are foreign firms on domestic organisations and agencies, both within and across sectors, the less likely are they to change prevalent patterns of behaviour.' This could potentially be significant as it may suggest that those firms which have tenuous links to state agencies may be less restricted in implementing practices which are at odds with host traditions. Therefore, there is a strong need for a representative picture of MNCs' HRM policies and practices in Ireland. Box 7.1 provides details of the methodology from a recent project conducted at the University of Limerick (McDonnell et al., 2007; Lavelle et al., 2009) which has attempted this task.

Box 7.1: Towards a Representative Picture of HRM in MNCs Operating in Ireland

In order to address the deficiencies of existing Irish research examining MNCs and to offer a better assessment of the landscape, a representative survey of MNCs was conducted by a team at the University of Limerick (cf. McDonnell et al., 2007; Lavelle et al., 2009). In order to provide definitional clarity a distinction was made between foreign and domestically owned MNCs as follows:

- All foreign-owned MNCs operating in Ireland, with 500 or more employees worldwide and 100 or more in their Irish operation.
- All Irish-owned MNCs with 500 or more employees worldwide and at least 100 overseas.

With respect to developing a total MNC population, a series of sources were consulted. These included the Industrial Development Agency of Ireland (IDA Ireland); Forfás; a private consultancy firm, Bill Moss Partnership; Enterprise Ireland; Kompass; *Major Companies of Europe 2005* (a directory of companies in Europe); company websites; and the *Irish Times* top 1,000 companies. Stratified sampling was then employed which led to the selection of a total of 414 MNCs. A total of 260 MNCs participated in the survey, representing a response rate of 63 per cent. This compares most favourably with organisational-level surveys of this type (Baruch and Holtom, 2008). The questionnaires focused on five substantive areas of human resource management/employment relations (the HR function; pay and performance management; employee representation and consultation; employee involvement and communication; and training, development and organisational learning), as well as encompassing a section on company background and other key attributes.

Once collected and inputted, the data were analysed by means of descriptive and binary logistical regression analysis. Employing binary logistical regression analysis allows the prediction of the presence or absence of a particular characteristic based on the values of a set of independent variables. For each of the regression analyses, a number of statistical tests were run to ensure this type of analysis was suitable. For example, all of

---

> the independent variables used were tested for multicollinearity, whilst the Hosmer–Lemeshow Goodness-of-Fit Test, a robust test for overall fit of a logistic regression model, was also employed. Each of the tests showed up as satisfactory.

Findings from the University of Limerick study indicate that there are a number of differences between Irish-owned, US-owned and other foreign-owned MNCs with respect to human resource (HR) practices. An overview of key descriptive results using cross tabulations is presented in Table 7.1. Differences are most pronounced in the areas of performance management and industrial relations. In the area of rewards, we find significant differences between Irish, US and other foreign MNCs in relation to a policy of paying managers above the median (in comparison to market comparators), employee share ownership schemes for both managers and the largest occupational group (LOG), and share options for managers. In the area of performance management we find significant differences between Irish, US and other foreign MNCs across all measures, with the exception of the use of 360 degree feedback. US MNCs were much more likely to report the use of performance appraisal for both groups, the use of forced distribution for both groups and 360 degree feedback for managers. These differences are most pronounced in relation to the use of forced distribution, with US MNCs differing considerably from Irish and other foreign MNCs. Similarly, there are a number of differences in relation to industrial relations within Irish, US and other foreign MNCs. US MNCs are less likely to recognise a trade union, less likely to report high levels of union density within the MNC, more likely to recognise just a single trade union, more likely to have a non-union structure of collective representation and also more likely to report the presence of a European Works Council. In relation to involvement and communication there are fewer differences between Irish, US and other foreign MNCs. Nonetheless, US MNCs are more likely to report the use of problem-solving groups, attitude or opinion surveys, systematic use of the management chain to cascade information and a company intranet. Finally, with regard to training and development within MNCs, US MNCs are more likely to report the use of management development programmes.

Table 7.1: Descriptive Results of University of Limerick MNC Survey

	Irish Owned	US Owned	Other Foreign Owned	N
Rewards				
Pay policy above the median (LOG)	31.7%	37.1%	43.9%	245
Pay policy above the median (managers)	54.8%	42.9%	57.9%	247
Follow the national level wage agreements for managers	60.0%	43.5%	57.1%	85
Follow the national level wage agreements for LOG	77.8%	57.6%	69.7%	171
Variable pay (LOG)	60.0%	70.0%	67.0%	257
Variable pay (managers)	87.0%	91.0%	92.7%	255
Employee share ownership (LOG)	30.4%	40.2%	19.8%	254
Employee share ownership (managers)	34.8%	43.9%	20.2%	253
Profit sharing (LOG)	26.2%	30.8%	23.3%	236
Profit sharing (managers)	34.1%	34.1%	34.6%	236
Share options (LOG)	14.3%	27.4%	25.0%	241
Share options (managers)	44.4%	65.6%	35.0%	244
Performance management				
Performance appraisal (LOG)	60.0%	82.0%	68.8%	257
Performance appraisal (managers)	87.0%	97.0%	91.1%	259
Forced distribution (LOG)	7.7%	40.7%	14.7%	182
Forced distribution (managers)	12.8%	43.8%	17.0%	235
360 degree feedback (LOG)	23.1%	27.5%	23.3%	179
360 degree feedback (managers)	38.5%	61.1%	44.4%	233
Industrial relations				
Trade union recognition	80.9%	41.6%	69.6%	260
Multiple unions	72.2%	47.6%	54.5%	155
Single union	27.8%	52.4%	45.5%	155
Low union density	43.2%	58.5%	42.3%	156

(Continued)

Table 7.1: (*Continued*)

	Irish Owned	US Owned	Other Foreign Owned	N
High union density	29.7%	9.8%	34.6%	156
Non-union representative structures	25.5%	41.0%	27.7%	259
European Works Council	17.0%	42.9%	46.7%	252
Employer association	89.4%	94.1%	91.1%	260
Involvement and communication				
Formally designated teams	47.6%	53.1%	57.7%	251
Problem-solving groups	61.9%	83.8%	70.3%	252
Attitude or opinion surveys	32.6%	84.0%	67.0%	258
Suggestion schemes	44.4%	59.0%	54.5%	257
Regular meetings between senior managers and the workforce	63.6%	90.0%	69.1%	254
Team briefings	97.8%	98.0%	98.2%	257
Newsletters or emails	89.1%	94.0%	95.5%	256
Systematic use of the management chain to cascade information	69.6%	89.0%	88.2%	256
Company intranet	66.7%	84.8%	77.5%	255
Project teams	60.0%	66.1%	53.4%	172
Training and development				
Training spend	16.7%	26.7%	22.4%	226
Succession planning	61.7%	72.0%	62.2%	258
Management development programme	57.8%	80.0%	69.6%	257
Organisational learning policy	27.9%	59.4%	49.1%	245

The descriptive results illustrate the value of a nuanced, representative understanding of the nature of MNCs, highlighting important differences between Irish, US and other foreign MNCs. These can be considered in a more in-depth and robust fashion by logistical regressions. This enables tests for differences across all variables whilst also being able to control for issues such as employment size, sector, the main occupation of the LOG and trade union recognition in the case of a certain number of variables. As reported in Table 7.2, the vast majority of differences reported in the descriptive findings remain in the logistical regression analysis, with some additional insight. In relation to rewards, the findings point towards little difference between Irish, US and other foreign MNCs, with the exception of the following policies and practices: paying the LOG above the median and variable pay for managers (other foreign) and employee share ownership scheme for the LOG (US). Where there are significant differences, these tend to be significant at the weaker 10 per cent level.

Again it is with regard to performance management that there are significant differences between Irish, US and other foreign MNCs. Here the findings indicate significant differences between Irish- and US-owned MNCs in relation to performance appraisal for both managers and the LOG, the use of forced distribution for both managers and the LOG, and the use of 360 degree feedback for managers. For example, US MNCs are ten and four times more likely to have performance appraisal for managers and the LOG respectively and almost eight and six times more likely to have forced distribution for the LOG and managers respectively. Similarly, there are significant differences in relation to industrial relations. Predictably, US MNCs are less likely than Irish MNCs to recognise a trade union and report high levels of union density. We find that US MNCs, when compared to Irish-owned MNCs, are eight times more likely to report the incidence of a European Works Council, over four times more likely to be a member of an employer association and almost three times more likely to have a non-union structure of collective employee representation

Table 7.2: Logistical Regression Results

	US Owned	Other Foreign Owned	N
Rewards			
Pay policy above the median (LOG)		2.242*	244
Pay policy above the median (managers)			246
Follow the national level wage agreements for managers			85

(Continued)

Table 7.2: (*Continued*)

	US Owned	Other Foreign Owned	N
Follow the national level wage agreements for LOG			170
Variable pay (LOG)			255
Variable pay (managers)		2.939*	253
Employee share ownership (LOG)	2.155*		254
Employee share ownership (managers)			252
Profit sharing (LOG)			236
Profit sharing (managers)			236
Share options (LOG)			240
Share options (managers)			242
Performance management			
Performance appraisal (LOG)	4.017***		255
Performance appraisal (managers)	10.301**		257
Forced distribution (LOG)	7.764**		181
Forced distribution (managers)	5.928***		234
360 degree feedback (LOG)			178
360 degree feedback (managers)	2.853**		232
Industrial relations			
Trade union recognition	-0.136***		260
Multiple unions			154
Single union			154
Low union density	4.012**		155
High union density	(-0.180)**		155
Non-union representative structures	2.765**		256
European Works Council	8.365***	8.463***	250
Employer association	4.660**		257
Involvement and communication			
Formally designated teams			250
Problem-solving groups	3.829***		251

(*Continued*)

Table 7.2: (*Continued*)

	US Owned	Other Foreign Owned	N
Attitude or opinion surveys	14.792***	6.235***	256
Suggestion schemes			255
Regular meetings between senior man-agers and the workforce	3.860***		252
Team briefings			255
Newsletters or emails			254
Systematic use of the management chain to cascade information	5.522***	5.099***	254
Company intranet	4.024***	2.636**	253
Project teams			170
Training and development			
Training spend			223
Succession planning	2.732**		255
Management development programme	6.294***	3.267***	254
Organisational learning policy	4.714***	3.012**	243

Reference category: Irish-owned
Controls: LOG occupation, employment size, sector and union recognition
Levels of significance: *** 1%, ** 5% and * 10%

There are some differences between Irish, US and other foreign MNCs in relation to involvement and communication practices. Specifically, there are differences in relation to the use of problem-solving groups, attitude or opinion surveys, regular meetings between senior managers and the workforce, systematic use of the management chain to cascade information and a company intranet. In some instances the differences are vast, for example US MNCs are almost fifteen times more likely and other foreign MNCs six times more likely to report the use of attitude or opinion surveys compared to Irish-owned MNCs. Finally, in relation to training and development the results indicate significant differences on three out of the four measures. For example, US MNCs are almost three times more likely than Irish MNCs to report the use of succession planning and six times more likely to have a management development programme in place.

Analysis and Insights

As noted above, significant debate has developed in Ireland over the last 30 years in relation to whether foreign-owned MNCs adapted to the local HRM traditions. The earlier literature pointed towards foreign-owned MNCs conforming to the prevailing HRM traditions. The more recent literature, however, referred to the development of a 'new orthodoxy', whereby foreign-owned MNCs no longer conformed to the prevailing traditions, but rather introduced HRM policies and practices that were different to those existing in indigenous companies – pointing and referring to the growing dominance of 'country of origin' effects. The evidence presented in this chapter has contributed to this debate by presenting findings from a study which has comprehensively examined HRM policies and practices in foreign- and also Irish-owned MNCs. In so doing it provides a clear profile of HRM within foreign- and Irish-owned MNCs via a carefully selected methodology which has sought to address traditional deficiencies when examining MNCs' activity in Ireland (McDonnell et al., 2007).

The findings of this chapter provide support for the contention that foreign-owned MNCs do behave differently to Irish-owned MNCs (Roche and Geary, 1996; Geary and Roche, 2001; Gunnigle et al., 2005; Collings et al., 2008; Lavelle, 2008). Indeed, quite a number of significant differences between Irish, US and other foreign MNCs were found to exist across HR domains – out of the 40 HR measures explored, significant differences occur in 22 of those measures. Where we find differences between MNCs, it was by and large between US and Irish MNCs – pointing towards country of origin effects among US MNCs. Differences are particularly pronounced between Irish and US MNCs, and with respect to the practice areas of performance management and industrial relations. This would find support within more general research, which has found conservatism amongst Irish firms in the domains of performance management, in part due to institutional context (Roche and Turner, 1998). For example, US MNCs are more likely to have performance appraisals, use forced distribution in appraisals, offer high levels of direct communication and participation practices, and are less likely to recognise a trade union (Almond and Ferner, 2006).

Furthermore, our data point to strong evidence that there is no convergence of HRM practices among MNCs operating in Ireland.

In a recent review of US, German and Japanese MNCs, Pudelko and Harzing (2007) found evidence of a convergence of HRM practices around US-style HRM. However, despite the predictions of a convergence towards US-style HRM practices or a global standard HRM style, we find no evidence to support this contention (Brewster et al., 2008). Indeed, our findings illustrate the utility of using home *and* host country effects to explain variation within MNCs and their HRM practices.

Finally, Geary and Roche (2001) predicted that there would likely be a spill-over effect from MNCs to Irish-owned companies, suggesting that host country practices would converge towards foreign MNCs' practices. If this was to occur, we would most likely see this convergence occurring between Irish- and foreign-owned MNCs. Yet our results showed little evidence of this spill-over effect from foreign-owned MNCs to Irish-owned MNCs, with many distinct differences as to how HRM appears in their respective organisations.

Conclusions

This chapter has examined the HRM practices that MNCs pursue in response to the internationalisation process (Scullion, 1995). In so doing it has highlighted the theoretical and methodological complexities of research in an area where HRM contributions have been surprisingly underrepresented (Morley et al., 2006). The findings indicate clear distinctions between the HRM practices of Irish MNCs and those of US and foreign MNCs. However, it is important to avoid overly simplistic claims of either convergence or divergence, or host country versus country of origin effects. Arguably, there are a range and interplay of effects to be explored, so that influences may not be mutually exclusive – for example Belanger et al. (2013) point toward the need to account for a broader set of relationships both inside and outside the operations of foreign MNCs. Likewise, there may be host country or country of origin patterns in the combinations of practices deployed as opposed to the incidence of individual practices (Ferner and Almond, 2013). From a practitioner standpoint, this chapter highlights the importance of being attentive to key influences and the broader cultural fit of specific HRM practices. It also suggests that best practice HRM may equate to universal principles, whereas the specifics of practice will respect local contingencies. Ultimately, key insights are likely to come from longitudinal survey research which can examine key trends over time, complemented with in-depth case analysis to explore why and how key international influences take effect. Both lines of research are of importance as the power of MNCs, coupled with the reality of emerging markets, means this is an area of ongoing significance.

References

Almond, P. and Ferner, A. (2006), *American Multinationals in Europe: Managing Employment Relations across National Borders*, Oxford: Oxford University Press.

Baruch, Y. and Holtom, B.C. (2008), 'Survey Response Rate Levels and Trends in Organizational Research', *Human Relations*, 61(8): 1139–1160.

Belanger, J., Lévesque, C., Jalette, P. and Murray, G. (2013), 'Discretion in Employment Relations Policy among Foreign-Controlled Multinationals in Canada', *Human Relations*, 66(3): 307–332.

Brewster, C., Wood, G. and Brookes, M. (2008), 'Similarity, Isomorphism or Duality? Recent Survey Evidence on the Human Resource Management Policies of Multinational Corporations', *British Journal of Management*, 19(4): 320–343.

Butler, R.A. (2006), 'Corporations Agree to Cut Carbon Emissions', *Mongabay.com*, 20 February, available from: <http://news.mongabay.com/2007/0220-roundtable.html>.

Collings, D.G. (2008), 'Multinational Corporations and Industrial Relations Research: A Road Less Travelled', *International Journal of Management Reviews*, 10(2): 173–193.

Collings, D.G., Gunnigle, P. and Morley, M.J. (2008), 'Between Boston and Berlin: American MNCs and the Shifting Contours of Industrial Relations in Ireland', *International Journal of Human Resource Management*, 19(2): 242–263.

Collinson, S. and Rugman, A. (2010), 'Case Selection Biases in Management Research: The Implications for International Business Studies', *European Journal of International Management*, 4(5): 441–463.

Dundon, T., Curran, D., Maloney, M. and Ryan, P. (2006), 'Conceptualising the Dynamics of Employee Voice: Evidence from the Republic of Ireland', *Industrial Relations Journal*, 37(5): 492–512.

Dundon, T., Wilkinson, A., Marchington, M. and Ackers, P. (2004), 'The Meanings and Purposes of Employee Voice', *International Journal of Human Resource Management*, 15(6): 1149–1171.

Edwards, T. and Ferner, A. (2002), 'The Renewed "American Challenge": A Review of Employment Practices in US Multinationals', *Industrial Relations Journal*, 33(2): 94–111.

Edwards, T. and Rees, C. (2006), 'The Transfer of Human Resource Practices in Multinational Companies' in T. Edwards and C. Rees (eds), *International Human Resource Management: Globalization, National Systems and Multinational Companies*, Harlow: Pearson Education, 66–88.

Edwards, T., Tregaskis, O., Edwards, P., Ferner, A. and Marginson, P. (2007), 'Charting the Contours of Multinationals in Britain: Methodological Challenges Arising in Survey-Based Research', *Warwick Papers in Industrial Relations*, 86(November): 1–32.

Enderwick, P. (1986), 'Multinationals and Labour Relations: The Case of Ireland', *Journal of Irish Business and Administrative Research*, 8(2): 1–11.

Fenton-O'Creevy, M., Gooderham, P. and Nordhaug, O. (2008), 'Human Resource Management in US Subsidiaries in Europe and Australia: Centralization or Autonomy?', *Journal of International Business Studies*, 39(1): 151–166.

Ferner, A. (1997), 'Country of Origin Effects and HRM in Multinational Companies', *Human Resource Management*, 7(1): 19–37.

Ferner, A. and Almond, P. (2013), 'Performance and Reward Practices in Foreign Multinationals in the UK', *Human Resource Management Journal*, 23(3): 241–261.

Ferner, A. and Quintanilla, J. (1998), 'Multinationals, National Business Systems and HRM: The Enduring Influence of National Identity or a Process of "Anglo-Saxonization"', *International Journal of Human Resource Management*, 9(4): 710–731.

Ferner, A. and Quintanilla, J. (2002), 'Between Globalisation and Capitalist Variety: Multinationals and the International Diffusion of Employment Relations', *European Journal of Industrial Relations*, 8(3): 243–250.

Geary, J. and Roche, W. (2001), 'Multinationals and Human Resource Practices in Ireland: A Rejection of the "New Conformance Thesis"', *International Journal of Human Resource Management*, 12(1): 109–127.

Gennard, J. and Steuer, M.D. (1971), 'The Industrial Relations of Foreign Owned Subsidiaries in the United Kingdom', *British Journal of Industrial Relations*, 9(2): 143–159.

Gunnigle, P. (1995), 'Collectivism and the Management of Industrial Relations in Greenfield Sites', *Human Resource Management Journal*, 5(3): 24–40.

Gunnigle, P., Collings, D.G. and Morley, M.J. (2005), 'Exploring the Dynamics of Industrial Relations in US Multinationals: Evidence from the Republic of Ireland', *Industrial Relations Journal*, 36(3): 241–256.

Gunnigle, P., Flood, P., Morley, M.J. and Turner, T. (1994), *Continuity and Change in Irish Employee Relations*, Dublin: Oak Tree Press.

Gunnigle, P., Morley, M.J., Clifford, N., Turner, T., Heraty, N. and Crowley, M. (1997), *Human Resource Management in Irish Organisations: Practice in Perspective*, Dublin: Oak Tree Press.

Kelly, A. and Brannick, T. (1985), 'Industrial Relations Practices in Multinational Companies in Ireland', *Journal of Irish Business and Administrative Research*, 7(1): 98–111.

Lavelle, J. (2008), 'Charting the Contours of Union Recognition in Foreign-Owned MNCs: Survey Evidence from the Republic of Ireland', *Irish Journal of Management*, 29(1): 45–64.

Lavelle, J., McDonnell, A. and Gunnigle, P. (2009), *Human Resource Practices in Multinational Companies in Ireland: A Contemporary Analysis*, Dublin: Labour Relations Commission.

McDonnell, A., Lavelle, J., Gunnigle, P. and Collings, D.G. (2007), 'Management Research on Multinational Corporations: A Methodological Critique', *Economic and Social Review*, 38(2): 235–258.

Morley, M., Heraty, N. and Collings, D. (eds) (2006), *International Human Resource Management and International Assignments*, London: Palgrave Macmillan.

National Centre for Partnership and Performance (2004), *The Changing Workplace: A Survey of Employers' Views and Experiences*, Dublin: NCPP.

Pudelko, M. and Harzing, A.W. (2007), 'Country-of-Origin, Localization, or Dominance Effect? An Empirical Investigation of HRM Practices in Foreign Subsidiaries', *Human Resource Management*, 46(4): 535–559.

Rees, C. and Edwards, T. (2011), 'Globalization and Multinational Companies' in T. Edwards and C. Rees (eds), *International Human Resource Management: Globalization, National Systems and Multinational Companies*, second edition, Harlow: Pearson Education, 11–32.

Roche, W.K. and Geary, J. (1996), 'Multinational Companies in Ireland: Adapting To or Diverging From National Industrial Relations Practices and Traditions', *Irish Business and Administrative Review*, 17(1): 14–31.

Roche, W.K. and Turner, T. (1998), 'Human Resource Management and Industrial Relations: Substitution, Dualism and Partnership' in W.K. Roche, K. Monks and J. Walsh (eds), *Human Resource Strategies: Policy and Practice in Ireland*, Dublin: Oak Tree Press, 67–108.

Rosenzweig, P.M. and Nohria, N. (1994), 'Influences on Human Resource Management Practices in Multinational Corporations', *Journal of International Business Studies*, 25(2): 229–242.

Scullion, H. (1995), 'International Human Resource Management' in J. Storey (ed.), *Human Resource Management: A Critical Text*, London: Routledge, 352–382.

Turner, T., D'Art, D. and Gunnigle, P. (1997a), 'Pluralism in Retreat: A Comparison of Irish and Multinational Manufacturing Companies', *International Journal of Human Resource Management*, 8(6): 825–840.

Turner, T., D'Art, D. and Gunnigle, P. (1997b), 'US Multinationals: Changing the Framework of Irish Industrial Relations?', *Industrial Relations Journal*, 28(2): 92–102.

United Nations Conference on Trade and Development (UNCTAD) (2006), *FDI from Developing and Transition Economies: Implications for Development*, New York, NY and Geneva: United Nations.

United Nations Conference on Trade and Development (UNCTAD) (2007), *World Investment Report 2007: Transnational Corporations, Extractive Industries and Development*, New York, NY and Geneva: United Nations.

United Nations Conference on Trade and Development (UNCTAD) (2008), *World Investment Report 2008: Transnational Corporations and the Infrastructure Challenge*, New York, NY and Geneva: United Nations.

United Nations Conference on Trade and Development (UNCTAD) (2009), *World Investment Report 2009: Transnational Corporations, Agricultural Production and Development*, New York, NY and Geneva: United Nations.

Whitley, R. (1999), *Divergent Capitalisms: The Social Structuring and Change of Business Systems*, Oxford: Oxford University Press.

CHAPTER 8

HRM in Small and Medium-Sized Enterprises (SMEs)

Brian Harney and Ciara Nolan

Introduction

While it is increasingly acknowledged that human resource management (HRM) is critical to competitive success, debate has rarely
extended to encompass small and medium-sized enterprises
(SMEs). This neglect is surprising given that SMEs dominate the
industrial landscape, contributing to over 55 per cent of gross
domestic product (GDP) and 65 per cent of total employment in
high-income countries (Organisation for Economic Co-Operation
and Development, 2005). This chapter examines HRM in SMEs in
Ireland. The chapter begins by exploring definitions of SMEs and
examining the significance of SMEs as the forgotten backbone of
economic and social development. The chapter then draws on
international evidence to consider the key characteristics of SMEs
and the implications these have for the type of HRM practices they
employ. With this understanding, the chapter then turns to existing
Irish research on HRM in the SME context. The chapter concludes
by examining key implications and mapping out pathways for
future research.

Small and Medium-Sized Enterprises: Definition and Significance

Reaching a consensus on what constitutes an SME is not without difficulty. The most basic common denominator is that SMEs are 'clearly not large' (Storey, 1994: 8). A key point is that not all SMEs equate to entrepreneurial start-up firms; many simply inherit or replace existing, proven forms of small business. It follows that the respective contexts of either newness or smallness will each yield specific human resource (HR) challenges (Cardon and Stevens, 2004). Even in the event of greater conceptual clarity, the task of offering a rigorous definition of what actually lies behind the label 'SME' is an onerous one. The typical response has been recourse to numbers employed as the most relevant measure of size (Kalleberg and Van Buren, 1996). One central problem with employment-based, numerical definitions is that actual categories used to distinguish between large and small firms can be somewhat arbitrary and may vary across sectors. There are also distinct national differences, with United States (US) studies defining small as up to 500 employees (Raby and Gilman, 2012). Within the European Union (EU) a consensus has emerged which serves as useful framing device. The EU definition disaggregates between *micro* firms (fewer than ten employees), *small* businesses (10–49 employees) and *medium*-sized enterprises (50–249 employees). In addition, this definition uses eligibility dimensions concerning annual turnover and ownership which ensure that the status of firms as non-subsidiary and independent is also invoked (see European Commission, 2005). Ultimately, however, size is a continuous as opposed to a discrete variable (Storey, 1994). Equally, formal criteria of 'numbers employed' can prove difficult where there is a transient, casual or undeclared workforce.

Irrespective of the precise definition that is applied, the numerical and economic significance of SMEs cannot be overstated. In Ireland SMEs account for 99.8 per cent of enterprises, 69 per cent of private sector employment, and 51 per cent of gross value added (Central Statistics Office, 2012). However, there are dangers in using figures in a homogenous and deterministic way. Under the umbrella of SMEs live a huge variety of organisations. Moreover, in Ireland 40 per cent of all SMEs are not actually 'companies' but rather 'sole proprietorships' with no other employees (Enterprise Strategy Group, 2004), while it estimated that the majority of SMEs are family owned (Birdthistle and Fleming, 2007). Overall, the SME sector is described as a 'vital fulcrum' of job creation in Ireland with its fate recognised as having 'major national economic implications' (Expert Group on Future Skills Needs, 2006: 25). More indirectly, SMEs also serve to disperse wealth and employment and can play a critical role as part of the supply chain and networks of larger firms. Allied to this is an ideological argument which sees SMEs as key mechanisms to counter the dominance of big business, thereby sustaining notions of competition and affording space for innovation and risk taking. As captured by the Irish Small Business Forum (2006: 4), 'the health of the small business sector is both an indicator of the condition of the whole economy and a determinant of that condition.' In more recent times, the indigenous SME sector is regarded as an important catalyst to sustainable economic and employment recovery (Lawless et al., 2012).

Characteristics of SMEs: Small Is?

SMEs have a number of unique characteristics that are likely to have specific HR implications. These include the role of concentrated ownership, proximity to external environmental forces, a hierarchically contracted structure which means close relations between management and employees, and a large degree of informal practice (Dundon et al., 2001). Much work in this area has taken these characteristics and collapsed them to represent opposite ends of a spectrum. Early work proposed a 'small is beautiful' thesis whereby jobs in SMEs were seen to be characterised by personalised authority relationships and informal job rotation yielding job enrichment and intrinsic satisfaction (Bolton, 1971; Ingham, 1967). SMEs were thought to exhibit better communication and greater flexibility as well as little bureaucracy. In contrast, from the 'small is bleak house' perspective informality and flexibility were judged as conductors of uncertainty resulting in employee insecurity and instability (e.g. Curran and Stanworth, 1981). This argument held that it was overly simplistic to equate low unionisation and lack of industrial disputes with conflict-free relations. Instead, SMEs were seen to be characterised by authoritarian regimes, job insecurity and exploitation of workers via limited voice and poor pay and conditions (Rainnie, 1989).

The legacy and ideological baggage of the beautiful/bleak house stereotype means that it still forms a key referent for research on SMEs (e.g. Wiesner and Innes, 2010). However, over time the dichotomy has been exposed as an overly simplistic reading. For example, a paternalistic managerial style may just as easily be a vehicle facilitating silent exploitation of workers (Wilkinson, 1999). Family ideology and low absenteeism may reflect exploitation and fear as much as unwavering commitment and employee buy-in. In terms of bleak house assessments, ethnographic research by Ram (1994) found that, even in extremely competitive conditions, employment relations in SMEs were mediated by familial, ethnic and gender relations so that employees were able to influence the dynamic of the effort–reward bargain in their favour. Overall, while conceptually elegant, the 'small is' polarisation forces a false homogeneity upon SMEs while assuming that the impact of certain characteristics (e.g. informality, paternalistic style) can be neatly read. In addition, it offers limited insight into the nature of HR practices actually in place in SMEs (whether formal or informal), and the key contextual factors that may shape these, e.g. strategy, sector and labour market (Saridakis et al., 2013).

HRM in SMEs

The labour-intensive nature of SMEs, coupled with their resource poverty, means that they offer a fruitful context in which to examine HRM interventions (Barrett and Mayson, 2008). However, it is evident from the brief review of the characteristics of SMEs that they are complex and heterogeneous organisations. Research examining HRM in SMEs has tended to pursue one of two broad approaches. The first tends to 'denature' SMEs, judging them as indistinct from larger firms. This involves taking the sophisticated HRM practices found in larger firms and assessing their impact on performance in the SME context. By contrast, the second approach acknowledges SME 'specificity' (Curran, 2006) and explores how the dynamics of the SME context may result in unique HRM challenges and practices.

Indicative of the denaturing approach, studies by Way (2002) and Hayton (2003) surveyed 'high performance work systems' (HPWS) in US small firms and found that embracing self-directed teams, group-based performance pay and formal training led to beneficial performance outcomes. Another study examining the diffusion of HPWS in Spanish firms concluded that 'adoption is likely to vary neither on the size nor on the age of the firm' (Ordiz-Fuertes and Esteban, 2003: 522). Similarly, SMEs have been found to be innovative in HRM and have largely similar HR practices to their large firm counterparts (Golhar and Deshpande, 1997). Others more cautiously highlight the merits of investment in sophisticated HRM in specific circumstances, such as facilitating growth trajectories (Kotey and Slade, 2005).

The denaturing stream of research has been important as it has extended traditional HRM research to embrace the neglected context of SMEs. However, it is not without limitation. First, the treatment of size is problematic. Research frequently selects the generous upper limit of 500 employees, while there is a tendency to omit those firms employing less than 100 (e.g. Hayton, 2003; Ordiz-Fuertes and Esteban, 2003). Second, the actual financial cost of introducing HRM practices (e.g. sophisticated recruitment practices) and their pragmatic viability (e.g. formal communication mechanisms) in the SME context is not considered. Finally, the dominant method of survey research is limited in a context where informal practices prevail. Overall, the denaturing argument holds that HRM practices as traditionally conceived have a universal relevance. Consequently, studies abstain from theoretical reflection and perpetuate a HRM large firm bias by either uncritically deploying established research instruments and/or by casting the smaller firm as lacking or deficient if it fails to meet the normative ideals.

The alternative stream of research acknowledges SME 'specificity' by critically examining how HR practices actually operate in this context, e.g. recruitment (Behrends, 2007), workplace learning (Kitching, 2007) and employee involvement (Wilkinson et al., 2007). Key findings include the limited diffusion of best practice ideals, difficulties in meeting legislative requirements and a prevalence of informal practice. In many cases sophisticated HR practice was not a prerequisite for desired outcomes. This is exemplified by Drummond and Stone's (2007) research on the *Sunday Times* (2007: 196) '50 best small companies to work for' where each firm 'adopted a distinct bundle of workforce related practices, based upon its own perceived needs and priorities'. It is also clear from research that size *per se* is not the sole determinant of HR practice. Drawing upon the extensive British Work Employment Relations Survey, Bacon and Hoque (2005) found that the nature of the workforce and value chain relations – either developmental or exploitative – were especially likely to predict the nature of HRM in place in SMEs.

Research has also explored key contingencies related to HRM in SMEs in more depth. Formality has been found to be important in enabling growth beyond, although research has found limited fit with stage models of growth (Rutherford et al., 2003). Ownership is also a dimension that has been found to impact significantly upon HR. A study of high-tech start-ups in the US found that the 'the founder's blueprint' had a lasting imprint on how people were managed, irrespective of the age, strategy or growth trajectory of the firm (Baron and Hannan, 2002). This work is reflective of recent attempts to build typologies of SMEs to better understand not only the characteristics that may render them distinct from large firms but also those that capture diversity across SME types (Edwards et al., 2006).

Overall, discussions concerning HRM in SMEs are broadly informed by assumptions related to denaturing or SME specificity. An important basis for advancing understanding may come from studies of employees working in SMES. Here it has been found that although employees are generally subject to less sophisticated HR practices, lower pay and poorer terms and conditions, they typically exhibit greater levels of trust, engagement and satisfaction compared to their larger firm counterparts (Forth et al., 2006). Indeed, research has indicated that up to certain size thresholds, formal HR practices can actually decrease satisfaction (Tsai et al., 2007).

HRM in SMEs: The Irish Evidence

Irish research on HRM has experienced something of an 'MNC bias' (Geary, 1999: 872). While a number of Irish studies do include SMEs as part of their overall research sample, it is rare that SMEs form a dedicated focus of research. This section will first draw on macro-level survey data and insights from policy reports to shed some broad empirical light on the extent of diffusion of HR practice to SMEs. Grounded by this understanding, the review will then explore organisational-level research which has been able to offer greater insight into the operation and determinants of HRM in Irish SMEs. This progression broadly mirrors the logic of denaturing and specificity.

Macro-Level Insights

Following a series of SME focus groups and stakeholder interviews, the Expert Group on Future Skills Needs (2006: 31) noted 'a distinct weaknesses in the sphere of human resource management'. Drawing on evidence from 2,668 private sector employers, the National Employer Survey conducted by the National Centre for Partnership and Performance (NCPP) (Watson et al., 2010) found that, relative to large and foreign-owned firms, Irish SMEs exhibited limited co-working practices (team-working) and were especially deficient in human capital development (staff training, formal performance reviews). However, SMEs were more likely than larger firms to have employee involvement practices (direct involvement in decisions, discretion in carrying out work). Examining the impact of bundles of practices, the NCPP data indicates that SMEs which adopt combinations of all three of these employment practices see benefits in terms of innovation, albeit not as great as for medium to large firms, suggesting a lower costs–benefit ratio for SMEs (Watson et al., 2010). Closer examination of the data also reveals significant variance *within* the SME category, both with respect to the diffusion of HR practices and likely outcomes. One concern related to the NCPP data is that it does not distinguish between SMEs that have multiple sites and/or may be part of a larger firm and independent SMEs, nor does it examine the age of the firm.

Details of independent status, numbers employed and age are provided by firms responding to the Heffernan et al. (2008) survey examining HRM practice in Ireland, resulting in 51 of the 165 respondents being allocated as SMEs. These SMEs had a mean age of 43.7 years, with only one established in the last five years, so the HR issues identified will be reflective of 'smallness' rather than 'newness'. Despite the small sample, examination of the diffusion of HR practices amongst the SME respondents is generally consistent with analysis of United Kingdom Workplace Employment Relations Survey (WERS) data (Forth et al., 2006). The most common practice was access to a formal grievance/complaint resolution policy (85.24 per cent) with the least common being administered employment tests (15 per cent) and options to obtain shares (6 per cent). With respect to the implementation of bundles of practices, evidence also points to limited diffusion with SMEs scoring an average HRM index of 36.9 (s.d. 16.24) out of a possible

100 in comparison to 51.50 (s.d. 15.88) for large firms (Harney, 2010). This echoes earlier findings from the University of Limerick/Cranfield surveys, which incorporated SMEs and similarly found that diffusion and formalisation of HR were positively correlated with organisational size (Gunnigle et al., 1994; MacMahon, 1995). Other research has usefully surveyed the impact of ownership, finding that family firms typically lag behind their non-family counterparts in implementing HRM, favouring informal, internal and less costly interventions (Birdthistle and Fleming, 2007; Reid et al., 2002).

Organisational Level Research

Empirical evidence from Ireland was early in countering overly simplistic 'small is beautiful' claims. Gunnigle and Brady's (1984: 23) study of 25 small manufacturing firms found minimal incidents of strike activity but argued that this was 'not necessarily indicative of good industrial relations'. A strong unitarist frame of reference has been frequently associated with owner-managers of SMEs who are often hostile to trade unions, collective bargaining and regulation because they feel that these impinge on their freedom to manage. This is one reason why trade union influence and presence is largely diluted in SMEs (Gunnigle and Brady, 1984). D'Art and Turner (2006) present details of an SME where attempts at union recognition to address grievances related to communication and conditions were de-railed by intimidation tactics and the isolation of union activists. Cullinane and Dundon's (2012) SME-rich sample yielded little evidence of paternalism or diffusion of sophisticated HR practices. Their interpretation echoes that of earlier case study work by MacMahon (1995), where it was argued that the 'social harmony' thesis neglects the wider context of SMEs and the impact of external variables. Box 8.1 similarly illustrates the complexity of employment relations in SMEs.

Box 8.1: Dynamics of Paternalism at Packaging Co.

Packaging Co. is an independent manufacturer and printer of packaging for the food industry which currently employs 67 people. Packaging Co. has a simple structure of an active owner-manager who continues to oversee all activities, although he is supported by long-serving staff in the form of a sales director, production manager and financial controller. There is little emphasis on formal rules regulating work activities. For example, in

---

terms of recruitment, Packaging Co. relies on local labour markets, typically sourcing candidates through contacts of its existing workforce. The owner-manager at Packaging Co. retains control over key decisions, and his paternalistic and informal style has engendered a certain degree of loyalty. Of the 67 employees, over half have over fifteen years' experience working for the organisation and many who leave to gain experience elsewhere eventually return. However, the appearance of organisational harmony is also accompanied by an authoritarian streak evident in the owner-manager's assertion that 'the buck stops with me' and his nickname of 'The General'. The long-term nature of working relations has also expanded the scope for personal control. The nature of control, and the impact of harsh competitive realities and lower pay, is in some respects ameliorated by the work atmosphere and informal relations that enable a certain amount of 'banter' and 'give and take'.

Source: Harney (2010)

With respect to HRM practices in Irish SMEs, Harney and Dundon's (2006) study of six SMEs found that HRM was not the coherent set of practices typically identified in the literature, but rather was frequently informal and emergent. Other research which has focused on single practices, most notably training and development, has similarly found a preference for informal interventions (Garavan et al., 2004; MacMahon and Murphy, 1999). Nolan (2002: 95) examined the service-intensive and densely SME populated hospitality sector and concluded that 'a formal approach to HRD may be inappropriate' with on-the-job training and multi-skilling across functional roles likely to leverage as much benefit. The Small Firms Association refers to the 'scale advantages' that come from small firm size, including more flexible jobs and multi-skilling and less 'pigeon holing' than might be found in larger firms (Small Firms Association, 2008). Likewise, MacMahon (1995) found informal communication to be more viable in this context.

HRM decisions in SMEs are typically the remit of the owner-manager or family members (Harney and Dundon, 2007). The result is that owner-managers can impose objectives directly and personally determine the adoption of practices. O'Dwyer and Ryan's (2000) study of micro firms indicates how owner-managers resisted the idea of management development, understanding it to be a large firm phenomenon of little relevance. MacMahon and Murphy (1999: 33) unearthed a paradox in that owner-managers may complain of being spread too thin, but not delegate activities, or alternatively view problems as externally imposed (e.g. difficulty in recruitment) when the root cause may be more internal (e.g. retention). In examining the role of the owner-manager, Keating and Olivares (2008) replicated the Baron and Hannan (2002) 'founder's blueprint' study amongst 55 Irish high-tech start-ups. In the main there were significant degrees of formalisation (e.g. job descriptions and performance evaluations), thereby aligning the firms studied with Baron and Hannan's (2002) engineering typology. This suggests that, in addition to internal factors, HRM is likely to be informed by sector, the diffusion of standards, levels of state agency and legislative intervention.

This point is picked up in research which has deployed a more integrative and holistic approach in exploring the multiple factors likely to shape HR in SMEs (MacMahon, 1995; Harney and Dundon, 2006). The proximity of SMEs to the external environment means that HRM will invariably be informed by key dimensions such as industrial sector, value chain pressures and legislation. McMahon's (1995) research on small manufacturing firms found that relations between small and large companies have a major bearing on employment practices in the former. Harney and Dundon (2006) found that size was not the key determinant of HRM, rather a complex interplay of external structural factors and internal dynamics shaped HRM in each of the SMEs studied. The sophistication and relative formality of HRM in some SMEs could only be adequately appreciated by reference to their competitive environments and the nature of their service offering, as well as managerial structure. Similarly, the nature of informality at a number of firms was not indicative of the substance of HRM but rather informality was dynamic, reflecting unique responses to the structural forces that shaped the parameters of feasible HRM options. Informality is a variable rather than a fixed characteristic and, as with formality, can be a means of legitimising authority and behaviour to meet key requirements (Gunnigle and Brady, 1984: 23). This is illustrated in Box 8.2.

Box 8.2: Informality as Advantage at Design Co.

Design Co. operates in the creative space of industrial design, designing consumer products for mass production. The organisation describes itself as a 45-person 'multidisciplinary team' working from an open-plan office. Design Co. is a relatively large-sized company for the industry and has a

---

flat structure with people management shared evenly across the directors. The managerial style deployed at Design Co. is open and participatory with employees afforded a high degree of autonomy. This has been shaped by the collaborative and non-routine nature of work tasks, and the desire to foster creativity. Employees face pressure to deliver not from formal, managerially determined rules but rather from vocational norms, peer pressure and a personal desire to 'exceed client expectations'.

People management at Design Co. centres on 'nurturing talent' through empowerment. Design Co. relies on extremely talented and creative individuals with very specific expertise, and so utilises specialist channels (online forums) and occupational networks to source staff. Staff are highly educated, technically competent and immersed in the values of the profession. One consequence is that training takes the form of informal mentoring by more senior staff. Whilst pay is relatively high at Design Co., employees also gain intrinsic satisfaction from design activities and the realisation of ideas. From the perspective of the directors, nurturing talent through the 'intangible stuff' of personal recognition and affirmation is deemed critical. Reflective of this, performance appraisals are conducted on a six-monthly basis. Nonetheless, there are no formalised criteria for these appraisals. In regard to communications, an informal weekly meeting is held for all staff every Friday. Design Co. has little desire to grow or introduce more formal practices; this is in part due to the belief that creative output is a function of its size and unique culture.

Source: Harney (2010)

HRM in SMEs: Analysis and Insights

This chapter has provided an overview of key themes emerging from international evidence examining HRM in SMEs, coupled with an exploration of the relatively limited Irish evidence available. A number of issues emerge. First, survey evidence suggests a generally limited diffusion of sophisticated HRM to SMEs. One reading of this might echo the sentiment of the Expert Group on Future Skills Needs (2006: 20) that SMEs 'have made relatively limited progress towards the adoption and implementation of modern HRM practices'. However, this is where the denaturing argument finds limitation as deviation from large firm ideals might not automatically imply HR deficiency. Case study evidence suggests that some formal practices may not be viable or necessary in the SME context; SMEs are likely to be natural work groups (Geary, 1999: 881) and adopt direct employee involvement practices, including discretion in carrying out work (Watson et al., 2010). Thus, while one explanation for the limited adoption of HRM may point to the resource poverty inherent to SMEs, this should be accompanied by consideration of the possibility that it may be strategically sensible not to adopt certain practices. The NCPP employee workplace data find employees in SMEs likely to be more satisfied and committed (O'Connell et al., 2010), suggesting less of a requirement for formal practice to induce or reinforce these outcomes. Arguably, when it comes to HRM in SMEs, comparisons with large firm ideals should form the beginning, rather than the end, of analysis.

Another key point concerns definitions. If SMEs are to be accommodated, a broader, more inclusive definition of HRM is required. Useful here is an analytical definition of HRM which 'takes account of the way that management actually behaves and therefore privileges understanding and explanation over prediction' (Boxall et al., 2007: 4). Boxes 8.1 and 8.2 illustrate the dynamic nature of informality as a basis for control, empowerment or accommodation, emphasising that its operation should be understood in context. Relatedly, research needs to better differentiate within the SME category. The SMEs in Harney and Dundon's (2006) study are better described as medium-sized firms, while the SMEs in the research of Reid et al. (2002) are closer to small organisations. Similarly, a line of research has begun to explore the learning needs of micro firms (Reinl and Kelliher, 2010). In addition, there is rich scope for differentiation between the respective contexts of smallness and newness, growth and stability, single and multi-site SMEs, etc. This is likely to lead to more focused and useful lines of enquiry, and consequently more sensitive and targeted policy advice.

Conclusions

This overview has indicated both the complexity and value of exploring HRM in SMEs. Arguably, greater attention to SMEs may have pre-empted areas only recently finding prominence in HRM, including the importance of management philosophy, local commitment and factors facilitating employee engagement. For research to advance in this area it will be important to avoid premature conceptual closure; rather than simply focusing on the form that HRM takes in SMEs *per se*, research should explore explanations for *why* it takes that particular form. This would allow for the seemingly conflicting evidence on the nature and form of HRM adopted in SMEs, providing one way out of the barren choice between support for the universal applicability of HRM (cf. *denaturing*) or being over-simplistic in declaring its irrelevance (cf. *specificity*) (Curran, 2006).

The current Irish focus on training and learning interventions would benefit from being complemented by research which examines recruitment and performance management in SMEs. Linked to this is the requirement for greater analytical depth and systematic research to explore the relevance of various typologies (Edwards et al., 2006) for particular types of SMEs, operating in particular contexts. Critically, research has paid little direct attention to exploring employee experiences of work and working in SMEs. This risks leaving those likely to have the greatest insights outside the research frame (Sheehan, 2013). Allied to this is an absence of research pursuing more in-depth ethnographic approaches which might better illuminate the dynamics and complexities of HR in this context (e.g. Ram, 1994).

Finally, in terms of practice there is much value to be leveraged from networks and forums where owner-managers can reflect on current HR practice and future challenges (Garavan and Ó Cinnéide, 1994). Local and sector-specific learning networks are likely to offer demand-driven targeted advice or tools. This exposes the flaws of universal supply-side solutions which are drawn exclusively from large firms and/or assume SMEs to constitute a homogenous sector.

References

Bacon, N. and Hoque, K. (2005), 'HRM in the SME Sector: Valuable Employees and Coercive Networks', *International Journal of Human Resource Management*, 16(11): 1976–1999.

Baron, J. and Hannan, M. (2002), 'Organizational Blueprints for Success in High-Technology Start-Ups: Lessons from the Stanford Project on Emerging Companies', *Californian Management Review*, 44(3): 8–37.

Barrett, R. and Mayson, S. (eds) (2008), *International Handbook of Entrepreneurship and HRM*, London: Edward Elgar.

Behrends, T. (2007), 'Recruitment Practices in Small and Medium Sized Enterprises', *Management Revue*, 18(1): 55–74.

Birdthistle, N. and Fleming, P. (2007), 'Under the Microscope: A Profile of the Family Business in Ireland', *Irish Journal of Management*, 28(2): 136–170.

Bolton, J.E. (1971), *Report of the Committee of Enquiry on Small Firms* (the Bolton Report), London: Her Majesty's Stationery Office.

Boxall, P., Purcell, J. and Wright, P. (eds) (2007), 'HRM: Scope, Analysis and Significance' in P. Boxall, J. Purcell and P. Wright (eds), *Handbook of Human Resource Management*, Oxford: Oxford University Press, 1–16.

Cardon, M. and Stevens, C. (2004), 'Managing Human Resources in Small Organisations: What Do We Know?', *Human Resource Management Review*, 14(3): 295–323.

Central Statistics Office (2012), *Business in Ireland 2009, Discussion Paper*, Dublin: CSO.

Cullinane, N. and Dundon, T. (2012), 'Unitarism and Employer Resistance to Trade Unionism', *International Journal of Human Resource Management*, DOI: 10.1080/09585192.2012.667428.

Curran, J. (2006), '"Specificity" and "Denaturing" the Small Business', *International Small Business Journal*, 24(2): 205–210.

Curran, J. and Stanworth, J. (1981), 'A New Look at Job Satisfaction in the Small Firm', *Human Relations*, 34(5): 343–365.

D'Art, D. and Turner, T. (2006), 'Union Organising, Union Recognition and Employer Opposition: Case Studies of the Irish Experience', *Irish Journal of Management*, 26(2): 165–183.

Drummond, I. and Stone, I. (2007), 'Exploring the Potential of High Performance Work Systems in SMEs', *Employee Relations*, 29(2): 192–207.

Dundon, T., Grugulis, I. and Wilkinson, A. (2001), 'New Management Techniques in Small and Medium-Sized Enterprises' in T. Redman and A. Wilkinson (eds), *Contemporary Human Resource Management*, London: Prentice Hall, 432–464.

Edwards, P., Ram, M., Sen Gupta, S. and Chin-Ju, T. (2006), 'The Structuring of Working Relationships in Small Firms: Towards a Formal Model', *Organization*, 13(5): 701–724.

Enterprise Strategy Group (2004), *Ahead of the Curve: Ireland's Place in the Global Economy*, Dublin: Enterprise Strategy Group.

European Commission (2005), *The Activities of the European Union for Small and Medium Sized Enterprises (SMEs)*, Brussels: Commission of the European Communities.

Expert Group on Future Skills Needs (2006), *SME Management Development in Ireland*, Dublin: Expert Group on Future Skills Needs.

Forth, J., Bewley, H. and Bryson, A. (2006), *Small and Medium-Sized Enterprises: Findings from the 2004 Workplace Employment Relations Survey*, July, London: Economic and Social Research Council/Advisory, Conciliation and Arbitration Service/Policy Services Institute, 1–127.

Garavan, T.N., McCarthy, A., McMahon, J. and Gubbins, C. (2004), 'Management Development in Micro and Small Firms in Ireland' in

J. Stewart and G. Beaver (eds), *HRD in Small Organisations*, London: Routledge, 285–311.

Garavan, T.N. and Ó Cinnéide, B. (1994), 'Entrepreneurship Education and Training Programmes: A Review and Evaluation', *Journal of European Industrial Training*, 18(11): 13–21.

Geary, J.K. (1999), 'The New Workplace: Change at Work in Ireland', *International Journal of Human Resource Management*, 10(5): 870–890.

Golhar, D. and Deshpande, S. (1997), 'HRM Practices of Large and Small Canadian Manufacturing Firms', *Journal of Small Business Management*, 35(3): 30–38.

Gunnigle, P. and Brady, T. (1984), 'The Management of Industrial Relations in the Small Firm', *Employee Relations*, 6(5): 21–25.

Gunnigle, P., Flood, P., Morley, M. and Turner, T. (1994), *Continuity and Change in Irish Employee Relations*, Dublin: Oak Tree Press.

Harney, B. (2010), 'HRM in Smaller Firms: A Theoretical and Empirical Exploration of Practices, Patterns and Determinants', Unpublished PhD thesis, University of Cambridge.

Harney, B. and Dundon, T. (2006), 'Capturing Complexity: Developing an Integrated Approach to Analysing HRM in SMEs', *Human Resource Management Journal*, 16(1): 48–73.

Harney, B. and Dundon, T. (2007), 'An Emergent Theory of HRM: A Theoretical and Empirical Exploration of Determinants of HRM among Irish Small to Medium Sized Enterprises', *Advances in Industrial and Labor Relations*, 15: 109–159.

Hayton, J. (2003), 'Strategic Human Capital Management in SME', *Human Resource Management*, 42(4): 375–391.

Heffernan, M., Harney, B., Cafferkey, K. and Dundon, T. (2008), 'People Management and Innovation in Ireland', CISC Working Paper, 27: 1–26.

Ingham, G.K. (1967), 'Organisational Size, Orientation to Work and Industrial Behaviour', *Sociology*, 1(3): 239–258.

Kalleberg, A. and Van Buren, M. (1996), 'Is Bigger Better? Explaining the Relationship between Organisational Size and Job Rewards', *American Sociological Review*, 61(1): 47–66.

Keating, M. and Olivares, M. (2008), 'Human Resource Management Practices in Irish High-Tech Start-Up Firms', *Irish Journal of Management*, 28(2): 171–192.

Kitching, J. (2007), 'Regulating Employment Relations through Workplace Learning: A Study of Small Employers', *Human Resource Management Journal*, 17(1): 42–57.

Kotey, B. and Slade, P. (2005), 'Formal Human Resource Management in Small Growing Firms', *Journal of Small Business Management*, 43(1): 16–40.

Lawless, M., McCann, F. and McIndoe-Calder, T. (2012), 'SMEs in Ireland: Stylised Facts from the Real Economy and Credit Market', *Central Bank Quarterly Bulletin*, 02/April: 99–123.

MacMahon, J. (1995), 'Employee Relations in Small Manufacturing Firms' in T. Turner and M. Morley (eds), *Industrial Relations and the New Order: Case Studies in Conflict and Co-Operation*, Dublin: Oak Tree Press, 171–200.

MacMahon, J. and Murphy, E. (1999), 'Managerial Effectiveness in Small Enterprises: Implications for HRD', *Journal of European Industrial Training*, 23(1): 25–35.

Nolan, C. (2002), 'Human Resource Development in the Irish Hotel Industry: The Case of the Small Firm', *Journal of European Industrial Training*, 26(2/3/4): 88–99.

O'Connell, P., Russell, H., Watson, D. and Delma, B. (2010), 'The Changing Workplace: A Survey of Employees' Views and Experiences', *The National Workplace Surveys: Research Series*, 7(2): Dublin: NCPP.

O'Dwyer, M. and Ryan, E. (2000), 'Management Development Issues for Owners/Managers of Micro-Enterprises', *Journal of European Industrial Training*, 24(6): 345–353.

Organisation for Economic Co-Operation and Development (2005), *Small and Medium Sized Enterprises and Entrepreneurship Outlook*, Paris: OECD.

Ordiz-Fuertes, M. and Esteban, F. (2003), 'High-Involvement Practices in Human Resource Management: Concept and Factors that Motivate Their Adoption', *International Journal of Human Resource Management*, 14(4): 511–529.

Raby, S. and Gilman, M. (2012), 'Human Resource Management in Small and Medium Sized Enterprises' in R. Kramar and J. Syed (eds), *Human Resource Management in a Global Context: A Critical Approach*, London: Palgrave Macmillan, 424–448.

Rainnie, A. (1989), *Industrial Relations in Small Firms: Small Isn't Beautiful*, London: Routledge.

Ram, M. (1994), *Managing to Survive: Working Lives in Small Firms*, Oxford: Blackwell.

Reid, R., Morrow, T., Kelly, B. and McCartan, P. (2002), 'People Management in SMEs: An Analysis of Human Resource Strategies in Family and Non-Family Businesses', *Journal of Small Business and Enterprise Development*, 9(3): 245–259.

Reinl, L. and Kelliher, F. (2010), 'Cooperative Micro-Firm Strategies: Leveraging Resources through Learning Networks', *Entrepreneurship and Innovation*, 11(2): 141–150.

Rutherford, M., Buller, P. and McMullen, P. (2003), 'Human Resource Management Problems over the Life Cycle of Small to Medium-Sized Firms', *Human Resource Management*, 42(4): 321–335.

Saridakis, G., Torres, R.M. and Johnstone, S. (2013), 'Do Human Resource Practices Enhance Organizational Commitment in SMEs with Low Employee Satisfaction?', *British Journal of Management*, 24(3): 445–458.

Sheehan, M. (2013), 'Human Resource Management and Performance: Evidence from Small and Medium-Sized Firms', *International Small Business Journal*, DOI: 10.1177/0266242612465454.

Small Business Forum (2006), *Small Business Is Big Business: Report of the Small Business Forum*, Dublin: Forfás.

Small Firms Association (2008), *SFA National Absenteeism Report*, Dublin: SFA.

Storey, D. (1994), *Understanding the Small Business Sector*, London: Routledge.

Tsai, C.J., Sengupta, S. and Edwards, P. (2007), 'When and Why Is Small Beautiful? The Experience of Work in the Small Firm', *Human Relations*, 60(12): 1779–1807.

Watson, D., Galway, J., O'Connell, P. and Russell, H. (2010), *The Changing Workplace: A Survey of Employers' Views and Experiences*, Dublin: National Centre for Partnership and Performance.

Way, S. (2002), 'High Performance Work Systems and Intermediate Indicators of Firm Performance within the US Small Business Sector', *Journal of Management*, 28(6): 765–785.

Wiesner, R. and Innes, P. (2010), 'Bleak House or Bright Prospect? HRM in Australian SMEs over 1998–2008', *Asia Pacific Journal of Human Resources*, 48(2): 150–184.

Wilkinson, A. (1999), 'Employment Relations in SMEs', *Employee Relations*, 21(3): 206–217.

Wilkinson, A., Dundon, T. and Grugulis, I. (2007), 'Information But Not Consultation: Exploring Employee Involvement in SMEs', *International Journal of Human Resource Management*, 18(7): 1279–1297.

CHAPTER 9

HRM in Knowledge-Intensive Firms

Kathy Monks, Edel Conway, Grainne Kelly and Na Fu

Introduction

This chapter examines human resource management (HRM) in knowledge-intensive firms (KIFs) in Ireland. We first draw on international evidence to consider the nature of KIFs and the knowledge workers they employ before examining research that has considered the operation of HRM within these knowledge-intensive contexts. We then turn our attention to research that has been undertaken within Ireland and evaluate this research against the backdrop of the international evidence. Finally, we conclude by considering some of the issues that have emerged from our analysis as well as their research and practice implications.

Knowledge-Intensive Firms

In defining a knowledge-intensive firm (KIF), it is useful first of all to consider classifications of different types of organisations. Lowendahl (1997: 21, cited in McGrath, 2005) suggests that there are three broad types of organisations: labour-intensive, capital-intensive and knowledge-intensive. Knowledge-intensive firms are subdivided into three types: (i) professional services (e.g. consulting), (ii) non-professional services (e.g. gourmet restaurants, schools) and (iii) products (e.g. computer software). Even this broad classification is fraught with difficulties as some kinds of larger organisations might display characteristics of one or more of these broad types within their overall remit. For example, while organisations such as consultancy firms, advertising agencies, high-tech companies, law or accountancy firms, or firms engaged in research and development (R&D) might generally be classified as KIFs (Swart et al., 2003), at the same time many individuals within such firms may also be engaged in routine work. Thus, such firms may have pockets of knowledge-intensive activity in areas such as R&D, while other areas could more correctly be described as labour-intensive. Other insights are offered by Starbuck (1992: 716–719), who suggests that the terms 'capital', 'labour' and 'knowledge' may be used to describe either the inputs or the outputs of firms. In his analysis of how KIFs might be differentiated, he suggests that it is 'exceptional and valuable expertise' that will predominate, rather than 'commonplace knowledge'. He goes on to distinguish 'an expert from a professional and a knowledge-intensive firm from a professional firm' while also differentiating between 'a knowledge-intensive firm' and 'an information-intensive firm'. Finally, he sees 'knowledge as a property of physical capital, social capital, routines, and organizational cultures, as well as individual people' (Starbuck, 1992: 736). While the KIF is viewed as a modern concept, McGrath (2005) presents an alternative perspective in his fascinating comparison of the structure and functioning of contemporary KIFs, as exemplified in professional services firms, with those of early Irish monastic communities.

Knowledge Work and Knowledge Workers

Within KIFs, the principal resource is identified as the competence of the workforce (Alvesson, 1993, 1995, 2000) and knowledge and expertise are seen as 'trading assets which they seek to sell to their clients' (Swart et al., 2003: 1). This 'knowledge work' is seen by Frenkel et al. (1995: 773) as a shift towards 'people-centredness characterised by an emphasis on theoretical knowledge, creativity and the use of analytical and social skills'. Benson and Brown (2007: 125) develop this distinction further by suggesting that knowledge work has three distinct but interrelated attributes: 'variation and the dynamic nature of the work undertaken (Scarbrough, 1999)'; 'the degree of reciprocal interdependence of work with other tasks being performed in the organisation (Cortada, 1998; Scarbrough, 1999)'; and 'the degree of autonomy employees have in carrying out their work (Kubo and Saka, 2002)'. They also suggest that 'knowledge workers will need to make numerous judgements about a variety of job-related issues and it is this uncertainty in the decision-making process that is a key characteristic of knowledge work' (Mohrman et al., 1995: 17, cited in Benson and Brown, 2007: 125). Other insights into the nature of knowledge work are provided by Alvesson (1993), who notes that the work of knowledge workers is more aptly characterised as ambiguity-intensive rather than knowledge-intensive. There is general agreement that knowledge workers are well educated, with Starbuck (1992: 719) defining the notion of 'well-educated' quite precisely in stating that employees within KIFs must comprise at least one third 'experts' and that an 'expert' denotes 'someone with a formal education and experience equivalent to a doctoral degree'.

HRM in KIFs

It is apparent from this short overview of the nature of KIFs that they are complex organisations that require highly educated individuals to undertake the demanding nature of the work. Given this complexity, it is not surprising to find that researchers of KIFs have moved away from traditional ways of viewing the operation of HRM as the series of functional activities that is depicted in standard textbooks. Studies that have been designed to capture the nature of HRM in KIFs have focused on issues such as job design (Benson and Brown, 2007; Foss et al., 2009); individual and organisational learning (Kang and Snell, 2009; Swart and Kinnie, 2010); and knowledge creation, exchange and combination (Collins and Clark, 2003; Collins and Smith, 2006). Studies have also focused on viewing people management issues from perspectives such as human, relational and organisational capital and 'knowledge assets' (Swart and Kinnie, 2003, 2012).

Despite the differing approaches used in researching HRM within KIFs, there is still the need for a human resource (HR) function as well as a set of practices to manage knowledge workers. In the case of the HR function, research indicates that HR departments within these types of organisation may not operate according to standard models. For example, Finegold and Frenkel

(2006: 2–3), in their analysis of HRM in eight United States (US) and Australian biotech start-up firms, suggest that 'HR managers play a strategic role as knowledge brokers, advisors and change agents in constantly moving the organization forward to the next best practice frontier' and that HR professionals need to be 'at the centre of the organization, analysing, building and reinforcing a corporate culture and core competencies' as 'knowledge creation, knowledge sharing and learning become keys to future success'. In the case of HR practices, the factors that have been identified as important in the management of knowledge workers include high levels of pay; the intrinsic nature of the work itself such as the challenge it presents and the opportunities it provides for learning and the development of transferable skills; as well as promotion options, the opportunity to influence work decisions and relationships with co-workers (May et al., 2002). Other factors that have been identified include development interventions that allow access to challenging projects that will enhance and expand skill sets and performance management systems (Swart et al., 2003). These practices, which may be broadly labelled 'high commitment', are believed to 'foster social climates that facilitate the development of employee-based capabilities – such as the ability to combine and exchange information to create new knowledge – that in turn create competitive advantage (Bowen and Ostroff, 2004; Collins and Clark, 2003)' (Collins and Smith, 2006: 546). At the same time, such approaches to HRM have to be tempered by the reality that many knowledge workers' loyalties will lie with their profession rather than their organisation and that extensive training and development may enhance transferable skills that are enticing to other employers (Swart, 2007).

HRM in KIFs: The Irish Evidence

Several studies of HRM in KIFs have been undertaken in Ireland over the last number of years. The studies follow the trend within the international literature discussed above of viewing KIFs and the knowledge workers they employ as distinctive types of entities, and the issues of learning, knowledge sharing, human capital, HR system design and the management of knowledge workers emerge as key themes. Most of the research to date has been focused at an employee level but there are also some industry-level and firm-level studies that provide insights into facets of HRM within KIFs. These three levels of analysis are therefore used as an organising framework for presenting the findings from the various studies which must also be viewed against the backdrop of the dramatic and often devastating changes in the economic climate that have occurred in Ireland in recent times.

Industry Level

A multi-level study of KIFs was undertaken in both Ireland and the United Kingdom (UK) between 2008 and 2010. This was funded by research agencies in both Ireland (Irish Research Council for Humanities and Social Sciences (IRCHSS)) and the UK (the Economic and Social Research Council (ESRC))[1] and explored how Ireland and the UK differ in their approaches to industrial policy and labour market planning and the impact of these differences on HRM policies and practices at the level of the firm. At an industry level, Hannon et al.'s (2011) analysis shows how the approach to industrial policy that has been adopted by the Irish government and its various development agencies has led to a strategic focus on the pharmaceutical industry. This, in turn, has led to large-scale investment at government level in doctoral-level programmes in science, technology and engineering to support an ongoing pipeline of knowledge workers for the sector. At the same time, knowledge workers who were interviewed in the four companies that are described in Hannon et al.'s work indicated that although their job descriptions demanded master's or PhD level qualifications, in many cases they were unable to utilise this expertise in their everyday work, leading to feelings of job dissatisfaction. This can largely be explained by the fact that the companies for which they were working were engaged mainly in manufacturing rather than in the R&D which would have provided more opportunities to use their education and training. The findings demonstrate how industrial policy can shape HR strategies through its impact on the availability and utilisation of skills in the sector. At the same time, they also illustrate how tensions may occur when government-level strategies to promote a knowledge economy by investment in postgraduate education are not matched with a widespread availability of knowledge-based job opportunities.

Firm Level

At a firm level, the IRCHSS/ESRC study indicated the existence of two quite different types of HR systems (productivity based and commitment based) operating within the information and communications technology (ICT) firms that formed part of the sample of KIFs. Here it was found that HR practices were designed and delivered to reinforce an overarching philosophy of how people might be managed (Monks et al., 2013). However, in the firms with productivity-based HR systems, the outcomes of such practices were not necessarily positive for the knowledge workers at the receiving end (see Box 9.1).

Box 9.1: Productivity-Based HRM in an ICT Firm

ICT2 employs 90 staff and is primarily engaged in software solutions. Performance permeates all aspects of the HR system, from the ways in which the jobs are designed through to the processes through which the HR practices are delivered. With regard to job design, the emphasis is on standardisation of tasks and activities and there is little discretion allowed in relation to how jobs are performed. The work is intensive and closely monitored and high levels of output are demanded. The focus on performance in the delivery of HR practices is exemplified in the HR manager's description of the performance management system as the 'key HR practice' within the firm. This system encompasses both rewards and training with the performance-related pay system having a dual role in both rewarding, when performance is high, and punishing (by withdrawing pay or threatening dismissal) when underperformance occurs. Training is used to reinforce the high performance, results-based culture, and is designed to ensure that employees can deliver solutions to specific customer problems rather than to enhance the skill set of the employees themselves. Communication is top-down and centres on encouraging productivity. There is little involvement on the part of employees in the design of work processes.

Employee reactions to these practices include job dissatisfaction and low morale. They also experience stress as a result of the intensive and competitive work environment and express frustration at the lack of opportunities to contribute new ideas or to engage in broader skills-based training or career development.

Source: Monks et al. (2013)

Another firm-level study undertaken in 120 professional service firms (Fu et al., 2013) applied concepts from the literature on high performance work systems (HPWS) to explore the linkages between HR practices and high performance. There was evidence in these firms of the adoption of high performance work practices that included selective recruitment, internal promotion, regular and multiple-source-based performance appraisal, above market levels of remuneration, information sharing, continuous training and mentoring. The study's findings suggest that HPWS influence performance by helping to build the firm's resources of human, social and organisational capital, which create value for the firm when they are effectively utilised.

Employee Level

Research within Ireland has been focused in particular at employee level and has concentrated on how HR practices are used in the management of knowledge workers. In the late 1990s an employee-level study of 402 knowledge workers was undertaken of eleven organisations in the high technology, manufacturing and financial services sectors in Ireland (Flood et al., 2001). The study examined the relationship between knowledge workers and their employers through the lens of the psychological contract and concluded that for knowledge workers, 'equitable rewards affect whether their expectations have been met which, in turn, affect the com-mitment of employees towards their organization' (Flood et al., 2001: 1163). The perception by knowledge workers that employers are fulfilling their part of the psychological contract meant that they are more likely to remain committed and less likely to leave the company, even when offered better employment conditions elsewhere.

Flood et al.'s (2001) study was conducted at a time when Ireland's economy was booming and issues of retention were problematic for all types of firms. More recent employee-level research has been undertaken in a very different economic environment where job opportunities are scarce and employers are focused much more on cost-cutting and retrenchment. The findings from these studies present a more mixed picture of the nature of the relationship between employers and knowledge workers.

In 2007, an in-depth ethnographic study was undertaken of knowledge workers employed by a multinational corporation operating in Ireland that is a world-renowned provider of high technology, knowledge-based, premium price products and services. Part of the study focused on exploring the relationship between HR practices, commitment, work and employment relations (Cushen and Thompson, 2012: 79–90) and was undertaken from a critical management perspective. The research revealed an interesting dichotomy between firm-level and employee-level perceptions of HR practices. On the one hand, the firm believed that 'in its search for committed, high-performing employees it was doing everything "by the textbook"' as it had invested in 'the brand, vision and extensive communication mechanisms, the bundles of interrelated, best practices; and an HR department at the core of its strategy and operations' (p. 89). Yet, the research found that 'the outcome was scepticism and often barely disguised contempt from the kind of employees we are told are particularly open to the charms of soft, culture-led practices' and 'knowledge workers' commitment to and engagement with the company was low' (p. 89). However, this scepticism did not translate into low levels of performance; indeed underperformance was of no concern within the firm. Thus 'anger at the company did not produce (at least overt) resistance or prevent positive attitudes to work performance' (p. 90) and the researchers suggest that 'skilled technical workers in knowledge-intensive firms can be uncommitted, angry and high-performing at the same time' (p. 79).

The contradictions that emerge from the Cushen and Thompson (2012) study of knowledge workers also surface in the IRCHSS/ESRC study. Here the employee-level analysis provides insights into careers within both the pharmaceutical and ICT sectors. In the pharmaceutical sector (Kelly et al., 2011), the study focused on understanding the richness and complexity of specialist and generalist human capital and its relevance for organisational learning. It also explored the experiences of knowledge workers within the pharmaceutical sector in relation to the training and development which has been identified as an important HR practice in the management of knowledge workers (e.g. Swart et al., 2003). It was apparent from the knowledge workers who were interviewed that there were wide variations in both the access they had to training and development and the ways in which they utilised opportunities that did arise and how their careers varied as a result (see Box 9.2). A later analysis of male and female careers across both the pharmaceutical and ICT sectors (Truss et al., 2012) showed that these training and development opportunities were gender-bound. It was found that while male and female knowledge workers held similar qualifications and work experience, female knowledge workers were more likely to hold lower-level positions than their male colleagues. This suggests that female knowledge workers in KIFS find themselves in a vicious circle as organisations are more likely to provide generalist training for knowledge workers holding more senior roles and individuals in these roles are more likely to be able to display the innovative behaviour necessary for career advancement.

Box 9.2: Specialist and Generalist Careers in a Pharmaceutical Firm

Pharma1 is a large multinational pharmaceutical company involved in manufacturing and R&D with sites and business units spread throughout the UK, Europe and the US. It employs knowledge workers in a range of scientific, technical and managerial positions that require the use of both specialist and generalist knowledge and skills. The company operates a graduate training scheme and attracts graduates with bachelor's, master's or PhD degrees in disciplines such as chemistry or engineering. Many of the graduates then work in the company's laboratories or manufacturing plant where they utilise their discipline-based, specialist expertise. The company provides training and development for these graduates in a number of ways. First, it provides on-the-job skills training in specific techniques, particularly in areas that relate to the highly regulated environment within which the pharmaceutical sector operates. Second, it supports the graduates' attendance at external scientific conferences or seminars that further enhance their specialist knowledge. Third, as part of the graduate training scheme, some graduates are identified as potential 'stars' (Groysberg and Lee, 2009) and are singled out for the types of education, training and development that will prepare them for future higher-level management roles. This process may involve these graduates studying for additional qualifications in different specialist areas to those of their original degrees; for example obtaining a qualification in engineering if they graduated in chemistry. This focus on cross-disciplinary expertise reflects the complexity of the manufacturing and R&D processes within the pharmaceutical industry and the need for senior management to understand the processes underpinning its operation. In addition, these graduates obtain management expertise through involvement in the organisation-wide management development programme and/or through obtaining an MBA qualification.

This multi-faceted approach to education, training and development pro-motes the development of generalist expertise in this cadre of graduates.

The focus on the creation of either specialist or generalist expertise has a number of outcomes at both individual and company levels. For the graduates who became specialists, the outcome at a personal level is a limiting of promotion possibilities to a scientific career track while at an organisational level their increasing specialisation leads to difficulties in sharing knowledge with those working in other areas. For the graduates who become generalists, the types of responsibilities that the management roles demand are sometimes a source of frustration as these knowledge workers are increasingly divorced from the scientific activity with which they had originally engaged. However, from an organisational perspective, their generalist expertise leads to increased opportunities for knowledge creation and sharing not simply across their own company but across the organisation as a whole.

Source: Kelly et al. (2011)

Further evidence of the fact that there may be a lack of fit between the HR systems designed to manage knowledge workers and the knowledge workers' high levels of education and specialist knowledge is found in a study undertaken by Harney et al. (2011). This study undertook research on 40 university research scientists working across five university research centres in Ireland. Most employees of these centres were educated to doctoral level and thus epitomise Starbuck's (1992) notion of a knowledge worker. Knowledge workers are generally considered 'core' employees as they 'possess valuable and firm-specific human capital' (Kang et al., 2007: 243). Yet the study found that many of the scientists working in these centres were only employed on contract, with contracts ranging from one to five years, and were dependent for the renewal of these contracts on the income that the centre might be able to raise from research grants. Given that knowledge work has gener-ally been regarded as a 'core' rather than a peripheral activity, these researchers experienced what the study describes as a 'Cinderella-like' status as university employees (Ackers and Oliver, 2007). Their contract status meant that they had no access to university-level HR practices such as promotion, performance management or career development. Yet these types of practices have been seen as vital in the management of knowledge workers (Collins and Smith, 2006; Swart et al., 2003) and were crucial to any career progression expec-tations that the research scientists might have.

HRM in KIFs: Analysis and Insights

This chapter has focused on providing a brief overview of the international literature on HRM in KIFs, as well as insights into the recent Irish research in the area. Several interesting issues emerge from this review. First, it is becoming evident from some of the more recent research that while high commitment HRM may have at one stage been the system of choice for many firms in their approach to managing their knowledge employees (e.g. Collins and Smith, 2006), this is no longer necessarily the case. There is evidence both internationally and within Ireland (Kang and Snell, 2009; Monks et al., 2013) that what have been labelled 'productivity-based' HR systems are also used in the management of such employees. In addition, there is also evidence that knowledge workers might be managed on the type of contract system that has been more usually assigned to peripheral workers (Harney et al., 2011). These approaches seem very much at odds with the previously accepted wisdom on the nature of knowledge work and the high levels of education that are held by knowledge workers. However, explanations of these trends can first of all be sought in the recent worldwide economic downturn that has created the need for firms to reduce costs and therefore rethink all aspects of management within their firms. The impact of this downturn has been particularly severely felt within Ireland, and in **Chapter 2** of this book Roche examines this in detail. It is also the case that the prior focus in HRM research on high commitment systems may have neglected the more pervasive impact of HR philosophy in determining approaches to the management of knowledge workers. In addition, the Irish research also points to the potential of small, university-based research centres as interesting research sites. Such sites, while encapsulating all the dimensions of a KIF as well as being populated nearly entirely by highly educated knowledge workers, have been somewhat neglected in prior analysis.

Second, the contradictions that have recently emerged with regard to the management of knowledge workers raise issues about synergy and fit in HR systems that have been the focus of considerable attention within the wider HRM literature (see Kepes and Delery, 2007 for an overview). Fit issues have been concentrated within firm-level research with limited attention paid to the impact on employees that contradictions or lack of fit might cause. However, the Irish research studies indicate the ways in which lack of fit may be created at an industry level and how this may then filter down to employee levels where it is exhibited in low levels of job satisfaction or high levels of discontent. This highlights tensions between the pursuit of high commitment and high productivity which have not been adequately captured to date.

Conclusions

The exploration of HRM in KIFs has indicated the complexity of both the organisations themselves and the approaches to HRM that are used in the management of the types of workers they employ. This complexity is mirrored in the approaches that have been adopted in researching and understanding HRM in KIFs. While these new approaches have provided a more nuanced understanding of HR issues, of knowledge workers and of the KIFs themselves, there are still avenues for additional research.

First, while definitions of the term 'knowledge worker' exist (e.g. Benson and Brown, 2007) there is perhaps a need to elaborate these definitions not only by reference to the type of work that is undertaken but also by the particular context within which it takes place. For example, Irish research has shown that individuals with doctoral level qualifications are not necessarily enjoying the access to employment opportunities that their skills levels might be expected to command or which fit with accepted wisdom on the working conditions that provide a motivating environment to engage in knowledge work. There may be a need for more research that focuses on particular types of KIF with the aim of providing a more nuanced understanding of the nature of KIFs, their knowledge workers and their HR systems.

Second, the interrelationships between the different levels of analysis that emerged from this Irish research suggests that the understanding of HRM in KIFs might benefit from more multi-level analyses that integrate industry, firm and employee level perspectives. Such an approach is in line with research that emphasises the need for attention to be paid to the contextual factors that influence HRM (e.g. Paauwe, 2004).

Finally, at a practice level, our analysis suggests that there are challenges for firms in designing HR systems to meet the needs of knowledge workers. There is evidence that high commitment HR systems, although not resulting in reductions in performance, may not necessarily be welcomed by knowledge workers (Cushen and Thompson, 2012). At the other end of the spectrum, where knowledge workers are exposed to productivity-based HR systems, performance may be maintained but in this case through a series of controls. The issue for KIFs is how a balance might be struck between the costs of these different types of HR system. There are employer-level costs of investment in high commitment HR systems and employee-level costs of experiencing a performance-driven system that creates widespread job dissatisfaction. In the latter case this may also translate into employer-level costs should economic conditions improve and employees decide to look for alternative employment. Overall, it is evident that many challenges remain for KIFs in the design and delivery of the HR systems that are crucial to their successful operation.

Notes

1   The financial support of the IRCHSS and the ESRC (RES-062-23-1183) in funding the research project is gratefully acknowledged.

References

Ackers, L. and Oliver, L. (2007), 'From Flexicurity to Flexsecquality? The Impact of the Fixed-Term Contract Provisions on Employment in Science Research', *International Studies of Management and Organization*, 37(1): 53–79.

Alvesson, M. (1993), 'Organizations as Rhetoric: Knowledge-Intensive Firms and the Struggle with Ambiguity', *Journal of Management Studies*, 30(6): 997–1015.

Alvesson, M. (1995), *Management of Knowledge-Intensive Companies*, Berlin: de Gruyter.

Alvesson, M. (2000), 'Social Identity and the Problem of Loyalty in Knowledge-Intensive Companies', *Journal of Management Studies*, 37(8): 1101–1124.

Benson, J. and Brown, M. (2007), 'Knowledge Workers: What Keeps Them Committed; What Turns Them Away', *Work, Employment and Society*, 2(1): 121–141.

Bowen, D. and Ostroff, C. (2004), 'Understanding HRM–Firm Performance Linkages: The Role of the "Strength" of the HRM System', *Academy of Management Review*, 29(2): 203–221.

Collins, C. and Clark, K. (2003), 'Strategic Human Resource Practices, Top Management Team Social Networks, and Firm Performance: The Role of Human Resource Practices in Creating Organizational Competitive Advantage', *Academy of Management Journal*, 46(6): 740–751.

Collins, C. and Smith, K. (2006), 'Knowledge Exchange and Combination: The Role of Human Resource Practices in the Performance of High Technology Firms', *Academy of Management Journal*, 49(1): 544–560.

Cortada, J. (1998), *Rise of the Knowledge Worker*, Boston, MA: Butterworth-Heinemann.

Cushen, J. and Thompson, P. (2012), 'Doing the Right Thing? HRM and the Angry Knowledge Worker', *New Technology, Work and Employment*, 27(2): 79–92.

Finegold, D. and Frenkel, S. (2006), 'Managing People Where People really Matter: The Management of Human Resources in Biotech Companies', *International Journal of Human Resource Management*, 17(1): 1–24.

Flood, P., Turner, T., Ramamoorthy, N. and Pearson, J. (2001), 'Causes and Consequences of Psychological Contracts among Knowledge Workers in the High Technology and Financial Services Industries', *International Journal of Human Resource Management*, 12(7): 1152–1165.

Foss, N., Minbaeva, D., Pedersen, T. and Reinholdt, M. (2009), 'Encouraging Knowledge Sharing among Employees: How Job Design Matters', *Human Resource Management*, 48(6): 871–893.

Frenkel, S., Korczynski, M., Donoughue, L. and Shire, K. (1995), 'Re-Constituting Work: Trends towards Knowledge Work and Info-Normative Control', *Work, Employment and Society*, 9(4): 773–796.

Fu, N., Flood, P., Bosak, J., Morris, T. and O'Regan, P. (2013), 'Exploring the Performance Effect of HPWS on Professional Service Supply Chain Management', *Supply Chain Management: An International Journal*, 18(3): 1–18.

Groysberg, B. and Lee, L. (2009), 'Hiring Stars and Their Colleagues: Exploration and Exploitation in Professional Service Firms', *Organization Science*, 20(4): 740–758.

Hannon, E., Monks, K., Conway, E., Kelly, G., Flood, P., Truss, K. and Mastroeni, M. (2011), 'The State and Industrial Policy in Ireland: A Case Study of the Irish Pharmaceutical Sector', *International Journal of Human Resource Management*, 22(18): 3692–3710.

Harney, B., Monks, K., Alexopoulos, A., Buckley, F. and Hogan, T. (2011), 'University Research Scientists as Knowledge Workers: Contract Status and Employment Status', *International Journal of Human Resource Management*, DOI:10.1080/09585192.2011.561241.

Kang, S., Morris, S. and Snell, S. (2007), 'Relational Archetypes, Organizational Learning, and Value Creation: Extending the Human Resource Architecture', *Academy of Management Review*, 32(1): 236–256.

Kang, S.C. and Snell, S. (2009), 'Intellectual Capital Architectures and Ambidextrous Learning: A Framework for Human Resource Management', *Journal of Management Studies*, 46(1): 65–92.

Kelly, G., Mastroeni, M., Conway, E., Monks, K., Truss, K., Flood, P. and Hannon, E. (2011), 'Combining Diverse Knowledge: Knowledge Workers' Experience of Specialist and Generalist Roles', *Personnel Review*, 40(5): 607–624.

Kepes, S. and Delery, J. (2007), 'HRM Systems and the Problem of Internal Fit' in P. Boxall, J. Purcell and P. Wright (eds), *The Oxford Handbook of Human Resource Management*, Oxford: Oxford University Press.

Kubo, I. and Saka, A. (2002), 'An Inquiry into the Motivations of Knowledge Workers in the Japanese Financial Industry', *Journal of Knowledge Management*, 6(3): 262–271.

Lowendahl, B. (1997), *Strategic Management in Professional Service Firms*, Copenhagen: Copenhagen Business School Press.

May, T., Korczynski, M. and Frenkel, S. (2002), 'Organizational and Occupational Commitment: Knowledge Workers in Large Organizations', *Journal of Management Studies*, 39(6): 775–801.

McGrath, P. (2005), 'Thinking Differently about Knowledge-Intensive Firms: Insights from Early Medieval Monasticism', *Organization*, 12(4): 549–566.

Mohrman, S., Cohen, S. and Mohrman, A. (1995), *Designing Team-Based Organizations: New Forms for Knowledge Work*, San Francisco, CA: Jossey-Bass.

Monks, K., Kelly, G., Conway, E., Truss, K., Flood, P. and Hannon, E. (2013), 'Understanding How HR Systems Work: The Role of HR Philosophy and HR Processes', *Human Resource Management Journal*, 23(4): 379–395.

Paauwe, J. (2004), *HRM and Performance: Achieving Long-Term Viability*, Oxford: Oxford University Press.

Scarbrough, J. (1999), 'Knowledge as Work: Conflicts in the Management of Knowledge Workers', *Technology Analysis and Strategic Management*, 11(1): 5–16.

Starbuck, W.H. (1992), 'Learning by Knowledge-Intensive Firms', *Journal of Management Studies*, 29(6): 713–740.

Swart, J. (2007), 'HRM and Knowledge Workers' in P. Boxall, J. Purcell and P. Wright (eds), *The Oxford Handbook of Human Resource Management*, Oxford: Oxford University Press.

Swart, J. and Kinnie, N. (2003), 'Sharing Knowledge in Knowledge-Intensive Firms', *Human Resource Management Journal*, 13(2): 145–156.

Swart, J. and Kinnie, N. (2010), 'Organisational Learning, Knowledge Assets and HR Practices in Professional Service Firms', *Human Resource Management Journal*, 20(1): 64–79.

Swart, J. and Kinnie, N. (2012), 'Managing Multidimensional Knowledge Assets: HR Configurations in Professional Service Firms', *Human Resource Management Journal*, 23(2): 160–179.

Swart, J., Kinnie, N. and Purcell, J. (2003), *People and Performance in Knowledge-Intensive Firms*, London: Chartered Institute of Personnel and Development.

Truss, K., D'Amato, A., Conway, E., Kelly, G., Monks, K., Hannon, E. and Flood, P. (2012), 'Knowledge Work: Gender Blind or Gender Biased?', *Work, Employment and Society*, 26(5): 735–754.

CHAPTER 10

HRM in Healthcare: A Focus on the Hospital Sector

Aoife M. McDermott and Mary A. Keating[1]

HRM in Healthcare: Saving Lives, Saving Cost

Why are healthcare organisations so difficult to manage? Few if any countries are satisfied with their health systems (Glouberman and Mintzberg, 2001). As a result, reforms are being contemplated worldwide to make health organisations more responsive to user needs as well as more financially accountable. A growing body of research has drawn attention to the potential of human resource management (HRM) to address these issues. HRM can help enhance the performance of health services, by impacting on the efficiency and effectiveness of patient care delivery. In theory, imperatives to reduce the costs of service provision and improve the quality of care, combined with the human-capital-intensive, high-skilled and high-impact nature of health service delivery, make healthcare an ideal context in which HRM can make a contribution.

The potential for HRM to influence efficiency is illustrated in the scale and centrality of the health sector to the Irish economy. According to the Department of Health (2011), total health expenditure accounted for 11.4 per cent of Irish gross national income in 2009, sixth highest of twenty-seven Organisation for Economic Co-Operation and Development countries. More than 107,000 whole-time-equivalent staff were employed by the health service in September 2011, with salary costs accounting for up to 70 per

191

cent of hospital expenditure. Beyond the efficiency concerns engendered by the scale of the sector, hospitals need to provide a good quality, safe service through the recruitment, retention and management of high calibre employees. This is challenging – and made more so by an increasingly globalised market for healthcare professionals. However, good people management is paramount. De Vries et al. (2008) have established that between 3.8 per cent and 16.6 per cent of all hospital in-patients internationally suffer avoidable harm during their care. Such harm ranges from healthcare-acquired infections to wrong or delayed diagnoses and medication errors, and is often rooted in people-related activities. This harm has personal, social and economic implications, with the United Kingdom's (UK) National Audit Office (2005) estimating that preventable adverse events cost approximately £3.5 billion per annum within the UK. The dual imperatives of saving lives and saving cost have led to sustained efforts to improve the delivery, efficiency, quality and safety of healthcare services through effective human resource management.

In this chapter we focus our attention on the provision of HRM in the hospital sector, although we note that similar challenges may be faced throughout the health service as a whole. We draw on Irish and international research throughout the remainder of this chapter. Having detailed the rationale for focusing on HRM in healthcare, we proceed to consider the role of the hospital human resource (HR) function and delivery structures; collate evidence on the relationship between HR and performance in hospitals; identify the structural, coordination, and union-related challenges to managing people in hospitals; and consider how current theoretical debates suggest these challenges might be addressed. We conclude by offering a critical commentary on the future of HRM in healthcare.

HRM in Hospitals: A Challenging and Constrained Imperative

HRM is concerned with the management of individuals and collectives of people at work. It delivers value to organisations at three levels: operational, managerial and strategic. At the operational level, HRM supports the efficient operation of an organisation by enabling the implementation of policies and standard HR practices on a daily basis. At the managerial level, these HR activities are managed and overseen by a HR management function. Finally, at the strategic level, HRM involves the planning and development of a HR strategy to underpin the delivery of an organisation's mission and strategy. We now focus on the managerial level and identify contextual challenges for hospital HRM before reviewing research on how the HR function supports the management of employees in hospitals.

Hospitals operate in complex political, structural and economic environments, where people management decisions and practices are constrained and impacted by a wide range of stakeholders. Decision-making regarding core HR practices, including pay, terms and conditions of employment, and certain aspects of union engagement, are centralised through the Health Service National Partnership Forum. Furthermore, professional representative bodies, including the Irish Medical Organisation and the Irish Nurses and Midwives Organisation, influence the training and development requirements for clinical staff and subsequent recruitment and selection criteria for posts.

The co-existence of multiple staff cohorts creates additional complexity for hospital HRM. Employee groups (e.g. doctors, nurses, allied health professionals (AHPs), porters, estates services and managerial employees) differ in terms of their uniqueness and value to the organisation (McDermott and Keating, 2011). As a result, despite working within the same hospital, employees within these groups have different employment relationships, union representation and collective agreements. The sector is therefore aptly described by Denis et al (2001: 809) as a 'classic pluralistic domain involving divergent objectives … and multiple actors'. The industrial relations context of the health sector in Ireland, as in Britain, is characterised by a multiplicity of unions and high union density. This context requires the HR function to provide support to, manage and cooperate with a range of employees and their representatives.

Lastly, we note that hospitals are predominantly professional organisations. They rely on the standardisation of skills among their operational core of clinical employees (doctors, nurses and allied health professionals) to deliver their services. The professional nature of clinical work raises issues regarding the legitimacy of HR practitioners in managing clinical staff. As a result, hospital HR managers require strong relationships with professionally trained managers to ensure that performance issues are identified and addressed. HR managers may need direct input from professionally trained colleagues, such as the medical director or director of nursing, to inform decisions regarding professional practice issues such as how clinically safe a work practice is, or whether an employee requires discipline or training after an adverse event.

In summary, HRM faces significant challenges and constraints in efforts to manage a complex array of external and internal stakeholders and support high quality service delivery. The decision-making capability and influence of the hospital HR management function is significantly constrained by national policy and centralised decision-making, the broad remit of professional bodies and the multi-union nature of the employee relations environment.

The Hospital HR Function

Reflecting these complexities, although HRM as a management practice has potential to contribute to organisational performance and patient outcomes, evidence from Ireland (McDermott and Keating, 2011; Conway and Monks, 2010) and the UK (Hyde et al., 2006) suggests that many hospital HR management functions are underdeveloped and lacking capacity. A core limitation is that aspects of HR (e.g. pay) are centrally controlled and managed. In Ireland, in spite of efforts to the contrary, many hospital HR functions play a marginal role, engaging in reactive strategising (McDermott and Keating, 2011) and acting as regulators of HR activities (e.g. absenteeism) (Conway and Monks, 2010).

In practice, the hospital HR function is driven by policy, administrative, industrial relations and compliance roles. The generation of clear managerial guidelines on how to implement specific HR practices, the translation of legislation and the generation of 'user-friendly' HR resources does add value for middle and line managers undertaking HR roles (Conway and Monks, 2010). However, hospital HR is still predominantly characterised by an administrative focus. It provides routine administrative and local industrial relations services and support to non-core, non-professional workforce groups. It struggles to play a strong role in the proactive management of professionals, or in the creation of strategy, planning or the implementation of change. The frustrations of one hospital HR manager in this regard are illustrated in Box 10.1.

Box 10.1: A HR Manager's Frustration at the Role of a Hospital HR Function

This example illustrates one HR manager's perspective on the role of the hospital HR function. The opinions were expressed in an interview that formed part of a multi-site study of the role of the hospital HR function.

The hospital HR manager expressed frustration at the difficulty of gaining external or internal support for his strategically oriented activities. His initial attempts to engage in strategic HR planning entailed detailed inputs into the hospital service plan. However, he had become disenchanted with the centralised nature of decision-making and a lack of feedback. Within the hospital, he also felt constrained. While he aimed to undertake strategic activities, he felt that HR doesn't 'have the clout, if you want to put it that way. It isn't seen as the role.' As a consequence, he described the role of the HR function as 'local, dealing with local small issues. ... The macro issues tend to be over your head.'

The activities of this HR function were therefore limited to a functional expert role. This included HR-related administration and implementing basic HR practices including industrial relations management; salary, pensions and increment administration; and recruitment. Salaries were established centrally but administered locally. Similarly, union negotiations were conducted centrally and recommendations implemented locally. The function was aiming to change a culturally embedded expectation that the HR function should undertake middle and line manager responsibilities, including dealing with absenteeism. However, devolution of people management was being resisted in the organisation, with the medical director noting, 'I have noticed a tendency for a lot of HR and personnel functions to devolve. ... And I have a tendency to devolve them back!'

Although the HR manager wished to move towards a strategic orientation, the HR function had low status and the culture of HR undertaking the duties of line managers placed significant strain on available resources. A movement towards a strategic orientation to workforce management appeared unlikely in the short to medium term.

Source: This box text draws on a Health Research Board funded study (PA-07-17) of the role of the hospital HR function, conducted by Aoife McDermott, Mary Keating and Louise Fitzgerald.

Although the HR function struggles to engage proactively in strategic management, hospitals do effectively provide large volumes of services and actively engage in service improvement, all of which necessitates the management of staff. Therefore, at the operational level, HRM as 'the management of people' is successfully practised daily – if not always led proactively by the HR function. This is related to the devolution of the practice of people management to middle and line managers within hospitals.

Devolved HRM in Healthcare: Professionals Managing Professionals

The management of professionals by professionals is a core characteristic of professional organisations such as hospitals, where the organisation surrenders power to and relies on high-skilled employees to complete its operational tasks. This approach is in line with the best practice devolved model of HRM. Devolved HRM positions line managers as the pivotal delivery point for the enactment of HRM policy and practices. The rationale for devolvement includes the fact that the attitudes, behaviours and practices of line managers affect the quality of people management outcomes, as line managers are closest to the workers. It has also been argued that devolution speeds up people-related decision-making and reduces costs. There is an additional rationale within hospitals. The professional knowledge of clinicians requires that they are managed by individuals within their professional skill boundary – who understand and have legitimacy in managing their work. Increasingly, 'hybrid' managers – who undertake both clinical and managerial roles (e.g. a clinical nurse manager or clinical director) – are a strong feature of hospitals. However, one challenge has been to create medium- to longer-term career development opportunities for hybrid managers. This has been achieved for nurses in Ireland, but clear career paths are less evident for hybrid managers from other professions.

One important consequence of profession devolution in hospitals has been the development of sophisticated silos, with implications for how the HR function is structured. Medical, nursing and other more generic chains of command are now so embedded that they are reflected in the structure of the devolved HR function: medical manpower, nursing personnel and general HR services are typically managed separately. This is illustrated in Figure 10.1. The professional differentiation in the HR delivery model reflects both how HR practitioners have adapted to providing HR within the professional bureaucracy and historic differences in the perceived status and function of each of the clinical professions (especially medicine and nursing).

Figure 10.1: Professionally Oriented Devolved Model of HRM

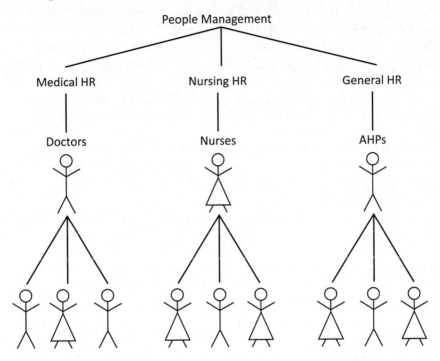

Source: This figure illustrates findings from a Health Research Board funded study (PA-07-17) of the role of the hospital HR function, conducted by Aoife McDermott, Mary Keating and Louise Fitzgerald.

Devolution has implications for the role, as well as the structure, of the HR function, which must support hybrid clinical middle and line managers as well as engage in broader HR activities. Three factors have been identified as supporting the effective devolution of HR within the hospital environment. These factors involve middle/line managers' (i) understanding of the rationale for their involvement, (ii) belief in the value of this involvement, and (iii) role clarity and capability for sophisticated enactment of the HR role (Conway and Monks, 2010). In addition to these factors, the HR function must ensure coordination between professionals who are managed independently. This challenge underpins the effective delivery of healthcare and is a theme to which we will return later.

In summary, the HR function has replicated the structural divisions in the management of professional staff and is therefore distanced from the managerial and clinical workforces (McDermott and Keating, 2011). Although the HR function has faced challenges regarding its status and power across a range of industries, scope to develop HRM in healthcare has been said to be limited by historic scepticism among professional staff regarding hospital management, the limited credibility of the HR function, its focus on a narrow operational contribution and its peripheral position in the professional organisation (Barnett et al., 1996). The delivery of HRM in hospitals poses the following challenges for HR professionals:

- Adapting to the professional structure of hospitals
- Achieving horizontal coordination among the hybrid clinical line managers delivering frontline HR and among frontline staff delivering services
- Dealing with multiple employee groups and their representatives

Prior to examining how these challenges might be addressed, we consider recent and more positive research evidence pertaining to the relationship between HR practice and performance in healthcare.

The Relationship between HR Practice and Performance in Healthcare: Early Evidence and Growing Understanding

HR Practices Supporting Organisational Outcomes

HRM as a discipline is comprised of a number of core activities or practices, including recruitment and selection, training and development, performance appraisal and management, reward, employee welfare and security, and employee relations. How these practices interact to support organisational outcomes has been a focus of HR research for some time. A growing body of research has evidenced potential for high performance work systems (HPWS) to enhance the effectiveness (West et al., 2006) and cost efficiency of health care (Bartram et al., 2007). The human capital intensity of healthcare delivery has led to the widespread adoption of HPWS, which typically focus on the effective selection, engagement, utilisation and development of employees to improve their performance and associated organisational outcomes (Garman et al, 2011). West et al. (2006) distinguished between the technical aspects of care, referring to the appropriate application of professional knowledge and skills, and the interpersonal aspects of care, referring to relationships between patients and care providers. HR practices found to influence both these aspects of care include performance appraisal and training, employment security, teamwork, decentralisation, and participatory mechanisms and team-based structures. West et al. (2006) argue that, together, performance appraisal/management and teamwork enable employees to be clear about their roles and to enhance their knowledge and skills. These HR practices work in combination with employment security to ensure that skills and knowledge are retained. Lastly, decentralisation, participatory mechanisms and team-based structures promote knowledge sharing. In summary, a combination of HR practices bundled together as a HPWS can support healthcare organisations to provide and improve patient-centred care. Next we move to consider the broader role of HR practices and the HR function in supporting employees' commitment to change initiatives – a key support for service improvement in healthcare.

HR's Role in Supporting Employees' Commitment to Change

Research on the role of HR practices in supporting commitment to change initiatives in the Irish health service has considered whether the HR practices valued by employees, rather than those valued by managers, are helpful in achieving organisational goals (Conway and Monks, 2008, 2009). Conway and Monks (2008) emphasised that basic HR practices, including communications, staffing and rewards, influence employee commitment to change. Communications-related interventions refer to top-down information mechanisms, rather than the high involvement HR practices often considered in the HR literature. Conway and Monks (2008) argue that one rationale for employees' concern with basic HR practices is that, in times of change, they may need reassurance regarding the status of their employment relationship (communication), whether there will be sufficient staffing to undertake new working arrangements (staffing) and whether the reward system will be amended to take account of new responsibilities incurred by a change initiative (rewards). These findings suggest that when organisations are undertaking change initiatives, HR functions need to ensure that the implications for the basic components of the employment relationship are explicitly considered, and that employees are kept informed. Importantly, their study also suggests that employees are more likely to take an interest in, and become committed to, change that has local benefits and that has immediate implications for their own roles and working conditions. As a result, there may be a significant role for HR in translating national, regional and organisational initiatives into organisational implications that employees can easily make sense of in their own work roles and environments. Box 10.2 considers the role of the HR manager in supporting change, while ensuring ongoing quality in the delivery of patient care.

Box 10.2: The Role of HR in Managing Change while Ensuring the Delivery of Patient Care

Mount Carmel private hospital was founded and built by a religious order of nuns, the Sisters of the Little Company of Mary, in 1949. Throughout its history the philosophy of the hospital has been to create an excellent patient experience supported by the highest quality of medical and nursing care.

In 2006, due to a decline in vocations, the nuns sold the hospital as a going concern. The hospital was acquired by Harlequin Healthcare Group, chaired by property developer Gerry Conlon. Initially, rumours were rife that the hospital would close and that Mr Conlon would develop apartments on the site. However, Harlequin subsequently announced plans to invest €30 million in upgrading facilities and in expanding the maternity service at Mount Carmel. New management was installed. The hospital expanded its services and made many changes in staffing and work practices.

Meanwhile, the Beacon private hospital opened in close proximity to Mount Carmel. Some of the consultants from Mount Carmel moved to provide their services from there. Concurrently, private health insurance costs soared and the number of private patients, and especially maternity cases, declined. The most recent set of accounts for the Mount Carmel Medical Group (South Dublin) Ltd, which operates the hospital, show that it had net liabilities of €32 million in 2008. Mr Conlon was one of the so-called 'Maple 10' group of Anglo Irish Bank clients who were lent money by the bank to buy shares in it. His borrowings, including those associated with Mount Carmel, have been taken over by the National Asset Management Agency (NAMA).

The hospital underwent another management change as NAMA installed a management team to run the hospital. In 2010 the staff at the hospital threatened to go on strike over pay cuts. In 2012, rumours began circulating that St James Hospital is involved in talks to take over or manage Mount Carmel hospital.

The hospital HR team now face a number of challenges. They must try to minimise threats to the continuity and quality of service delivery caused by industrial unrest. This requires working to improve staff morale and minimise turnover among valuable professional staff. This is particularly challenging in an environment characterised by pay cuts and uncertainty regarding the hospital's future.

We will now focus on the issues of coordination, knowledge sharing and teamwork in health service delivery. These themes pre-empted the development of the relational coordination construct, increasingly recognised as a key mechanism underpinning the relationship between HR and performance in healthcare.

Achieving Coordination between Healthcare Groups: The Role of Relational Coordination in Supporting Healthcare Performance

The primary purpose of the hospital is to provide highly specialised care, delivered by independently practising professionals: clinicians, nurses and allied health professionals. Their work is enabled by the support of non-clinical support staff and technical services. The work of the different employee cohorts is delivered through different bureaucratic structures – specifically the professional bureaucracy for clinical specialists and the machine bureaucracy for managerial and support employees (Mintzberg, 1981). One of the major criticisms of these functional structures is that they reinforce divisions between clinical professions – and also between these professions and management. This has meant that ensuring interaction and coordination among the employees responsible for delivering all aspects of a patient's care is a particular challenge in hospitals. Despite the fact that professional groups must interact to achieve organisational goals, social boundaries are 'created by well developed professional roles, identities and traditional work practices' (Ferlie et al., 2005: 128), for example between doctors, nurses, midwives and physiotherapists, even where they share multidisciplinary team membership.

A focus on coordination, knowledge-sharing and teamwork is therefore particularly important in healthcare. Horizontal and lateral linking mechanisms are the principal means of coordinating activities across structures: silos, units or divisions. In terms of organisation design, balancing the amount of lateral coordination with different types and amounts of process is a strategic and policy challenge. In general, it is accepted that the higher the need for lateral coordination, the more formal the process and/or structure to deal with it. Hospitals use a range of strategies to coordinate and manage interdependencies among their employees. These include using routines, including protocols and patient pathways (specifying tasks and links between tasks); introducing hybrid boundary-spanning roles to liaise between different professional groups; and using uni- and multidisciplinary team meetings to enhance interactions among clinical professionals through multi-stakeholder involvement in decision-making. Such interventions emphasise that conceptions of coordination have moved from a focus on information processing and sharing towards a focus on coordination as a relational process, involving shared understandings of work and the work context, among workers who perform interdependent tasks (c.f. Gittell, 2002; Gittell et al., 2008). In turn, this understanding has led to the emergence of the relational coordination construct which identifies seven factors influencing the quality of communication and the relationships underpinning communication. These factors, illustrated in Figure 10.2, are the (i) frequency, (ii) timeliness, (iii) accuracy and (iv) focus on problem-solving rather than blaming in communication. These factors are dependent on the quality of underpinning relationships and the extent to which actors have (v) shared goals, (vi) shared knowledge and (vii) mutual respect (Gittell et al., 2008).

Figure 10.2: Relational Coordination

Quality of Communication		**Quality of Relationship**
Frequency		Shared goals
Timeliness	⬅➡	Shared knowledge
Accuracy		Mutual respect
Problem-solving orientation		

Source: Derived from Gittell et al. (2008)

Relational coordination supports integration by helping employees understand how tasks fit together in the work process; in determining shared goals driven by the overall work process, rather than their personal job roles (Gittell, 2002); and in showing how shared goals allow employees to value the contributions of others. Gittell et al. (2010) detail a series of work practices to improve relational coordination, which include:

- Selecting and training employees for relational competence
- Performance management that takes account of overarching and relational goals
- Proactive conflict management to support high quality relationships and understandings of how the service fits together
- Job design to support task interdependence and the frequency, nature and quality of interactions among workers

Relational coordination in healthcare has been found to improve critical indicators of hospital effectiveness and efficiency, including employee satisfaction, the quality of care experienced by patients and (reduced) length of hospital stay (Gittell et al., 2010).

In this section we have discussed several important ways in which HR can support performance. These include how bundles of HR practices work together to support hospital outcomes, specifically the technical, interpersonal and improvement oriented aspects of care. Beyond ensuring employees' commitment to change, the role of HR in supporting service improvement through organisation development and other improvement methods is noted, although not developed in this context. Finally, to summarise these core themes, a visual overview of the role of HR in supporting patient care and service delivery is provided in Figure 10.3. This synthesises the research discussed in the chapter to date, and summarises the role of specific HR practices in ensuring: (i) that individual employees possess and appropriately apply technical skills and knowledge; (ii) that all employees involved in a work process coordinate and share their knowledge through productive working relationships; and (iii) that knowledge, relationships and service-improvement capacity become embedded in hospitals. We now turn to consider emerging theoretical debates, and how these might shape the future of hospital HRM.

Figure 10.3: Using HR Practices to Support Service Delivery and Improvement in Healthcare

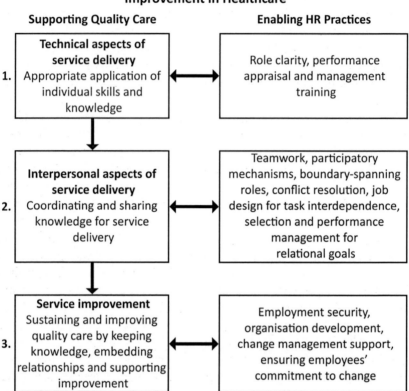

Where To From Here? Current and Emerging Theoretical Debates in HRM in Healthcare

In this section we discuss two current and emerging trends pertaining to HRM in healthcare: the integration of HR and management systems and the move from a professional to a service orientation in HR delivery, by integrating people management into clinical directorate structures.

Integrating HR and Management Systems: The Emergence of Human Resource Strategy

One emerging theme in the HRM literature is the increasing integration of organisational performance management systems

(OPMS) and HPWS. OPMS traditionally provide information on key performance indicators. This information is then used to inform structural and process interventions (e.g. total quality management, supply chain management) to improve task performance. The coherent and systematic use of HPWS to support contextually relevant social drivers of performance can also enhance the performance of healthcare organisations (Garman et al., 2011; West et al., 2006). In Ireland the move towards the systematic measurement of organisational performance has been supported by HealthStat, which provides monthly measures of access (e.g. waiting times for services), integration (whether services are patient-centred) and resourcing (how staff and financial resources are being used). Further, a new CompStat system is being designed, which will also integrate measures of clinical quality. Crucially, there is increasing recognition of the potential for such operational and people management systems to be mutually reinforcing (see Birdi et al., 2008). This is captured in popular management expressions, such as 'what gets measured gets managed.' This development signals a more strategic approach to the alignment of human resource management and organisational goals and objectives.

Integrating HR into Clinical Directorate Structures?

Within hospitals, the introduction of clinical directorate (CD) structures is intended to achieve lateral coordination between clinicians and management. CDs are management sub-units that move away from professionally oriented functional hospital structures towards either (i) a divisional design, derived from grouping pre-existing services such as 'medicine' and 'surgery' or (ii) an institute design, where the CD is structured around the patient pathway. From an operational perspective, CDs tend to be managed by a tripartite management team with a clinical director (a doctor generally of senior status), supported by a nurse manager and business manager. Key stakeholder groups therefore share management responsibility for service delivery, development and resource allocation in clinical sub-units. One potential model for restructuring HR in healthcare is to provide HR support to clinical directorates – rather than to professional silos. This would enable a more strategic and service-oriented focus.

Where Next? Moving to Support Patient-Centred Services rather than Clinical Professions

While we have identified the centrality of human capital to service delivery in healthcare, we have highlighted that HR operates in a complex and constrained environment influenced by a variety of stakeholders. Irish hospitals are pluralist and highly unionised workplaces which face coordination challenges both across the professional and machine bureaucracy structures and between different employee cohorts.

Research evidence suggests that the historical structure of hospitals has a dominant impact on the management of HR. Operational HR practice is devolved to hybrid clinical line managers, in keeping with best practice. Further, research evidence concludes that HPWS can both enable healthcare organisations to deliver organisational outcomes and facilitate employees' commitment to ongoing change. Despite these positive research findings, Irish research has suggested that the hospital HR management function is somewhat distanced from the devolved practice of HR by line managers. It faces challenges in integrating HR staff and frontline employees across the separate devolved divisions (McDermott and Keating, 2011).

Once organisational structures are in place, they typically exist for long periods of time, and only change when absolutely necessary or extremely advantageous to the organisation or its stakeholders (Miller, 1986). To date, management research has focused on the design of HR practices within the hospital structure rather than on how the HR architecture should be structured to support the delivery of high performance healthcare. Hospital organisations need to reconsider the design of their HR functions, strategy and systems. In our view, it is now both necessary and advantageous for the hospital HR structure to change to support services rather than professions. In so doing it would support the shift towards patient-centred care. In this chapter we have made two suggestions to enable this transition: integrating HR into operational management systems and integrating HR into clinical directorate structures. However, the paucity of research into hospital HR, particularly in Ireland, suggests that future research may provide further insight into how HRM can further enhance its contribution to healthcare. There is huge scope for future research to explore the enacted practice of operational HRM, adopting a

HR-as-practice orientation. Similarly, we have illustrated that there is scope to explore and expand the role of the HR function in professional service firms such as healthcare. Lastly, we emphasise the latent potential contribution of a more strategic orientation to HRM in a healthcare context.

Notes

[1] Acknowledgements: We note our thanks to the Health Research Board and the Irish Research Council for the Humanities and Social Sciences for funding our research in this area.

References

Barnett, S., Buchanan, D., Patrickson, M. and Maddern, J. (1996), 'Negotiating the Evolution of the HR Function: Practical Advice from the Health Care Sector', *Human Resource Management Journal*, 6(4): 18–37.

Bartram, T., Storm, P., Leggat, S., Casimir, G. and Fraser, B. (2007), 'Lost in Translation: Exploring the Link between HRM and Performance in Healthcare', *Human Resource Management Journal*, 17(1): 21–41.

Birdi, K., Clegg, C., Patterson, M., Robinson, A., Stride, C., Wall, T. and Wood, S. (2008), 'The Impact of Human Resource Management and Operational Management Practices on Company Productivity: A Longitudinal Study', *Personnel Psychology*, 61(3): 467–501.

Conway, E. and Monks, K. (2008), 'HR Practices and Commitment to Change: An Employee-Level Analysis', *Human Resource Management Journal*, 18(1): 72–89.

Conway, E. and Monks, K. (2009), 'Unravelling the Complexities of High Commitment: An Employee-Level Analysis', *Human Resource Management Journal*, 19(2): 140–158.

Conway, E. and Monks, K. (2010), 'The Devolution of HRM to Middle Managers in the Irish Health Service', *Personnel Review*, 39(3): 361–374.

Denis, J.L., Lamothe, L. and Langley, A. (2001), 'The Dynamics of Collective Leadership and Strategic Change in Pluralistic Organizations', *Academy of Management Journal*, 44(4): 809–837.

Department of Health (2011), *Health in Ireland: Key Trends 2011*, Dublin: Department of Health, available from: <http://www.dohc.ie/publications/key_trends_2011.html>.

De Vries, E., Ramrattan, M. and Gouma, D. (2008), 'The Incidence and Nature of In-Hospital Adverse Events: A Systematic Review', *Quality and Safety in Health Care*, 17(3): 216–223.

Ferlie, E., Fitzgerald, L., Wood, M. and Hawkins, C. (2005), 'The Non-spread of Innovations: The Mediating Role of Professionals', *Academy of Management Journal*, 48(1): 117–134.

Garman, A.N., McAlearney, A.S., Harrison, M.L., Song, P.H. and McHugh, M. (2011), 'High-Performance Work Systems in Health Care Management, Part 1: Development of an Evidence-Informed Model', *Health Care Management Review*, 36(3): 201–213.

Gittell, J.H. (2002), 'Coordinating Mechanisms in Care Provider Groups: Relational Coordination as a Mediator and Input Uncertainty as a Moderator of Performance Effects', *Management Science*, 48(11): 1408–1426.

Gittell, J.H., Seidner, R. and Wimbush, J. (2010), 'A Relational Model of How High-Performance Work Systems Work', *Organization Science*, 21(2): 490–506.

Gittell, J.H., Weinberg, D., Pfefferle, S. and Bishop, C. (2008), 'Impact of Relational Coordination on Job Satisfaction and Quality Outcomes: A Study of Nursing Homes', *Human Resource Management Journal*, 18(2): 154–170.

Glouberman, S. and Mintzberg, H. (2001), 'Managing the Care of Health and the Cure of Disease — Part I: Differentiation', *Health Care Management Review*, 26(1): 56–69.

Hyde, P., Boaden, R., Cortvriend, P., Harris, C., Marchington, M., Pass, S., Sparrow, P. and Sibbald, B. (2006), *Improving Health through Human Resource Management: Mapping the Territory*, London: Chartered Institute of Personnel and Development.

McDermott, A. and Keating, M. (2011), 'Managing Professionals: Exploring the Role of the Hospital HR Function', *Journal of Health Organization and Management*, 25(6): 677–692.

Miller, D. (1986), 'Configurations of Strategy and Structure: Towards a Synthesis', *Strategic Management Journal*, 7(3): 233–249.

Mintzberg, H. (1981), 'Organization Design, Fashion or Fit?', *Harvard Business Review*, 59(11): 103–116.

National Audit Office (2005), *A Safer Place for Patients: Learning to Improve Patient Safety*, London: The Stationery Office.

West, M.A., Guthrie, J.P., Dawson, J.F., Borrill, C.S. and Carter, M. (2006), 'Reducing Patient Mortality in Hospitals: The Role of Human Resource Management', *Journal of Organizational Behavior*, 27(7): 981–1002.

Section 4

Challenges

CHAPTER 11

Careers and Career Development

Sue Mulhall

Introduction

This chapter examines the domain of careers and career development, an area that is particularly important in an Irish context given changing demographics and a government-level emphasis on developing human capital and a knowledge-based economy agenda that emphasises new career opportunities and career types. In examining these issues, this chapter first of all explores government policies that have brought the notion of career into sharper focus. Following on from this, the chapter reviews the varying, and sometimes contradictory, definitions and conceptualisations of careers. The chapter then examines organisational support and practice, outlining the empirical evidence, and concludes with key implications of the analysis for future research and practice.

Policies and Positions

Numerous reports emphasise that Ireland needs to build an innovative knowledge-based economy that provides sustainable employment opportunities (see, for example, Department of Education and Skills, 2011; Department of Enterprise, Trade and Employment, 2009). This agenda is set against the backdrop of the

European Union's (EU) growth strategy, 'Europe 2020', which antic-ipates smart, sustainable and inclusive economies delivering high levels of employment, productivity and social cohesion (European Commission, 2010). The intention of the EU's employment objec-tive is to create conditions for modernising labour markets with a view to raising employment and productivity levels, whilst safe-guarding exiting social models. This entails, *inter alia*, empowering people through the acquisition of additional proficiencies, thereby enabling the current and future workforce to adapt to changing conditions and potential career shifts. Initiatives have, therefore, been developed to ensure that European citizens are equipped to manage labour market changes more effectively, by affording opportunities to develop skills and gain access to information, advice and guidance, thus assisting people to make well-informed career choices (Cedefop, 2008). As a result, national and interna-tional employment policy reinforces the long-held contention of career scholars that those seeking employment opportunities require lifelong learning and development to acquire a portfolio of competence and competencies to manage their careers in fluid, fast-paced settings (Arnold and Cohen, 2008; Arthur et al., 1999; Arthur and Rousseau, 1996; Briscoe and Hall, 2006; Hall, 1976, 1996; King, 2004).

The Nature of Career Management

Individuals do not, however, undertake their careers in a vacuum, as decisions about future trajectories need to be considered within the context of the broader world (Herr, 2008; King, 2004). Facili-tating this decision-making is the process of career management, which has been defined as an 'ongoing problem-solving process in which information is gathered, awareness of oneself and the envi-ronment is increased, career goals are set, strategies are developed to attain those goals, and feedback is obtained' (Greenhaus et al., 2009: 18). Career management, therefore, involves 'the analysis, planning and action that can be taken by an individual at any stage of their career – and ideally throughout it – to actively increase the chance of doing well' (Forsyth, 2002: 3). In essence, success has to be proactively sought and job seekers need to have a clear idea of what they mean by success and how to achieve it. Whilst striving for this career success people face a number of developmental tasks and challenges. If individuals understand these activities, they can formulate strategies that are most appropriate to a particular period in their careers. To support this, organisations attuned to the unfolding pattern of a career over an employee's employment lifespan can design developmental programmes suitable for the different stages of an individual's career (Greenhaus et al., 2009). This emphasises the interplay between career management and career development, a theme discussed later in the chapter. It also highlights that understanding and conceptualising careers is a critical task bridging the levels of national policy, organisation practice and individual expectations.

Preparation for and engagement in career management and the career development process necessitates an understanding of the contemporary career and its diverse depictions over time. Examining the historical meanings ascribed to the definition of 'career' unearths the shifting sands of emphasis over the past century. Table 11.1 outlines the evolutionary journey of the career concept characterised as four distinct stages:

- Stage 1 – The roots of career development derived from Parsons' (1909) three-step formula for choosing a career that involved the matching of personal requirements with the external environment.
- Stage 2 – The Chicago School of Sociologists, epitomised by Hughes (1937, 1958), took an expansive life perspective approach, underscoring the relationship between professional and personal biographies.
- Stage 3 – At this stage, the concept of career returned to a more restricted occupational and organisational orientation, situating career within the context of stable employment structures (e.g. Super, 1957, 1980; Wilensky, 1961), typified by linear, upward progression across a limited number of firms with a focus on extrinsic rewards and organisational career management.
- Stage 4 – This reflects a movement to a more contemporary understanding of career, exemplified by broader, experienced-focused, post-organisational descriptions, attempting to replicate how individuals enact their career in a changing world (e.g. Arthur et al., 1989; Arthur and Rousseau, 1996; Sullivan and Baruch, 2009).

Table 11.1: Key Contributors to the Career Concept, in Chronological Order

Stage	Author(s)	Definition of Career
1	Parsons (1909)	'In the wise choice of a vocation, there are three broad factors: (1) a clear understanding of yourself, your aptitudes, abilities, interests, ambitions, resources, limitations, and their causes; (2) a knowledge of the requirements, conditions of success, advantages and disadvantages, compensation, opportunities and prospects in different lines of work; (3) true reasoning on the relations of these two groups of facts.' (p. 5)
2	Hughes (1937)	'In a highly and rigidly structured society, a career consists, objectively, of a series of status and clearly defined offices. In a freer one, the individual has more latitude for creating his own position or choosing from a number of existing ones.' (p. 409) … 'Subjectively, a career is the moving perspective in which the person sees his life as a whole and interprets the meaning of his various attributes, actions, and the things which happen to him. … The career is by no means exhausted in a series of business and professional achievements. There are other points at which one's life touches the social order, other lines of social accomplishment.' (p. 410) … 'It is possible to have a career in an avocation as well as in a vocation.' (p. 411)
	Hughes (1958)	'Subjectively, a career is the moving perspective in which persons orient themselves with reference to the social order, and of the typical sequences and concatenations of office.' (p. 67)
3	Wilensky (1961)	'A career is a succession of related jobs, arranged in a hierarchy of prestige, through which persons move in an ordered (more-or-less predictable) sequence.' (p. 523)
	Super (1980)	'A career is a sequence of positions held during the course of a lifetime, some of them simultaneously (Super, 1957); an occupational career is the sequence or combination of occupational positions held during the course of a lifetime.' (p. 286)

(Continued)

Table 11.1: (*Continued*)

Stage	Author(s)	Definition of Career
4	Arthur et al. (1989)	'Our adopted definition of career is the *evolving sequence of a person's work experiences over time.* A central theme in this definition is that of work and all that work can mean for the ways in which we see and experience other people, organizations, and society. However, equally central to this definition is the theme of time, along which the career provides a "moving perspective" (Hughes, 1958: 67) on the unfolding interaction between a person and society. ... The notion of a career also links matters internal to the individual with matters external, such as those concerning official position. ... The study of careers is the study of both individual and organizational change ... as well as of societal change.' (p. 8) [emphasis in original]
	Arthur and Rousseau (1996)	'CAREER Old meaning: a course of professional advancement; usage is restricted to occupational groups with formal hierarchical progression, such as managers and professionals. New meaning: the unfolding sequence of any person's work experiences over time.' (p. 372) [emphasis in original]
	Sullivan and Baruch (2009)	'We define a *career* as an individual's work-related and other relevant experiences, both inside and outside of organizations that form a unique pattern over the individual's lifespan. This definition recognizes both physical movement ... as well as the interpretation of the individual, including his/her perceptions of career events ... career alternatives ... and outcomes. Moreover, careers do not occur in a vacuum. An individual's career is influenced by many contextual factors ... as well as by personal factors.' (p. 43) [emphasis in original]

A consensus seems to have emerged, emanating from work by authors such as Arthur et al. (1989) and Arthur and Rousseau (1996), that a career constitutes the unfolding sequence of a person's work experiences over time (Arnold and Cohen, 2008; Arthur et al., 2005; Dries et al., 2008). The definitions offered in Table 11.1 illustrate that a career can be described in two different ways – objectively and subjectively (Arthur et al., 2005). There are objective careers, emulating the more or less publicly observable positions, situations and statuses that serve as benchmarks for gauging an individual's movement through society, comprising predictable stages and an ordered sequence of development (Dries et al., 2008). Associated criteria for assessing careers on this basis might include level of remuneration and promotion history coupled with position in the organisational hierarchy. Yet careers can also be understood on a more subjective basis, reflecting the individual's own sense of his/her career, defined by the personal interpretations and values that identity bestows on a person (Dries et al., 2008). Relevant here are dimensions such as job satisfaction, contentment with career opportunities and feeling self-confident at work. This reveals the inherent two-sidedness of the career concept (Arthur et al., 2005). Notably, the objective and the subjective aspects of careers are persistently dependent, and this interdependence occurs over time (Hughes, 1937, 1958). Such an appreciation provides a basis to better comprehend and evaluate contemporary conceptualisations of careers.

Contemporary Conceptualisations

In tandem with the changing definitions of career, new concepts have emerged, devised to reflect an altered environment, with increased globalisation, rapid technological advancements, growing workforce diversity and the expanding use of outsourcing and part-time and temporary employees (Arthur et al., 1999; Sullivan and Baruch, 2009). These changes have transformed traditional organisational structures, employer–employee relationships and the work context, creating divergence in how individuals enact their careers (Briscoe and Hall, 2006; Forsyth, 2002; Herr, 2008; Humphreys, 2013; Mulhall, 2011; Sullivan and Baruch, 2009). The demise of the traditional bureaucratic career, which entails employees progressing in an upward hierarchical manner within a small number of organisational structures, has been regularly noted (see, for example, Arthur et al., 1999; Hall, 2002; Sullivan and Arthur, 2006). This perspective is being replaced by more embracing notions of career, based on the accumulation of skills and knowledge and the integration of one's professional and personal life, with employees holding diverse roles in an array of settings.

Various career concepts and metaphors have been formulated to capture this metamorphosis, including such notions as the protean career (Briscoe and Hall, 2006; Hall, 1976, 1996), the boundaryless career (Arthur and Rousseau, 1996; DeFillippi and Arthur, 1994; Sullivan and Arthur, 2006), career profiles (Briscoe and Hall, 2006), hybrid careers (Granrose and Baccili, 2006), the post-corporate career (Peiperl and Baruch, 1997) and the kaleidoscope career model (Mainiero and Sullivan, 2005, 2006; Sullivan et al., 2009).

The protean and boundaryless concepts were developed to explain the variety of career patterns exhibited in today's dynamic work situations (Sullivan and Baruch, 2009). Based on the metaphor of the Greek god Proteus, who could adapt his shape at will, the protean careerist can rearrange and repackage his/her knowledge, skills and abilities to meet both the demands of a changing workplace and his/her need for self-fulfilment (Hall, 1976, 1996). The individual, not the organisation, is in control of his/her career management and development, requiring a high level of self-awareness and personal responsibility to succeed. Briscoe and Hall (2006) revised the concept by defining two dimensions (values-driven and self-directed career management attitudes) of the protean orientation. The boundaryless career describes a sequence of job opportunities that go beyond the scope of a single employer, so individuals are independent of, rather than dependent on, traditional organisational career arrangements (Arthur and Rousseau, 1996; DeFillippi and Arthur, 1994). In 2006, Sullivan and Arthur modified the concept by detailing varying levels of physical and psychological career mobility between successive employment situations. The reconceptualised boundaryless career is seen to be constituted of physical movements across employment types and employers, coupled with psychological progression in terms of enhanced self-awareness and fulfilment. This offers a richer conceptualisation captured by the degree of boundarylessness displayed by the career actor (Sullivan and Arthur, 2006).

More recent conceptualisations, including career profiles and hybrid careers, have been referred to as 'integrative frameworks' (Sullivan and Baruch, 2009), as they represent attempts to merge various ideas from the protean and boundaryless metaphors. Career profiles combine the two components of the boundaryless career (physical and psychological mobility), plus the two factors of the protean career (values-driven and self-directed career management attitudes), yielding sixteen potential career categories (Briscoe and Hall, 2006). The hybrid career emerged from the interpretations of research findings containing aspects of the traditional career, in addition to the protean and boundaryless career concepts (e.g. Granrose and Baccili, 2006).

The post-corporate career comprises careers occurring outside of large organisations whereby individuals enact a multitude of alternative options, including employment with smaller, more agile firms, self-employment, and/or working in compact project teams (Peiperl and Baruch, 1997). According to this perspective, people voluntarily or involuntarily leave large companies because they are unable or unwilling to pursue corporate careers due to the uncertainty that is inherent in them. Post-corporate careerists have, therefore, a permanent career, rather than a permanent job. Using the metaphor of a kaleidoscope, the kaleidoscope career model explains how individuals focus on three career parameters when making decisions, thereby reflecting the continually changing pattern of their careers (Mainiero and Sullivan, 2005, 2006; Sullivan et al., 2009). These parameters are authenticity, defined as being true to oneself; balance, described as the equilibrium between work and non-work demands; and challenge, characterised as stimulating work and career advancement. This representation purports to offer conceptualisations that are not an extension of either the protean or boundaryless concepts, but instead provide an alternative lens through which careers can be examined (Sullivan and Baruch, 2009).

In summary, an examination of the theoretical underpinnings of the discipline indicates that career experiences are more diverse than previously conceived, requiring individuals and organisations to respond proactively, rather than reactively, to this evolving environment. This theme is further explored in the next two sections of the chapter.

Organisational Support and Practice

While responsibility for career management and career development is perceived as resting largely with the individual, organisational support programmes are also considered to assist in satisfying personal career aspirations, whilst simultaneously meeting an employer's future skills and capability requirements (Cedefop, 2008). Managing change and meeting strategic objectives are viewed as the critical goals of organisational career management (Chartered Institute of Personnel and Development, 2011; King, 2004). Many organisations are therefore involved in examining how to design jobs that enable individuals to enhance their capacity to access career opportunities while simultaneously allowing the organisation to upskill the talent required to meet potential priorities and challenges. This entails finding solutions that are satisfactory for both parties so that an organisation's career management structure offers initiatives that reconcile organisational and individual perspectives, as illustrated in Figure 11.1.

Figure 11.1: Reconciling Organisational and Individual Career Perspectives

| Past | Present | Future |

Employee

Past experience, skills, knowledge and expertise → Current priorities for career → Future career and life goals

↓

Career management

↑

Employer

Combined skills, knowledge, abilities and expertise of people in the organisation → Current priorities for developing people within the organisation → Future talent needed to ensure viability and competitive advantage

Source: Adapted from King, Z. (2004: 7), *Career Management: A Guide*, London: CIPD with the permission of the publisher, the Chartered Institute of Personnel and Development, London (www.cipd.co.uk).

The building of individual capacity in parallel with organisational capacity is embodied in the Southside Partnership Training Network (SPTN) (see Box 11.1). This inter-organisational learning network supports knowledge acquisition and career development in the not-for-profit sector.

Box 11.1: A Useful Way of Developing Learning Networks

The SPTN is an initiative of Southside Partnership DLR, an organisation that tackles socioeconomic disadvantage in the Dún Laoghaire–Rathdown area of Dublin. The SPTN develops individuals to contribute to the organisations within their communities by facilitating local groups to learn from each other through networking and collaboration. It works with community groups operating with restricted budgets to promote ongoing sustainability beyond the funding provided by national agencies. The network invests in individuals whose leadership will assist in delivering organisational change. Since its commencement in 2007, it has provided quality, affordable accredited and non-accredited programmes, organising 200 training courses for over 3,000 people. Annual evaluations from the network's participants (trainees and managers) indicate that at least:

- 93 per cent believe that the training is applicable to their work and careers.
- 84 per cent state that the courses have advanced their knowledge.
- 83 per cent maintain that the programmes have positively changed their attitudes.
- 79 per cent contend that the developmental initiatives have increased their skill sets.

By investing in the expertise of practitioners through the provision of peer support, mentoring and the sharing of resources, the SPTN equips individuals with the competencies to progress their careers. This, consequently, enhances the capability of community groups to manage change within a resource-constrained environment, underlining the symbiotic relationship between organisational and individual career management.

Source: http://www.southsidepartnership.ie/.

A useful way of understanding the balancing of organisational and individual positions is within a framework that depicts the stages through which careers typically evolve. These stages include entry, early career, mid-career, later career and end career (Greenhaus et al., 2009). This life cycle commences with induction to the organisation where the new recruit begins the process of socialisation into the norms of the company, assisted by directed career planning.

The next phase encompasses progress within defined areas of work relevant to the job holder, where skills and aptitudes are developed through experience, training, coaching and performance management. By mid-career, some staff will have promotional prospects open to them, while others may have reached a plateau. Notwithstanding the trajectory, during this phase there is evidence that all individuals benefit from participation in developmental schemes such as role enrichment, role enlargement and job rotation. The penultimate stage, later career, involves reassuring employees that they can still contribute by providing opportunities to undertake new challenges. At the final juncture, end career, the possibility of phasing disengagement might be considered, such as offering part-time roles for a specified duration before an employee ultimately leaves the organisation. This career life cycle, though, needs to be underpinned by appropriate human resource strategies, involving, *inter alia*, deciding on the degree to which the company develops talent internally or hires it externally, establishing defined career routes, formulating succession management plans, integrating professional development planning as a crucial element of a performance management process, and devising systems and processes to achieve the advancement and dissemination of learning and knowledge across the company (Greenhaus et al., 2009). The achievement of these aims will also require the detailing of specific activities in the organisation's career management and career development policies and procedures. Examples include lateral moves to create cross-functional experience, *ad hoc* assignments, internal and external secondments, formal mentoring, career counselling, career workshops and retirement preparation programmes (Cedefop, 2008; King, 2004). Employees will also need to be supported by individual career plans delineating the routes that they can take to advance within an organisation. This career progression is usually described in terms of what people are required to know and be able to do to perform a sequence of jobs at increasing levels of responsibility in pre-designated competency bands, thus situating career management and career development within a competency-based framework.

Empirical Evidence

While textbooks suggest that career management and career development programmes should focus on sustained and long-term success (Armstrong, 2012; Greenhaus et al., 2009), research studies reveal mixed evidence on whether or not this actually takes place. A study by the coaching firm Fairplace (2012) of just over 2,000 employees indicates that almost two in five British workers (39 per cent) have never had a career conversation with their line manager, over a quarter (26 per cent) have no long-term career plan, and only one in ten (11 per cent) feel that they have the opportunity for long-term development within their current organisation. Research indicates that such perceptions can damage employee motivation and loyalty (Chartered Institute of Personnel and Development, 2012a), with one study of careers in the high-tech sector suggesting that formal and informal organisational policies are especially likely to adversely impact on women's managerial career aspirations (Cross and Linehan, 2008). A study by business consultants Insala (2012) found that the primary reason for career management and development programmes in the United Kingdom (UK) is to improve employee engagement (33 per cent), followed by succession planning (28 per cent) and employee retention (15 per cent). Factors such as the effective utilisation of human resources, retention of employees, the attraction of high quality candidates, and the management of employee career expectations have been found to be key influencers in Ireland (Heraty and Collings, 2006). This contrasts with a survey of over 2,000 respondents by the Chartered Institute of Personnel and Development (2011), which found that the most common career supports revolve around enabling individuals to improve their performance and widen the scope of their existing role, closely followed by measures that emphasise either the short term or attend to the next promotion.

The current recessionary climate is impacting on workers' career expectations and on the availability of organisational career opportunities, with the main barrier to the continuance of career development programmes being the lack of resources (Chartered Institute of Personnel and Development, 2011). Expenditure on career management and career development is contingent upon the size of the company's training and development budget. Based on a study of almost 340 private sector firms employing 115,000 staff, the Irish Business and Employers' Confederation (IBEC) found that the average percentage of payroll costs represented by training in 2010 was 2.6 per cent, but it was 3.3 per cent in 2008 (McGann and Anderson, 2010). The public service has also experienced a decline in funding for training and development, with a previous commitment to devote 4 per cent of payroll to this activity now radically revised downwards (Department of Finance, 2003). The impact of these cutbacks is evident within private sector companies. In a survey of 444 managers responsible for human resource management (HRM) in Irish enterprises, more than half of the firms have decreased their training and development budget (Roche et al., 2011). Where allocations were cut and only partial training carried out, it often involved the re-training or cross-training of staff to assume new tasks, with four out of ten companies training staff for new roles within the business. The research by Roche et al. (2011) highlights the fact that the commitment of organisations to developing their employees' skills and competencies has predominantly remained undiminished during the recession, countering the view proffered by some commentators of the 'hollowing out' of skills during an economic downturn (Humphreys, 2013). This is reflected in a recent comparative analysis studying European labour markets post-recession, including Ireland (Couch, 2011).

Roche et al. (2011) provide case studies highlighting the varying career management and career development experiences of companies during a recession. For example, when the Dublin Airport Authority introduced a voluntary redundancy programme, a career development centre was organised to facilitate the out-placing of middle managers at the company. This supports evidence from the UK indicating that even in a period of downsizing and retrenchment, half of the organisations making positions redundant in 2011 (51 per cent) utilised career transition services, which was an increase from the 34 per cent of the previous year (Chartered Institute of Personnel and Development, 2012b). Despite the economic downturn in Ireland, Medtronic, a global medical technology company, actively develops internal career paths, and, consequently, about half of its vacancies are filled from in-house staff pools annually (Roche et al., 2011). The Archangel case study (Box 11.2) describes how a company can manage the internal career paths of knowledge workers in a flexible manner, whilst simultaneously taking account of the vagaries of the external environment.

Box 11.2: Upskilling Knowledge Workers

Set up in 1997, 'Archangel' is a professional consulting company offering archaeological services such as excavation for national road schemes, environmental and cultural heritage impact studies, and educational field schools. During the Celtic Tiger, the company employed a core team of 26 archaeologists on contracts of indefinite duration (permanent staff), supplemented by an average of 100 archaeologists on short-term contracts (temporary staff) for every project. These numbers reduced in the recession. The majority of employees (permanent and temporary) are knowledge workers, requiring particular archaeological qualifications, experience, competence and competencies. The company utilises a project management structure whereby a permanent staff member manages each archaeological project, leading a team employed on temporary, short-term contracts. These team members are recruited within a defined career structure, hired as project managers, site directors, supervisors, assistants (two grades) and general operatives. During an assignment, temporary workers receive ongoing site-specific training, with their performance reviewed and assessed against pre-determined competencies on a periodic and prearranged basis. Successful performance on a project assists the temporary employee in being retained for the next suitable venture, with upward progression on the career hierarchy a distinct possibility. Permanent and temporary archaeologists employed at site director grade and above require a licence to practise from the National Monuments Service. Archangel expects temporary staff to self-fund this certification, presenting valid, up-to-date accreditation for every project, but the company finances the certification process for permanent staff. This permit is specific to the employee with the staff member, not the organisation, holding the intellectual property rights, underlining the portable nature of a knowledge worker's portfolio of skills. Archangel also pays for relevant continuous professional development activities that advance the archaeologists' learning, as their expertise is used to promote the company's services, which, in turn, influences profitability, emphasising what King (2004) views as the overlap between organisational and individual perspectives in career management and career development.

Source: Based on the author's consulting experience.

In conclusion, the empirical evidence underlines the fluid nature of careers within the contemporary workplace. It points to the realities that individuals need to continually adapt, upskill and re-train while organisations have to plan for short-, medium- and long-term success by providing programmes that meet current and future resource requirements.

Conclusions

Providing effective career management and career development programmes is a critical challenge for twenty-first century human resource practitioners and business leaders. Such programmes have an important role in building sustainable organisations and for offering employees a meaningful focus for their future. Organisations and employees, however, bring varying perspectives to the situation and one of the challenges in the career management process is how such differences might be recognised and resolved. A partnership approach (Cedefop, 2008; Chartered Institute of Personnel and Development, 2011; King, 2004) offers one possibility as this entails employers supporting employees to develop the skills they need tomorrow, but within a context that appreciates that individuals are different and will have diverse expectations and requirements from a career. The value of this collaborative approach is that it reflects the current and future capabilities required by the organisation to fulfil its strategy and meet its objectives, as well as satisfying the needs of individuals to build the competence and competencies to feel engaged with, and valued by, their organisation.

Reconciling organisational and individual needs necessitates integrating career management and career development within the broader business strategy. Short-term horizons and an emphasis on financial results mean that the requirement for effective career management and career development with its more intangible, enduring outcomes is often overlooked. Senior managers and human resource professionals require evidence to substantiate the benefits of focusing on long-term ongoing career management and career development measures, rather than transitory programmes, and this need provides several opportunities for researchers. For example, by using quantitative and qualitative longitudinal studies, career scholars could research the impact on organisational performance of embedding extended timelines into the performance, reward and development systems of companies. Such an approach would facilitate our understanding of how altering key human resource systems over time, like performance appraisal, contingent pay structures and learning initiatives, influence organisational career management and career development, and ultimately organisational performance. This could be conducted in tandem with exploring the effect of such measures on the individual career actor, providing both 'hard' and 'soft' data to support the organisation's business and human resource strategies.

Meeting the challenge of balancing the organisational and individual positions in career management and career development initiatives will become even more important as working patterns continue to evolve in our globalised world. To reflect contemporary conceptualisations of careers within the globalised labour market, research might usefully be conducted with underrepresented groups and within a variety of work experiences (Arnold and Cohen, 2008; Mulhall, 2011; Sullivan and Baruch, 2009). The incorporation into research agendas of a wider range of employment settings could augment our understanding of modern careers by mirroring the diversity of arrangements that individuals enact. For example, exploring the careers of part-time and temporary workers, those involved in double employment, and individuals who combine paid employment with self-employment. This would facilitate a more complete consideration of a person's career, incorporating the totality of the unfolding sequence of his/her work experiences over time.

References

Armstrong, M. (2012), *Handbook of Human Resource Management Practice*, twelfth edition, London: Kogan Page.

Arnold, J. and Cohen, L. (2008), 'The Psychology of Careers in Industrial and Organizational Settings: A Critical but Appreciative Analysis', *International Review of Industrial and Organisational Psychology*, 23: 1–44.

Arthur, M.B., Hall, D.T. and Lawrence, B.S. (1989), 'Generating New Directions in Career Theory: The Case for a Transdisciplinary Approach' in M.B. Arthur, D.T. Hall and B.S. Lawrence (eds), *Handbook of Career Theory*, Cambridge: Cambridge University Press, 7–25.

Arthur, M.B., Inkson, K. and Pringle, J. (1999), *The New Careers: Individual Action and Economic Change*, London: Sage.

Arthur, M.B., Khapova, S. and Wilderom, C. (2005), 'Career Success in a Boundaryless Career World', *Journal of Organizational Behavior*, 26(2): 177–202.

Arthur, M.B. and Rousseau, D. (1996), 'Introduction: The Boundaryless Career as a New Employment Principle' in M.B. Arthur and D.M.

Rousseau (eds), *The Boundaryless Career: A New Employment Principle for a New Organizational Era*, Oxford: Oxford University Press, 3–20.

Briscoe, J.P. and Hall, D.T. (2006), 'The Interplay of Boundaryless and Protean Careers: Combinations and Implications', *Journal of Vocational Behavior*, 69(2): 4–18.

Cedefop (2008), *Career Development at Work: A Review of Career Guidance to Support People in Employment*, European Centre for the Development of Vocational Training, Luxembourg: Office for Official Publications of the European Communities, 151: 1–135, available from: <http://www.cedefop.europa.eu/en/Files/5183_EN.PDF>.

Chartered Institute of Personnel and Development (2011), 'Managing Careers for Organisational Capability', Research report, November, London: CIPD, 1–31.

Chartered Institute of Personnel and Development (2012a), 'Emotional or Transactional Engagement – Does It Matter?', *Research Insight*, May, London: CIPD, 1–33.

Chartered Institute of Personnel and Development (2012b), *Resourcing and Talent Planning 2012: Annual Survey Report*, London: CIPD.

Couch, K.A. (2011), 'The Post-Recession Employment Situation: A Comparative Perspective', *Journal of Policy Analysis and Management*, 31(1): 153–195.

Cross, C. and Linehan, M. (2008), 'Organisational Barriers and the Female Managerial Career: Some Empirical Evidence from Ireland', *Journal of Workplace Rights*, 13(3): 245–258.

DeFillippi, R. and Arthur, M. (1994), 'The Boundaryless Career: A Competency-Based Perspective', *Journal of Organizational Behavior*, 15(4): 307–324.

Department of Education and Skills (2011), *National Strategy for Higher Education to 2030: Report of the Strategy Group*, Dublin: The Stationery Office.

Department of Enterprise, Trade and Employment (2009), *Entrepreneurship Education in Ireland*, Dublin: The Stationery Office.

Department of Finance (2003), *Framework for Civil Service Training and Development 2004–2008*, Dublin: The Stationery Office.

Dries, N., Pepermans, R. and Carlier, O. (2008), 'Career Success: Constructing a Multidimensional Model', *Journal of Vocational Behavior*, 73(2): 254–267.

European Commission (2010), *Europe 2020: A Strategy for Smart, Sustainable and Inclusive Growth*, Brussels: European Commission.

Fairplace (2012), 'Lack of Career Conversations Causing Workplace Disengagement', *Fairplace News and Events*, 6 November, available from: <http://www.fairplace.com/news/8/71/Lack-of-career-conversations-causing-workplace-disengagement.php>.

Forsyth, P. (2002), *Career Management*, Oxford: Capstone Publishing.

Granrose, C.S. and Baccili, P.A. (2006), 'Do Psychological Contracts Include Boundaryless or Protean Careers?', *Career Development International*, 11(3): 163–182.

Greenhaus, J.H., Callanan, V.M. and Godshalk, V.M. (2009), *Career Management*, fourth edition, Thousand Oaks, CA: Sage.

Hall, D.T. (1976), *Careers in Organizations*, Glenview, IL: Scott Foresman.

Hall, D.T. (1996), 'Long Live the Career' in D.T. Hall (ed.), *The Career Is Dead – Long Live the Career*, San Francisco, CA: Jossey-Bass, 1–12.

Hall, D.T. (2002), *Careers In and Out of Organizations*, Thousand Oaks, CA: Sage.

Heraty, N. and Collings, D.G. (2006), 'International Briefing 16: Training and Development in the Republic of Ireland', *International Journal of Training and Development*, 10(2): 164–174.

Herr, E.L. (2008), 'Social Contexts for Career Guidance Throughout the World' in J.A. Athanasou and R.V. Esbroeck (eds), *International Handbook of Career Guidance*, New York, NY: Springer, 45–68.

Hughes, E.C. (1937), 'Institutional Office and the Person', *American Journal of Sociology*, 43(3): 404–413.

Hughes, E.C. (1958), *Men and Their Work*, Glencoe, IL: Free Press.

Humphreys, J. (2013), 'The Way We Work Now', *Irish Times*, 12 January, 6.

Insala (2012), *Career Development Survey Report*, London: Insala, available from: <http://www.insala.com/website/whitepapers/09-17-2012-career-development-survey-report-2012.pdf>.

King, Z. (2004), *Career Management: A Guide*, London: CIPD.

Mainiero, L.A. and Sullivan, S.E (2005), 'Kaleidoscope Careers: An Alternative Explanation for the "Opt-Out Generation"', *Academy of Management Executive*, 19(1): 106–123.

Mainiero, L.A. and Sullivan, S.E. (2006), *The Opt-Out Revolt: How People Are Creating Kaleidoscope Careers Outside of Companies*, New York, NY: Davies-Black.

McGann, K. and Anderson, G. (2010), *IBEC Education and Skills Survey*, Dublin: IBEC.

Mulhall, S. (2011), 'CSI: Career Success Investigation', *Irish Journal of Management*, 30(2): 67–93.

Parsons, F. (1909), *Choosing a Vocation*, Boston, MA: Houghton Mifflin.

Peiperl, M. and Baruch, Y. (1997), 'Back to Square Zero: The Post-Corporate Career', *Organizational Dynamics*, 25(4): 6–22.

Roche, W.K., Teague, P., Coughlan, A. and Fahy, M. (2011), *Human Resources in the Recession: Managing and Representing People at Work in Ireland*, Dublin: Labour Relations Commission.

Sullivan, S. and Arthur, M.B. (2006), 'The Evolution of the Boundaryless Career Concept: Examining Physical and Psychological Mobility', *Journal of Vocational Behavior*, 69(1): 19–29.

Sullivan, S.E. and Baruch, Y. (2009), 'Advances in Career Theory and Research: A Critical Review and Agenda for Future Exploration', *Journal of Management*, 36(6): 1542–1571.

Sullivan, S.E., Forret, M., Carraher, S.C. and Mainiero, L. (2009), 'Using the Kaleidoscope Career Model to Examine Generational Differences in Work Attitudes', *Career Development International*, 14(3): 284–302.

Super, D.E. (1957), *The Psychology of Careers*, New York, NY: Harper.

Super, D.E. (1980), 'A Life-Span, Life-Space Approach to Career Development', *Journal of Vocational Behavior*, 16(3): 282–298.

Wilensky, H.L. (1961), 'Careers, Lifestyles, and Social Integration', *International Social Science Journal*, 12(6): 553–538.

CHAPTER 12

Broken Promises: Why Strategic HRM Does Not Always Work

Jean Cushen and Brian Harney

Introduction

Despite the widespread endorsement and diffusion of strategic human resource management (SHRM), numerous scholars argue the practice is beset with fundamental contradictions and tensions (Delbridge and Keenoy, 2010; Kochan, 2007; Thompson, 2012). This chapter grapples with these contradictions and tensions to show how they lie at the heart of SHRM prescriptions. First, we explore the limitations of SHRM and the consequences for SHRM's quest of realising and demonstrating human resources' (HR) strategic and performance impact. We then move on to explore why SHRM does not always deliver on its promises and why it is unrealistic to expect it to do so. Here we evaluate the definitive role that financial imperatives play in framing SHRM intent and activities and the consequences for employee dynamics. The chapter then evaluates these arguments with respect to the available Irish evidence. The chapter concludes with commentary on the implications for SHRM theory, methodology and practice.

SHRM: Progress or Castles in the Air?

Since SHRM entered managerial parlance, it has been commended by advocates on the basis of two key and connected promises. The first of these promises is that HR practices can be 'strategically aligned' to orientate people toward the achievement of business goals, thereby enhancing organisational performance. The second promise is that strategically aligned HR practices can create a 'unitarist' environment of mutual gains prompting individuals to work as a team to achieve shared goals (Geare et al., 2006; Janssens and Steyaert, 2009; Van Buren, 2011). A quick scan of textbooks, dedicated journals, educational provisions and academic positions indicates that SHRM is in a very healthy position; it remains a widely endorsed approach to people management. However, although the early promises of SHRM are intuitively appealing, it is becoming increasingly evident that they are founded upon an inherent contradiction which undermines both the performance and unitarist assertions: what is good for the organisation is not necessarily good for employees (Batt and Appelbaum, 2013; Cushen, 2013). This contradiction was noted in the early debates on SHRM and sparked ethical concerns that business realities meant SHRM placed a deceptive emphasis on the extent to which organisations cared about mutual gains and humanitarian values of self-actualisation at work (Drake and Drake, 1988; Legge, 1998). The contradiction was touched upon in early models of hard and soft human resource management (HRM), which highlighted that balancing the two was, at the very least, difficult (Legge, 1995; Watson, 2004). However, these concerns were downplayed by a unitarist revival manifest in interpretations of the SHRM function as an 'employee champion/advocate' or strategic partner (Ulrich and Brockbank, 2005) coupled with universalistic arguments concerning the beneficial impact of SHRM for both organisations and employees (Van Buren, 2011).

Whilst the dominance of performance and unitarist assertions have certainly brought legitimacy and visibility to SHRM, there are increasing signs of frustration concerning its progress and impact (see Kaufman, 2012; Guest, 2011). With respect to the HR profession, Kochan (2007: 603) bemoans the loss of the HR function's ability to challenge firms to better balance employee and organisational interests. Furthermore, the validity of studies proclaiming the positive impact of SHRM has been called into question. Boselie et al. (2009: 464) claim research on SHRM 'takes a single-country, best-practice view of HRM, and builds on unitarist notions built on the interests of the organizations' managers or shareholders'. In other words, SHRM is deemed to work if shareholders are satisfied and insufficient regard is given to the recipients of SHRM interventions, namely employees. Extensive content analysis of key SHRM studies finds a 'consensus' orientation underpinned by a unitarist outlook and a related bias to assess positive outcomes (Keegan and Boselie, 2006; Batt and Banerjee, 2012). Simply put, researchers have been slow to examine any negative consequences of SHRM. Assumptions of unitary outcomes and a tendency to treat organisations as functional entities operating in isolation have resulted in a failure to fully embrace the complexities of organisational life (Van Buren, 2011). In order to flesh out the prospective tensions and contradictions hidden beneath the surface of SHRM, the next section examines the socioeconomic context framing organisational and SHRM actions and subsequent employee dynamics. These provide a lens through which the realities of SHRM can be better appreciated.

Structural Constraints: Financial Capitalism

One of the most significant factors influencing contemporary organisations and social relations within them is the dominance of capital flows and financial institutions (Nolan, 2011). This current era of 'financialization' has brought with it an unprecedented movement of capital directed by institutional investors interested in short-term earnings and projections as manifest in metrics including 'earnings per share' (EPS), 'return on capital employed' (ROCE), 'economic value added' (EVA) and 'total shareholder return' (TSR). Organisational strategy is increasingly organised around achieving these financialized metrics in order to satisfy and engage investors (Froud et al., 2006). In this regard, the firm's primary purpose becomes one of maximising shareholder value (Kochan, 2012). To date, SHRM research has incorporated external influences (e.g. product markets) in a functional manner but has neglected the definitive role of investors and developments in capitalist investment patterns (Thompson, 2003, 2013). This failure of SHRM enthusiasts to consider the pressures generated by financial markets risks undermining the credibility of their prescriptions. This is because in this current era of capitalism firms are more orientated towards financial engineering to accumulate capital from financial markets over and above production and product markets (Thompson, 2013). Put simply, financial relationships external to the organisation are deemed to be defining the employment relationship (Appelbaum et al., 2013).

Top management are under increasing pressure to provide financial returns if they are to avoid divestment and hostile take-over, not to mention loss of personal remuneration. Financial returns can be realised through increasing revenue in the consumer market and/or cutting internal costs. However, not all consumer markets are amenable to ever-changing products and services and not all organisations can continuously cut costs without negative consequences for employees. Even in times of economic prosperity, consumer markets often fail to yield sufficient returns to satiate investor appetites and maintain share price. The ultimate conse-quence is a quest by top management for short-term financial gain resulting in cost-cutting, downsizing, taking on debt and limiting internal investment. The stock market reinforces this behaviour by no longer exacting a price penalty, and indeed rewarding cost-cutting and asset-stripping (Batt and Appelbaum, 2013; Kochan, 2012). Financialization therefore aligns with, and reinforces, broader trends of labour market insecurity, externalisation and internationalisation (Thompson, 2013). Moreover, the logic has been readily transferred beyond stock-listed companies to inform organisational behaviour, action and the terms of accountability not only in the private sector but also increasingly in the public and non-profit domains.

With respect to SHRM, financialized capitalism accentuates existing tensions to polarise the interests of top management and employees (Cushen, 2013). Top management are mandated to operate by investor rules, leaving little time for considerations of culture or development, resulting in a focus on 'reducing rather than transforming the workforce' (Thompson, 2005: 168). Quanti-tative studies demonstrate that prioritising the needs of investors results in significant losses for employees. Employees working within highly financialized economies experience greater job inse-curity, financial insecurity, work intensification, an erosion of benefits and a suppression of employee voice (see Cushen, 2013, for a review). At the extreme case of market servitude are examples such as 'dead peasants' insurance', where employers have taken out life insurance policies on employees without their knowledge or consent, resulting in them making a profit when the employee dies (Marinetto, 2011: 132). The elevation of profits and stock price to the role of ultimate arbiters in the evaluation of SHRM implicitly promotes the view that employee-focused practices or goals such as improving working conditions are only justifiable insofar as they deliver immediate financial gain (Adler et al., 2007; Rynes, 2004).

Employee Dynamics: High Performance and Mutual Gains?

A key premise of SHRM is that it fosters enhanced commitment and that employees derive a level of personal and material fulfilment upon the achievement of organisational goals. In practice, the unitary experience appears to be the exception with studies indicating a general decline in job satisfaction since the 1990s, low overall levels of employee engagement (Truss et al., 2013) and the emergence of substantial job inequality (Kochan, 2012). Compliance can substitute for commitment in a domain where 'high performance' work is largely a function of performance management and market discipline (Thompson, 2011). High performance strategic alignment can therefore translate into employees being judged as objects to be examined, benchmarked and modified in the task of realising business strategy. Innovative business analytics facilitate organisations to analyse their human resources to specifically identify those individuals who or positions that generate the most profit (Kiechel, 2012: 71). This is not to say that studies on high performance work systems (HPWS) do not position employees as important agents in the HPWS chain; the problem is that such studies often do not give due regard to the consequences of HPWS interventions on the supposedly important other aspect of the SHRM bargain, namely unitary outcomes of mutual gain.

Subsequent employee-related tensions are typically explained in terms of ineffective SHRM with the assumption that employee behaviour can simply be strategically re-aligned through leveraging a series of intrinsic and extrinsic levers. The problem is assumed to come from within the individual and not wider systemic tensions and contradictions that polarise the interests of different organisational agents. Even in organisations where the HR function has achieved something akin to a strategic partner role, employees have been found to experience feelings of frustration and isolation (Hope-Hailey et al., 2005). Moreover, the increased task autonomy of high involvement HRM can also result in pressure to perform and less overall control of working lives (Orlitzky and Frenkel, 2005). Indeed SHRM proponents have been criticised for neglecting critical HR-related trends which run counter to the unitarist perspective, such as outsourcing, trade unions, conflict management and top management fraud (Batt and Banerjee, 2012). In light of such trends, it is perhaps unsurprising that some find the very terminology of human 'resources' ethically fraught as it risks the humanness, dignity, rights and liberty of those managed by hollowing them to 'a narrow dimension of their whole selves' (Mintzberg, 2009: 61). Recognising that SHRM does not automatically improve performance outcomes or the employment experience has prompted some scholars to challenge the persuasive rhetoric, imagery and values of SHRM (Keenoy, 2009). Such works claim that the power of SHRM stems from the role it plays in perpetuating unitary myths that heighten managerial legitimacy. This post-structural viewpoint argues that SHRM paints a deceptive gloss over harsher business decisions in order to provide employees with a baselessly positive view of their worth to the organisation and to secure their subjective commitment even in times when the organisation is not committing to employees.

However, in the context of financialized capitalism, there is an argument that monolithic normative structures promoting commitment and shared product market visions are increasingly redundant, if not counterproductive (Cushen, 2013). Indeed, many question how proponents of SHRM can claim the approach is based on mutual commitment and enhancing the employment experience when this frequently sits alongside a lived reality of heightened employment insecurity prompted by prioritising the short-term financial interests of shareholders (Kochan, 2012; Marchington and Grugulis, 2000). In essence, market risks are increasingly being borne by employees whose 'ultimate allegiance is to their skills and careers and who have little reason to identify with their current, but probably temporary, employer' (Kunda and Ailon-Souday, 2005: 213).

Broken Promises? The Irish Evidence

Irish scholars have a strong record in uncovering the complexities of the employment relationship and how financial imperatives undermine the ideological undercurrents of some key SHRM concepts. This section will draw on studies which highlight how the aspirations of SHRM may reflect an ideological ideal as opposed to an empirical reality. In particular, it will detail research which may better explicate the status of SHRM in Ireland. The first section offers a broad overview of the socioeconomic context in Ireland. The second section explores organisational and employee-based research which has illuminated some of the complexities and tensions of SHRM as it is enacted in practice in Ireland.

Ireland and Financialized Capitalism

In many ways the Irish context and its economic turbulence serve as an ideal backdrop to examine the issues explored in this chapter. As a small, open economy, Ireland is firmly rooted within financialized capitalism and is vulnerable to its consequences. Indeed, early commentators noted that Ireland's adherence to free trade, free enterprise and foreign industrial domination exemplified how dependency-type mechanisms can thrive in a liberal, open market context (O'Hearn, 1989). Ireland is one of the largest per capita recipients of foreign direct investment (FDI) from market listed multinational corporations (MNCs) and has been referred to as the most globalised economy in the world (Collings et al., 2008). Dobbins (2010: 498) argues that Ireland's position as a very open economy characterised by permissive voluntarism leaves enterprises especially exposed to the contradictions of capitalism, with the consequence that employers are more likely to renege on workplace bargains with employees. In an examination of social partnership, McDonough and Dundon (2010) draw upon social structures of accumulation theory to explore how four constituent elements – globalisation, neoliberalism, weakened labour and financialization – intertwined to initially foster, but then subsequently fracture, the basis for social partnership. They conclude that 'Irish industrial relations cannot be understood in isolation from a broader analysis of the rise and fall of social structures of capitalist accumulation' (McDonough and Dundon, 2010: 544). From this understanding it is apparent that social partnership was never as stable or unitarist as was typically assumed (cf. Teague and Donaghey, 2009).

Other Irish authors have critiqued the trend towards an exclusively economic orientation to people management (Bolton and Houlihan, 2008), with an associated argument that national-level policy has replicated an emphasis 'on the resource dimension of the human rather than the human dimension of the resource' (Lee, 2002: 292). Looking at the SHRM concept of the psychological contract, Cullinane and Dundon (2006: 124) lament how a language of individualism, obligations and mutual reciprocity has refashioned the employment relationship in such a way that it 'manifestly ignores important structural, institutional and class-based dimensions of social relationships'. Incorporating such dimensions, Dundon et al. (2010) explore the mutually reinforcing roles of socialisation, education, vested interests and SHRM discourse in informing managerial hostility to trade unions. Whilst the vast economic expansion in Ireland during the Celtic Tiger years served to deflect attention away from the key contradictions of financialized capitalism (Roche, 2007; O'Riain, 2010), worrying trends emerged even in the 'good times'. Those especially vulnerable at the height of economic growth included older workers and women (D'Art and Turner, 2005). Immigrants to the country found very little of reality in the image of the Celtic Tiger (Dundon et al., 2007; Turner, 2010). Income inequality in Ireland expanded over the boom years as an increasing share of the wealth generated was returned to capital rather than labour (Flaherty and O'Riain, 2013). Kirby (2010: 190) captures the paradox inherent within the Irish model as 'relating to its core features – its highly dependent regime of capital accumulation and its very weak regime of distribution'.

Irish Organisations and Employees in an Era of Financialized Capitalism

Irish scholarship has long questioned the dominant streams of SHRM research and focused not on SHRM prescriptions but on understanding employee experiences of work (cf. Guest, 2011). This section will examine broad trends in employment before exploring research which has more directly connected the employee experience of SHRM to wider financial imperatives. Whilst some more recent trends are partly attributable to the onset of the financial crisis and the Irish recession, the evidence demonstrates how financial and performance goals have long defined the employment relationship and the SHRM agenda. Exposure to the pressures of capital accumulation is often combined with a growing 'elasticity of work' manifest in enhanced work demands and responsibilities coupled with a blurring of private and work life (Thompson, 2013). This certainly seems to be the case in Ireland where, starting more than twenty years ago, there has been a trend of growing intensity in the level and difficulty of tasks conducted by employees (Turner and Morley, 1995: 65). In a study examining 402 employees in manufacturing firms, Turner and Morley (1995) found that the majority of workers felt that they were working harder and operating under tougher conditions. Geary and Dobbins (2001) explored the introduction of teamwork in an Irish subsidiary of a large United States (US) pharmaceutical company. Respondents reported on the notable intensification of effort and pressure to achieve targets, although it was acknowledged that responses to teamwork were not uniform but contingent on expectations and previous experience. Recent research on work–life balance, drawing on a sample of 729 employees from 15 public and private organisations, found that achieving a desired balance is an endemic problem for Irish workers, irrespective of the category of employee or their respective career stage (Darcy et al., 2012). A comprehensive overview of employee experiences of work is provided in the National Workplace Surveys (O'Connell et al., 2010), the latest of which identifies an increase in work pressures and work intensification and a decrease in job security.

Comparing the 2009 workplace survey with a comparable national survey conducted in 2003, Russell and McGinty (2013) found a significant increase in work pressure. Increased work pressures were associated with key job changes such as pay cuts, increases in responsibility and monitoring. Staff reductions and company reorganisations in the previous two years also, unsurprisingly, contributed to increased work pressure and job insecurity.

Geary and Trif (2011) conducted an in-depth case study of a financial institution to explore the distribution of gains accruing from workplace partnership interventions. This study likewise uncovered increased work pressure in the form of additional responsibilities and work hours. Interestingly, senior management in this organisation were more likely than employees to assert that the gains from partnership were equally shared. This tendency of management to over-emphasise the unitary benefits of its SHRM practices has been documented in other studies. A project exploring workplace values and beliefs amongst over 300 employees in Ireland found that while those at managerial levels had a unitarist orientation with respect to their workplace, this was in marked contrast to the pluralist outlook found amongst employees (Geare at al., 2014). This distinction is likewise found in previous work which exposed significant gaps in the perceptions between management and workers with reference to whether they operate on the same side (Turner and Morley, 1995: 204) and with respect to the level of influence workers are permitted to have (Geary, 2007: 120). Ironically, the disseminators and recipients of SHRM are reporting widely different views of the same practices, practices which are specifically designed to cultivate cohesive unitary shared views. Furthermore, employees are aware of such differentials, as evidenced in a study examining modes of employee resistance in an advertising agency where humour served to subvert various forms of control, including gender norms and managerial authority (Kenny and Euchler, 2012).

An examination of trends relating to employee careers highlights how responsibility for careers and performance has switched from the organisation to the individual as manifest in the language of boundaryless and protean careers (see **Chapter 11**). Research on contingent work shows how trends in this area can be understood in terms of advanced capitalism and the 'intermeshed nature of the economic and the social' (Bolton et al., 2012: 123). In this context, Cullen (2010: 508) has argued that prominent self-help and career development books can be read 'as tools of domination in how they encourage individuals to maintain a malleable sense of selfhood which can be recombined and reconfigured to meet the needs of rapidly changing circumstances'. Even the most privileged of employees, namely those operating in knowledge-based positions, are not necessarily recipients of the type of sophisticated practices or developmental opportunities that best SHRM practice might prescribe (Harney et al., 2011; Kelly et al., 2011). Research by Cushen (2013) has expanded upon the experiences of knowledge workers by directly incorporating capital market pressures and examining the resulting tensions (see Box 12.1).

Box 12.1: Financialisation Trumps HRM in Avatar Ireland

'Avatar Ireland' is a subsidiary of a high technology, multinational corporation, 'Avatar Group'. Avatar Group is one of the most financially successful organisations in the world, consistently ranked high within publications listing the world's 'largest', 'most innovative', 'best known brands' and 'great places to work'. In the year the ethnographic study was conducted, 2007, Avatar Ireland's HR practices were ranked in the top 5 per cent of the Irish 'Great Place to Work' competition, reflecting its elaborate employee brand, people management strategy, award-winning communication mechanisms, bundles of interrelated best HR practices, and a large HR department at the core of strategy and operations. Despite this level of HR sophistication, employees at Avatar Ireland exhibited low levels of engagement, scepticism and often barely disguised contempt for HR practices; this from a cadre of knowledge workers who are supposedly particularly open to the charms of soft HRM.

In-depth interviews revealed that employees perceived that their employment was defined by financial, career and job insecurity. Avatar Group's desire to boost the share price meant cost-cutting was a regular feature of life in Avatar Ireland. Despite the levels of financial success, Avatar Ireland was frequently restructured and jobs were lost through centralisation, outsourcing and redundancies. Employees felt insecure, underpaid and undervalued. Far from glossing over these sentiments or easing the implementation of cost-cutting measures, HR practices were interpreted as a 'vanity' project that painted an excessively flattering picture of the organisation. Employees interpreted the gap between HR rhetoric and their lived reality as an affront to their ability to discern the material conditions of their employment. One employee summed up the common sentiment stating:

> It's very hard to swallow, they're telling you one day how important you are to them and the next day they're making more redundant. They're telling you there's not enough people to do the job, and they're agreeing that they're trying to do something about it. Then they're letting all these people go and they're not taking people on to replace them. It's just hypocrisy after hypocrisy.

Surveys in Avatar Ireland revealed that, for several years, while it was a high performing organisation, employee engagement was lower than the national average as benchmarked by the consulting company that the firm commissioned to conduct the survey. The Avatar Ireland case challenges the salience given to best practice HR as the sole source of positive workplace outcomes and employee performance. In fact, well-meaning attempts to

> convince employees that the organisation values them can have the con-
> tradictory effect of prompting employees to examine the gap between such
> rhetoric and their lived experience. Skilled knowledge workers can be high
> performing and simultaneously uncommitted and even angry towards the
> company.
>
> *Source:* Cushen (2013)

Cushen's (2013) in-depth ethnographic research into the subsidiary of a leading global organisation (Avatar), demonstrates
how financial markets can dominate the organisation of knowledge work over and above the product market, creating a distinct,
tension-filled, financialized knowledge labour process (Cushen,
2013). This research unbundles 'best practices', the conditions that
can undermine and sustain them, and the contradictory effects on
the employment experience and attitudes of employees (Cushen
and Thompson, 2012: 82).

SHRM's Broken Promises: Analysis and Insights

In a classic early contribution, Karen Legge took issue with the
dominance of the normative perspective on personnel management, 'removed from its context without recognising that, in
practice, it is the context in which it operates that is likely to con-
strain and mould the content of the function' (Legge, 1978: 1). This
criticism holds true of much work in SHRM today. Dominant
SHRM writings continue to abstract SHRM away from the context
of the broader structures which it both reflects and serves. The
current chapter highlights the importance of opening up theoretical and methodological pathways for a more balanced assessment
of the realities of SHRM. Theoretical viewpoints that understand
SHRM as a unitarist organisation-level practice that functions in
a vacuum, divorced from economic context, are not in a position
to uncover and explain the varied and contradictory lived experiences of SHRM that more pluralistic approaches identify. Of course
contemporary literature in SHRM does speak to the distinction
between intended and enacted practice but it assumes that this is a
gap that can be easily bridged, or constitutes a problem for which
there is a fixed menu of SHRM solutions. In order to avoid going
down this theoretical cul-de-sac, researchers and practitioners
need to give credence to the varied roles and experiences of the

range of stakeholders who effect and are affected by SHRM. This in turn draws attention to the impact and sustainability of SHRM interventions in the context of the broader socioeconomic system (Thompson, 2011). Clearly, SHRM can lead to complex and contradictory outcomes (Ehrnrooth and Björkman, 2012). However the 'structured antagonism' (Edwards, 1986: 5) that characterises work is frequently (conveniently) neglected in SHRM research. The tensions and contradiction inherent to the employment relationship mean that SHRM interventions can only ever be expected to deliver partial success (Townsend et al., 2013) or partial failure (Hyman, 1987). A consequence is that 'an understanding of how the employment relationship is structured and regulated and a concern with how managers manage such endemic potential conflicts *ought* to be at the heart of HRM' (Delbridge and Keenoy, 2010: 802, emphasis in the original).

With respect to methodology, the data presented in this chapter illuminate the value of in-depth methods to complement dominant positivist, large-scale survey approaches to understanding SHRM. Irish studies have highlighted how previous research has tended to ignore or downplay employees' subjective assessments (Geary and Trif, 2011), focus only on core groups (Geary and Dobbins, 2001) or offer surface-level snapshots rather than intensive, longitudinal explorations (Cushen, 2013). As Watson (2004: 464) articulates in his call for critical social science, 'it is only when close attention is given to the activities of "flesh and blood" organizational actors in "actual" organizational situations that the full extent of the interplay that occurs between interpretive and the broader socio-political processes becomes clear.' An exclusive reliance on positivism is particularly problematic as it operates by assuming a specific world order by way of variables or relationships and then maps reality back to fit that order (Harney, 2009). Typically absent is any serious situating of SHRM in the wider structural and cultural context of changing forms of capitalist political economy and the realities of societal and global power and inequalities (Thompson, 2012: 360; Watson, 2004). Perhaps more cynical is the suggestion by Keegan and Boselie (2006) that many academic journals actually favour a 'consensus' standpoint underpinned by a unitarist orientation and a related bias to assess positive, 'win-win' outcomes. Indeed, it may not be in a fledging field's interest to recognise the partial basis of its success or the indeterminacy inherent to the employment relationship; SHRM academic research is ultimately part of a system and serves its own masters of legitimacy, funding and publication.

Conclusions

Overall, Irish researchers have looked beyond the seductive rhetoric of SHRM. Concepts such as 'new realism', 'high performance work systems' and 'high commitment management' were subject to early empirical scrutiny with particular attention directed to the impact of SHRM on trade unions and the dynamics of performance management (Roche, 1999; Turner and Morley, 1995). This chapter has located the discussion of why SHRM may not realise its full promise within a broader socioeconomic context, whereby the circuit of capital is seen to shape both the enactment and experience of SHRM. In so doing we have avoided the term 'critical SHRM', on the basis that a suitably informed approach to SHRM should, by definition, not be seduced by simplistic prescriptions and instead should embrace the complexity of SHRM through exploring the structural context and the range of stakeholders and perspectives that shape the contemporary employment experiences. SHRM research should therefore incorporate the institutional interactions that frame SHRM decisions, including the competing logics of markets, consultants and stakeholders (Delbridge and Edwards, 2013).

It follows that further theory and research might be on more realistic ground by researching the actual practice and experience of SHRM within firms and by appreciating that SHRM interventions are simply the latest incarnation of century-old managerial attempts to manage the contradictions of control and consent rather than the means of eluding or absolving them (Barley and Kunda, 1992). SHRM in this guise may be best conceptualised as constant management of challenge (cf. Rumelt, 2011). This, in turn, may help generate a more helpful form of analysis which sees the broken promises of SHRM interventions as not necessarily a failing of the HR function or employees *per se*, but as a symptom of the tensions and contradictions that abound in the contemporary workplace. In terms of practice, this would caution against simplistic HRM interventions and expose the futility of naively adopting 'best practice'. The realities of business are such that SHRM simply cannot always be 'strategically aligned' and 'unitarist' at the same time, and to downplay this represents a considerable disservice to HR practitioners who often have the unenviable task of implementing tough management decisions on the one hand and maintaining high levels of employee engagement and motivation on the other. This is not to say that SHRM is redundant, we simply argue that HR stakeholders would be better served by advice and research that helps them to appreciate and navigate, rather than suppress and deny, the plurality of interests that shape the employment relationship.

References

Adler, P., Forbes, L. and Wilmott, H. (2007), 'Critical Management Studies', *Academy of Management Annals*, 1(1): 119–179.

Appelbaum, E., Batt, R. and Clark, I. (2013), 'Implications of Financial Capitalism for Employment Relations Research: Evidence from Breach of Trust and Implicit Contracts in Private Equity Buyouts', *British Journal of Industrial Relations*, 51(3): 498–518.

Barley, S.R. and Kunda, G. (1992), 'Design and Devotion: Surges of Rational and Normative Ideologies of Control in Managerial Discourse', *Administrative Science Quarterly*, 37(1): 363–399.

Batt, R. and Appelbaum, E. (2013), 'The Impact of Financialization on Management and Employment Outcomes', Upjohn Working Paper 13-191, Kalamazoo, MI: WE Upjohn Institute for Employment Research, available from: <http://research.upjohn.org/up_workingpapers/191/>.

Batt, R. and Banerjee, M. (2012), 'The Scope and Trajectory of Strategic HR Research: Evidence from American and British Journals', *International Journal of Human Resource Management*, 23(9): 1739–1762.

Bolton, S. and Houlihan, M. (2008), 'Beginning the Search for the H in HRM' in S. Bolton and M. Houlihan (eds), *Searching for the Human in Human Resource Management*, New York, NY: Palgrave Macmillan, 1–19.

Bolton, S., Houlihan, M. and Laaser, K. (2012), 'Contingent Work and Its Contradictions: Towards a Moral Economy Framework', *Journal of Business Ethics*, 111(1): 121–132.

Boselie, P., Brewster, C. and Paauwe, J. (2009), 'In Search of Balance – Managing the Dualities of HRM: An Overview of the Issues', *Personnel Review*, 38(5): 461–471.

Collings, D., Gunnigle, P. and Morley, M. (2008), 'Between Boston and Berlin: American MNCs and the Shifting Contours of Industrial Relations in Ireland', *International Journal of Human Resource Management*, 19(2): 240–261.

Cullen, J. (2009), 'How to Sell Your Soul and Still Get into Heaven: Stephen Covey's Epiphany-Inducing Technology of Effective Selfhood', *Human Relations*, 62(8): 1231–1254.

Cullinane, N. and Dundon, T. (2006), 'The Psychological Contract: A Critical Review', *International Journal of Management Reviews*, 8(2): 113–129.

Cushen, J. (2013), 'Financialization in the Workplace: Hegemonic Narratives, Performative Interventions and the Angry Knowledge Worker', *Accounting, Organizations and Society*, 38(4): 314–331.

Cushen, J. and Thompson, P. (2012), 'Doing the Right Thing? HRM and the Angry Knowledge Worker', *New Technology, Work and Employment*, 27(2): 79–92.

Darcy, C., McCarthy, A., Hill, J. and McCarthy, A. (2012), 'Work–Life Balance: One Size Fits All? An Exploratory Analysis of the Differential Effects of Career Stage', *European Management Journal*, 30(2): 111–120.

D'Art, D. and Turner, T. (2005), 'Union Recognition and Partnership at Work: A New Legitimacy for Irish Trade Unions?', *Industrial Relations Journal*, 36(2): 121–137.

Delbridge, R. and Edwards, T. (2013), 'Inhabiting Institutions: Critical Realist Refinements to Understanding Institutional Complexity and Change', *Organization Studies*, 34(7): 927–947.

Delbridge, R. and Keenoy, T. (2010), 'Beyond Managerialism?', *International Journal of Human Resource Management*, 21(6): 799–817.

Dobbins, T. (2010), 'The Case for "Beneficial Constraints": Why Permissive Voluntarism Impedes Workplace Cooperation in Ireland', *Economic and Industrial Democracy*, 31(4): 497–519.

Drake, B.H. and Drake, E. (1988), 'Ethical and Legal Aspects of Managing Corporate Cultures', *California Management Review*, 30(2): 107–123.

Dundon, T., González-Perez, M.A. and McDonough, T. (2007), 'Bitten by the Celtic Tiger: Immnigrant Workers and Industrial Relations in the New "Glocalized" Ireland', *Economic and Industrial Democracy*, 28(4): 501–522.

Dundon, T., Harney, B. and Cullinane, N. (2010), 'De-Collectivism and Managerial Ideology: Towards an Understanding of Trade Union Opposition', *International Journal of Management Concepts and Philosophy*, 4(3/4): 267–281.

Edwards, P. (1986), *Conflict at Work: A Materialist Analysis of Workplace Relations*, Oxford: Blackwell.

Ehrnrooth, M. and Björkman, I. (2012), 'An Integrative HRM Process Theorization: Beyond Signalling Effects and Mutual Gains', *Journal of Management Studies*, 49(6): 1109–1135.

Flaherty, E. and O'Riain, S. (2013), 'Labour's Declining Share of National Income in Ireland and Denmark: Similar Trends and Different Dynamics', Unpublished mimeo, Department of Sociology, National University of Ireland, Maynooth.

Froud, J., Johal, S., Leaver, A. and Williams, K. (2006), *Financialization and Strategy: Narrative and Numbers*, London: Routledge.

Geare, A., Edgar, F. and McAndrew, I. (2006), 'Employment Relationships: Ideology and HRM Practice', *International Journal of Human Resource Management*, 17(7): 1190–1208.

Geare, A., Edgar, F., McAndrew, I., Harney, B., Cafferkey, K. and Dundon, T. (2014), 'Exploring the Ideological Undercurrents of HRM: Workplace Values and Beliefs in Ireland and New Zealand', *International Journal of Human Resource Management*, forthcoming.

Geary, J. (2007), 'Employee Voice in the Irish Workplace: Status and Prospect' in R.B. Freeman, P. Boxall and P. Haynes (eds), *What Workers Say: Employee Voice in the Anglo-American Workplace*, Ithaca, NY: ILR Press, 97–124.

Geary, J. and Dobbins, A. (2001), 'Teamworking: A New Dynamic in the Pursuit of Managerial Control', *Human Resource Management Journal*, 11(1): 3–24.

Geary, J. and Trif, A. (2011), 'Workplace Partnership and the Balance of Advantage: A Critical Case Analysis', *British Journal of Industrial Relations*, 41(1): 44–69.

Guest, D. (2011), 'Human Resource Management and Performance: Still Searching for Some Answers', *Human Resource Management Journal*, 21(1): 3–13.

Harney, B. (2009), 'Exploring the Road Less Travelled in HRM-Performance Research: A Critical Realist Alternative to "Big Science"' *Proceedings of the Labor and Employment Relations Association 61st Annual Meeting*, Champaign, IL: LERA, available from: <http://www.lera.uiuc.edu/pubs/proceedings/2009/AP2009.pdf#page=15>.

Harney, B., Monks, K., Alexopoulos, A., Buckley, F. and Hogan, T. (2011), 'University Research Scientists as Knowledge Workers: Contract Status and Employment Status', *International Journal of Human Resource Management*, DOI:10.1080/09585192.2011.561241.

Hope-Hailey, V., Farndale, E. and Truss, C. (2005), 'The HR Department's Role in Organisational Performance', *Human Resource Management Journal*, 15(3): 49–66.

Hyman, R. (1987), 'Strategy or Structure? Capital, Labour and Control', *Work, Employment and Society*, 1(1): 25–55.

Janssens, M. and Steyaert, C. (2009), 'HRM and Performance: A Plea for Reflexivity in HRM Studies', *Journal of Management Studies*, 46(1): 143–155.

Kaufman, B. (2012), 'Strategic Human Resource Management Research in the United States: A Failing Grade after 30 Years?', *Academy of Management Perspectives*, 26(2): 12–36.

Keegan, A. and Boselie, P. (2006), 'The Lack of Impact of Dissensus Inspired Analysis on Developments in the Field of Human Resource Management', *Journal of Management Studies*, 43(7): 1491–1511.

Keenoy, T. (2009), 'Human Resource Management' in M. Alvesson, T. Bridgman and H. Wilmott (eds), *The Oxford Handbook of Critical Management Studies*, Oxford: Oxford University Press, 454–472.

Kelly, G., Mastroeni, M., Conway, E., Monks, K., Truss, K., Flood, P. and Hannon, E. (2011), 'Combining Diverse Knowledge: Knowledge Workers' Experience of Specialist and Generalist Roles', *Personnel Review*, 40(5): 607–624.

Kenny, K. and Euchler, G. (2012), '"Some Good Clean Fun": Humour, Control and Subversion in an Advertising Agency', *Gender, Work and Organization*, 3(19): 306–323.

Kiechel, W.I. (2012), 'The Management Century', *Harvard Business Review*, 90(11): 63–75.

Kirby, P. (2010), *Celtic Tiger in Collapse: Explaining the Weaknesses of the Irish Model*, New York, NY: Palgrave Macmillan.

Kochan, T. (2007), 'Social Legitimacy of the HRM Profession: A US Perspective' in P. Boxall, J. Purcell and P. Wright (eds), *Oxford Handbook of Human Resource Management*, Oxford: Oxford University Press, 599–619.

Kochan, T. (2012), 'A Jobs Compact for America's Future', *Harvard Business Review*, 90(3): 64–72.

Kunda, G. and Ailon-Souday, G. (2005), 'Managers, Markets and Ideologies: Design and Devotion Revisited' in S. Ackroyd, R. Batt, P. Thompson and P. Tolbert (eds), *Oxford Handbook of Work and Organization*, Oxford: Oxford University Press, 200–219.

Lee, J.J. (2002), 'Labour, Employment and Society in Twentieth Century Ireland' in P. Gunnigle, M. Morley and M. McDonnell (eds), *The John Lovett Lectures: A Decade of Developments in Human Resource Management*, Dublin: Liffey Press, 279–303.

Legge, K. (1978), *Power, Innovation and Problem-Solving in Personnel Management*, London: McGraw-Hill.

Legge, K. (1995), *Human Resource Management: Rhetoric and Realities*, London: Palgrave Macmillan.

Legge, K. (1998), 'Is HRM Ethical? Can HRM Be Ethical?' in M. Parker (ed.), *Ethics and Organizations*, London: Sage: 150–172.

Marchington, M. and Grugulis, I. (2000), 'Best Practice HRM: Perfect Opportunity or Dangerous Illusion?', *International Journal of Human Resource Management*, 11(4): 905–925.

Marinetto, M. (2011), 'Ethics, Philosophy and the Employment Relationship' in P. Blyton, E. Heery and P. Turnbull (eds), *Reassessing the Employment Relationship*, London: Palgrave Macmillan, 122–146.

McDonough, T. and Dundon, T. (2010), 'Thatcherism Delayed? The Irish Crisis and the Paradox of Social Partnership', *Industrial Relations Journal*, 41(6): 544–562.

Mintzberg, H. (2009), *Managing*, London: FT Prentice Hall.

Nolan, P. (2011), 'Money, Markets, Meltdown: The 21st-Century Crisis of Labour', *Industrial Relations Journal*, 42(1): 2–17.

O'Connell, P., Russell, H., Watson, D. and Byrne, D. (2010), *The Changing Workplace: A Survey of Employees' Views and Experiences*, Dublin: National Centre for Partnership and Performance.

O'Hearn, D. (1989), 'The Irish Case of Dependency: An Exception to the Exceptions?', *American Sociological Review*, 24(2): 169–197.

O'Riain, S. (2010), 'Addicted to Growth: Developmental Statism and Neoliberalism in the Celtic Tiger' in M. Bøss (ed.), *The Nation-State in Transformation: The Governance, Growth and Cohesion of Small States Under Globalisation*, Aarhus: Aarhus University Press.

Orlitzky, M. and Frenkel, S. (2005), 'Alternative Pathways to High-Performance Workplaces', *International Journal of Human Resource Management*, 16(8): 1325–1348.

Roche, W.K. (1999), 'In Search of Commitment-Orientated Human Resource Management Practices and the Conditions that Sustain Them', *Journal of Management Studies*, 36(5): 653–678.

Roche, W.K. (2007), 'Social Partnership in Ireland and New Social Pacts', *Industrial Relations*, 46(3): 395–425.

Rumelt, R. (2011), *Good Strategy/Bad Strategy*, London: Profile Books.

Russell, H. and McGinty, F. (2013), 'Under Pressure: The Impact of Recession on Employees in Ireland', *British Journal of Industrial Relations*, doi: 10.1111/bjir.12018.

Rynes, S.L. (2004), 'Where Do We Go from Here? Imagining New Roles for Human Resources', *Journal of Management Inquiry*, 13(3): 203–213.

Teague, P. and Donaghey, J. (2009), 'Why Has Irish Social Partnership Survived?', *British Journal of Industrial Relations*, 47(1): 55–78.

Thompson, P. (2003), 'Disconnected Capitalism or Why Employers Can't Keep Their Side of the Bargain', *Work, Employment and Society*, 17(2): 359–378.

Thompson, P. (2005), 'Section Introduction: Managerial Regimes and Employee Actions' in S. Ackroyd, R. Batt, P. Thompson and P. Tolbert (eds), *Oxford Handbook of Work and Organization*, Oxford: Oxford University Press, 165–175.

Thompson, P. (2011), 'The Capitalist Labour Process: Concepts and Connections', *Capital and Class*, 34(1): 7–14.

Thompson, P. (2012), 'The Trouble with HRM', *Human Resource Management Journal*, 21(4): 355–367.

Thompson, P. (2013), 'Financialization and the Workplace: Extending and Applying the Disconnected Capitalism Thesis', *Work, Employment and Society*, 27(3): 472–488.

Townsend, K., Wilkinson, A. and Burgess, J. (2013), 'Routes to Partial Success: Collaborative Employment Relations and Employee

Engagement', *International Journal of Human Resource Management*, DOI :10.1080/09585192.2012.743478.

Truss, C., Shantz, A., Soane, E., Alfes, K. and Delbridge, R. (2013), 'Employee Engagement, Organisational Performance and Individual Well-Being: Exploring the Evidence, Developing the Theory', *International Journal of Human Resource Management*, 24(14): 2657–2669.

Turner, T. (2010), 'The Jobs Immigrants Do: Issues of Displacement and Marginalisation in the Irish Labour Market', *Work, Employment and Society*, 24(2): 318–336.

Turner, T. and Morley, M. (1995), *Industrial Relation and the New Order: Case Studies in Conflict and Co-Operation*, Cork: Oak Tree Press.

Ulrich, D. and Brockbank, W. (2005), *The HR Value Proposition*, Boston, MA: Harvard Business School Press.

Van Buren III, H., Greenwood, M. and Sheehan, C. (2011), 'Strategic Human Resource Management and the Decline of Employee Focus', *Human Resource Management Review*, 21(1): 209–219.

Watson, T. (2004), 'HRM and Critical Social Science Analysis', *Journal of Management Studies*, 41(3): 447–467.

CONCLUSION

Towards the Future

Kathy Monks and Brian Harney

Introduction

The aim of this chapter is to explore the future of strategic human resource management (SHRM) in Ireland at both a research and practice level. In so doing, the authors are very well aware that they do not have a crystal ball at their disposal that can be guaranteed to predict what such a future may hold. At the same time, recent trends and developments do provide us with some opportunity to consider what issues might emerge and how researchers and practitioners might be best placed to either research or manage new developments. We examine emerging areas that we consider will provide interesting and fruitful lines of enquiry for researchers and managers alike. At an organisational level we explore the areas of SHRM and sustainability, 'green HRM' and e-HRM, while at an employee level we consider the broad area of the employment relationship, particular with regard to understanding the nature and management of skills and issues of employee well-being. Finally, at a more theoretical level, we consider emerging reconceptualisations of human resource management (HRM) that include the notion of human resource (HR) signals rather than practices.

SHRM and Sustainability: A New Extension of the SHRM and Performance Debate?

The starting point for our consideration of the future of research into SHRM emerges from the debates on the links between SHRM and performance. This topic has exercised the minds of many academics for a long number of years, although gaps in our understanding still remain and the actual mechanisms of the workings of the 'black box' that are at the centre of these debates are still somewhat elusive. For the most part, this stream of literature has been located at firm level, although more recently the focus of attention has switched to the employee as well as to the role of line managers (see **Chapter 1** of this book for an overview of SHRM and performance research). A smaller stream of research has considered the issue of SHRM and performance more widely. For example, the broader context within which SHRM operates was always to the fore in the minds of many European researchers such as Paauwe (2009) but has tended to be given less attention in the influential stream of research emerging from the United States.

There is now evidence of a shift in direction and a broadening of how the notion of performance might be interpreted. For example, a recent special edition of *Human Resource Management* (2012) focused on SHRM's role in sustainability. The definition adopted by the editors of this special edition is that 'business sustainability means adopting a "triple bottom line" perspective that focuses on the environmental, social and economic performance of an organization' (Taylor et al., 2012: 790). This notion not only extends the performance focus that has been at the heart of SHRM research for so long into a much broader landscape, but radically alters the notion of the landscape itself. The previously held view that the function of a business was simply to make profit is gradually eroded as it becomes evident that there is an insufficient supply of natural resources to fuel such a philosophy. The research on sustainability links to the emerging literature on 'green' SHRM. A recent review (Jackson et al., 2011, cited in Taylor et al., 2012) suggests a programme for SHRM research that interlinks aspects of SHRM with the area of environmental management. Similarly, another recent review (Renwick et al., 2013) uses the ability–motivation–opportunity (AMO) theory in developing a case for the integration of the separate literatures of environmental management and SHRM research. This review summarises the research gaps in our understanding of these issues, which range from how staff might be attracted, developed and motivated in line with a 'green' agenda (Bauer and Aiman-Smith, 1996) to the linking mechanisms between employee participation in green employee involvement schemes and positive employee and organisational outcomes.

This broadening of the scope of SHRM research to embrace the notion of a sustainable organisation provides exciting opportunities. Given Ireland's precarious economic position, it may also be particular apposite at this point in time. At the same time, the terrain is not without its perils for researchers keen to make a name for themselves in this area. Multi-level research is invariably complex (Klein and Kozlowski, 2000) and areas such as sustainability and the environment add another layer of complexity to the challenges of data collection and analysis, as well as requiring researchers to adopt a multi-disciplinary perspective in their perusal of relevant literature.

At a practice level, the incursion by the HR professional into these new areas will require a rethinking of the contribution that HR might make within the organisation and acquisition of a broader level of expertise. A recent survey in the United Kingdom indicates that HR managers increasingly see their contribution to the corporate responsibility agenda as vital. However, it also notes that the HR profession as a whole needs to articulate more persuasively why HR should have a central role in corporate responsibility (Ballinger et al., 2012). An article by Dubois and Dubois (2012) sets out a set of SHRM actions that they suggest will support the embedding of environmental sustainability into an organisation. They examine HR functional areas in considering the HR actions required and here it is interesting to note the terms used in their descriptions of functional areas and their accompanying practices. While the old reliables of training and development, performance management, and rewards and recognition appear in their list, these are joined by practices such as 'line management alignment', 'HRM system architecture development' and 'organization strategy participation', suggesting new areas of expertise may be required for HR managers. A distinction is also made between 'transformational HRM' activities that 'create a paradigm shift for all organisational members' (p. 816) and 'traditional HRM' that is undertaken 'with an eye to transformation' and to 'ensure vertical/horizontal alignment' (p. 817). This presents HR professionals with options in both approach and delivery of the new agenda.

E-HRM: The Domain of HR Professionals or IT Specialists?

A discussion of electronic human resource management (e-HRM) shares commonalities with our previous discussion of SHRM and sustainability in requiring the adoption of a multi-disciplinary perspective. Indeed, it is this multidisciplinary perspective that makes both HR academics and HR professionals somewhat uneasy with the domain of e-HRM as it is unclear the extent to which it belongs to information technology (IT) or HR experts. Additional complications come from the possibility that it may be viewed as a transactional rather than transformational activity and somewhat immutable to change, thus reducing further the interest level of possible protagonists (see Stone and Dulebohn, 2013).

A recent definition of e-HRM suggests that it consists of 'configurations of computer hardware, software and electronic networking resources that enable intended or actual HRM activities (e.g., policies, practices and services) through individual and group level interactions within and across organisational boundaries' (Marler and Fisher, 2013: 21). Marler and Fisher examined primary research studies into e-HRM that had been undertaken over a twelve-year period in order to describe and evaluate the evidence for the relationship between e-HRM and SHRM. Their findings suggest various research avenues that might be progressed. First, it appears that e-HRM is still at a very early stage of development when compared with either the information technology or the strategic management literatures. Second, despite the vast amount of literature on the SHRM and performance debates, Marler and Fisher could not find any study that had directly examined either the relationship between the adoption of e-HRM and organisational performance measures or the adoption of e-HRM and improved HR outcomes such as job satisfaction or turnover. Third, while research has been undertaken into specific areas of e-HRM, such as e-learning or e-recruiting, many areas remain untapped. For example, there is little known about the effectiveness of web-based selection systems, despite their evident popularity.

Venturing into the terrain of e-HRM will require researchers to grapple with the complexities of information technology and understand its various applications. Issues of professional identity will once again come to the fore as HR and IT specialists work to deliver effective HR solutions. At a practice level, there is a need for HR professionals to consider some of the ramifications of e-HRM systems on areas such as the employment relationship. For example, if employees are much more in command of the ways in which they manage their elements of this relationship through e-systems, how will the role of the HR professional alter? (See Aguinis and Lawal (2013) and Strohmeier (2013) for an overview of this issue and some proposed areas for research.) The boundaries of the employment relationship are also likely to reconfigure as technological advances make it easier to perform work remotely (Dewhurts et al., 2013). Indeed, experts project that, within a few years, more than 1.3 billion people will work virtually (Johns and Gratton, 2013). Finally, social networks open up a range of possibilities for problem-solving as employees can more readily draw upon the collective intelligence of their social network (Gorbis, 2013). While this makes managing the knowledge flows of an organisation all the more complex, it presents an important opportunity for the HR function to connect employees through technology (Ulrich et al., 2013).

The ways in which the employment relationship may change as a result of e-HRM brings us to the next section of our analysis, which moves to an employee level in considering some of the emerging issues surrounding the employment relationship.

Rethinking the Employment Relationship

In a recent article in *Human Resource Management Journal*, written as part of the 'Innovations in HRM Series', Peter Boxall (2013) assesses the quality of alignment in employment relationships. He suggests that research to date has been oriented towards exploration of the specific practices that comprise HRM, such as selection, training, appraisal or remuneration and that, as a result, 'the question of how to assess the quality of the whole – the employment relationship – has been poorly served' (p. 3). In common with research trends in sustainability and e-HRM already described, Boxall adopts a multidisciplinary perspective in exploring the issue of mutuality or alignment in the employment relationship. In this analysis he disputes widely-held views on notions of human resources as 'people employed in any organisation', instead adopting a much more wide-ranging definition that proposes them as: 'the resources that are intrinsic to human beings which they can apply to the various tasks of life'. In this definition he includes the 'knowledge, skills, networks and energies that people may deploy in their various roles' as well as 'the underpinning dynamic characteristics of people, including their physical and emotional health' (p. 4). Boxall moves on to provide a model of how the alignment in employment relationships might operate and proposes three tests of this alignment: whether there is a capability match, a commitment match and a contribution match (p. 6). Boxall's redefinition of human resources, together with his views on how alignment in employment relationships might be tested, is considered in light of interest at both research and practice levels in the notion of talent management and the underpinning stream of contemporary research on the nature of skills and performance. Some of these issues are considered in more detail below.

Managing Talent – or Optimising Skills?

A recent consultancy report by KPMG International (2012) identified many elements within the broad area of talent management as issues which HR executives identified as challenges for the future. These inter-related challenges included: 'managing, hiring and identifying talent globally while retaining important local insights'; 'managing a flexible and virtual workforce – but not at the cost of loyalty and career development'; and 'retaining the best talent – maintaining employee engagement in the face of a less committed, more flexible workforce' (p. 4). However, research within an Irish context (Shanks et al., 2013) suggests that Irish organisations may be facing somewhat more basic talent management problems. The survey of 1,000 employed and unemployed individuals and 100 organisations undertaken by Shanks et al. suggest that there are critical gaps between the skills that current and prospective employees possess and those that organisations actually require.

The centrality of talent management for both HR practitioners and HR researchers raises deep-seated issues that relate to the nature of skills within organisations. While researchers continue to tackle these issues (see Hunter et al., 2012 for the issues involved in hiring an innovative workforce), an article by Grugulis and Stoyanova (2011) explores the assumption that there is actually a link between skills and performance. In so doing, they unpack some of the issues involved in defining, evaluating and measuring these two complex constructs, as well as the problems in establishing satisfactory proxies for their use in research studies. The encompassing of both 'hard' and 'soft' elements within the domain of 'skills' gives some indications of the issues that must be considered in any deconstruction of the term. This becomes particularly difficult in unpacking the notion of 'soft skills'. Grugulis and Stoyanova (p. 522) point out that:

> ... the term 'soft skills' covers qualities that are so many and so varied that it is tempting to attribute either everything or nothing to them. This is, after all, a category that can incorporate (among others) smiling, problem-solving, customer service and self-confidence.

However, these reservations do not necessarily appear to be held by those at the practice end of SHRM. The KPMG International Report (2012) suggests that the ability to quantify skills through the use of data analytics will allow HR departments to 'collect clearer information on its supply chain of talent and where the most demand for particular skills lies', thus giving them 'the long-overdue chance to become more empirical, to provide hard evidence for their opinions, thereby gaining much-needed credibility at the highest levels of the business' (p. 11). However, how such data might then be linked to improvements in organisational performance that investment in skill development might warrant is as yet unclear. Grugulis and Stoyanova's (2011) analysis of research that purports to examine some elements of the skill and performance equation indicates the limitations of research in this regard, particularly given its failure to find a causal relationship between the two (Guest, 2011). In suggesting how research might progress this area, Grugulis and Stoyanova propose as a good starting point a focus on firms or sub-sectors where theory suggests a link might be found and identify several studies that provide good exemplars of successful models (e.g. Keep and Mayhew, 2004; Felstead et al., 2005, 2009). At a practice level, several research-based consultancy reports offer steps that HR professionals and organisations might take to tackle problems with skill gaps (Shanks et al., 2013; Smith et al., 2012; KPMG International, 2012).

Optimising Skills – or Intensifying Work? Considering Employee Well-Being

Discussions of skills and skill enhancement within the employ-ment relationship lead on to consideration of more deep-seated issues such as work intensification and employee well-being. One clearly identified trend in recent years in Ireland is the intensifica-tion of work in both the public and private sectors (O'Connell et al., 2009). While discussions about skills and skills development might appear removed from those on work intensification, such issues are intertwined as long working hours and pressures on performance, including pressures to enhance skills, affect employees' well-being (Bacon et al., 2010; Brown, 2012; Dekas et al., 2013). In addition, there is not as yet a consensus within the SHRM and performance literature on the outcomes for employees of engagement with high-performance work systems.

A recent review by Van De Voorde et al. (2012) examines evidence for the competing perspectives of 'mutual gains' and 'conflicting outcomes'. Their analysis suggests that 'the appropriate perspec-tive on employee well-being depends on the type of well-being that is studied' (p. 401) and points to several avenues for future research. First, they suggest research to bring together the mutual gains and conflicting outcomes perspectives, rather than contrasting them as has been the trend to date, with the high involvement work systems literature (Boxall and Macky, 2009) perhaps serving as an appro-priate starting point. Second, they suggest that 'in trying to balance well-being, research on HRM and employment relationships needs to consider various aspects of well-being' (Van De Voorde et al., 2012: 402). Third, they advance the need for what they term a 'dif-ferential approach' (p. 403) so that there is better 'discrimination between HR practices required because of external pressures, those basic HR process-related practices involved in employing staff, and those HR practices that really propel the workforce towards spe-cific goals' (p. 403). These suggestions, while applied to the area of well-being in their analysis, would appear to be valuable areas of research that would enhance understanding of SHRM across several domains. For practitioners they raise issues about how both employee well-being *and* organisational performance might be achieved.

Reconceptualising SHRM

In our final section, we consider some of the ways in which the discipline of SHRM itself might be reconceptualised. We are cognisant of the fact that such reconceptualisations run the risk of being simply 'old wine in new bottles', but we suggest that they can also offer new ways of looking at SHRM and therefore new opportunities for both researchers and practitioners.

Our starting point for this analysis is a book chapter by Haggerty and Wright (2010: 101), which suggests that:

> … conceptualizing HRM as a practice or set of practices not only ignores important aspects of context, it may in fact lead to the development of HR functions that base their contribution to the business on practices or bundles (benchmarking), not on business results.

They propose that SHRM should be reconceptualised as 'signals from management to employee groups and individuals' (p. 101). Interestingly, Haggerty and Wright's rationale for a reconceptualisation begins with the practice of SHRM and its implementation and with the need for improved skills for HR professionals, a starting point which is not necessarily always adopted by those researching SHRM issues. At this practice level, Haggerty and Wright identify a range of competencies that HR professionals must acquire. Most of their list is little different in many ways from the skills advocated by a range of writers, perhaps most notably Ulrich (1997), over the years. However, they do suggest that HR must adopt a 'more complete systems orientation', a 'process that must be closely linked to the aspirational principle that people are an important (if not the most important) asset in the organization' (p. 112). While not necessarily breaking new ground, such an orientation does return employees to the heart of SHRM practice and therefore the central focus of the attentions of HR professionals. Concern with employees' role in the employment relationship had lost favour over the years with many HR professionals: the 'business partner' role holding far greater promise for career advancement than anything that an 'employee champion' (see Ulrich, 1997) might bring.

At a theoretical level, Haggerty and Wright's (2010) analysis emanates from and extends Bowen and Ostroff's (2004) work on the strength of the HR system. Their extension of the Bowen and Ostroff arguments lies in their suggestion that 'the strength of the HR system is leveraged more on the process and less on the content of HRM' (Haggerty and Wright, 2010: 106). Bowen and Ostroff's (2004) work is widely cited and has proved extremely influential in debates on HR systems. However, little empirical work has been undertaken into Bowen and Ostroff's core concepts and their highly elaborated arguments would provide fruitful avenues for exploration. A study that does pursue this line of enquiry has recently been undertaken in a hospital context (Townsend et al., 2012) and provides interesting insights how 'strong signals' might operate within the different hierarchical levels of a hospital environment. This study also provides a reminder of the critical role that key intermediaries such as line managers can play in enacting SHRM, something increasingly recognised by researchers and practitioners alike (Freeney and Fellenz, 2013; Shanks et al., 2013).

Conclusions

In our attempt to identify emerging trends and developments, we have taken an eclectic and wide-ranging look at the area of SHRM. It is evident from the chapters that comprise this book, as well as our concluding remarks, that the discipline of SHRM comprises a very broad array of topics and that this poses considerable difficulties for researchers and practitioners alike. Its multi-disciplinary underpinnings and operation means that researchers cannot remain safely cocooned within the boundaries of one discipline area. For practitioners, this translates into ever-changing demands to update their knowledge base and to explore new avenues in which SHRM contributions will benefit both employers and employees. While such demands are not without their costs, they at the same time make both the research and the practice of SHRM valuable and exciting domains that will continue to intrigue and challenge researchers and practitioners both in Ireland and internationally.

References

Aguinis, H. and Lawal, S. (2013), 'eLancing: A Review and Research Agenda for Bridging the Science–Practice Gap', *Human Resource Management Review*, 23(6): 6–17.

Bacon, N., Blyton, P. and Dastmalchian, A. (2010), 'The Impact of Organizational Change on Steelworkers in Craft and Production Occupational Groups', *Human Relations*, 63(8): 1223–1248.

Ballinger, C., Gifford, J. and Miller, J. (2012), 'The Role of HR in Corporate Responsibility: Stewardship, Leadership and Governance', CIPD research report, February, London: Chartered Institute for Personnel Development.

Bauer, T. and Aiman-Smith, L. (1996), 'Green Career Choices: The Influence of a Firm's Ecological Stance on Perceived Company Attractiveness', *Journal of Business and Psychology*, 10(4): 445–458.

Bowen, D.E. and Ostroff, C. (2004), 'Understanding HRM–Firm Performance Linkages: The Role of the "Strength" of the HRM System', *Academy of Management Review*, 29(2): 203–221.

Boxall, P. (2013), 'Mutuality in the Management of Human Resources: Assessing the Quality of Alignment in Employment Relationships', *Human Resource Management Journal*, 23(1): 3–17.

Boxall, P. and Macky, K. (2009), 'Research and Theory on High-Performance Work Systems: Processing the High-Involvement System', *Human Resource Management Journal*, 19(2): 3–23.

Brown, M. (2012), 'Responses to Work Intensification: Does Generation Matter?', *International Journal of Human Resource Management*, 23(17): 3578–3595.

Dekas, K., Bauer, T., Welle, B., Kurkoski, J. and Sullivan, S. (2013), 'Organizational Citizenship Behaviour, Version 2.0: A Review and Qualitative Investigation of OCBs for Knowledge Workers at Google and Beyond', *Academy of Management Perspectives*, 27(3): 219–237.

Dewhurts, M., Hancock, B. and Ellsworth, D. (2013), 'Redesigning Knowledge Work', *Harvard Business Review*, 91(1): 59–64.

Dubois, C. and Dubois, D. (2012), 'Strategic HRM as Social Design for Environmental Sustainability in Organization', *Human Resource Management*, 51(6): 799–829.

Felstead, A., Fuller, A., Jewson, N. and Unwon, L. (2009), *Improving Working and Learning*, London: Routledge.

Felstead, A., Fuller, A., Unwin, L., Ashton, D., Butler, P. and Lee, T. (2005), 'Surveying the Scene: Learning Metaphors, Survey Design and the Workplace Context', *Journal of Educational and Work*, 18(14): 359–383.

Freeney, Y. and Fellenz, M. (2013), 'Work Engagement, Job Design and the Role of the Social Context at Work: Exploring Antecedents from a Relational Perspective', *Human Relations*, 66(11): 1427–1445 .

Gorbis, M. (2013), 'The New Kind of Worker Every Business Needs', *Harvard Business Review Blog Network*, 22 April, available from: <http://blogs.hbr.org/2013/04/the-new-kind-of-worker-every-business/>.

Grugulis, I. and Stoyanova, D. (2011), 'Skills and Performance', *British Journal of Industrial Relations*, 49(3): 515–536.

Guest, D. (2011), 'Human Resource Management and Performance: Still Searching for Some Answers', *Human Resource Management Journal*, 2(1): 3–13.

Haggerty, J. and Wright, P. (2010), 'Strong Situations and Firm Performance: A Proposed Reconceptualisation of the Role of the HR Function' in A. Wilkinson, N. Bacon, T. Redman and S. Snell (eds), *The Sage Handbook of Human Resource Management*, London: Sage.

Hunter, S., Cushenberry, L. and Friedrich, T. (2012), 'Hiring an Innovative Workforce: A Necessary yet Uniquely Challenging Endeavour', *Human Resource Management Review*, 22(4): 303–322.

Jackson, S.E., Renwick, D.W.S., Jabbour, C.J.C. and Muller-Carmen, M. (2011), 'State-of-the-Art and Future Directions for Green Human Resource Management: Introduction to the Special Edition', *Zeitschrift für Personalforschung*, 25(2): 99–116.

Johns, T. and Gratton, L. (2013), 'The Third Wave of Virtual Work', *Harvard Business Review*, 91(1): 66–73.

Keep, E. and Mayhew, K. (2004), *Can Employers Be Persuaded that Training Pays?*, Glasgow: Futureskills Scotland, Highlands and Islands Enterprise, Scottish Enterprise.

Klein, K. and Kozlowski, E. (2000), *Multilevel Theory, Research, and Methods in Organizations*, San Francisco, CA: Jossey-Bass.

KPMG International (2012), 'Rethinking Human Resources in a Changing World', *KPMG*, available from: <http://www.kpmg.com/Global/en/IssuesAndInsights/ArticlesPublications/hr-transformations-survey/Documents/rethinking-human-resources-2012v2.pdf>.

Marler, J. and Fisher, S. (2013), 'An Evidence-Based Review of e-HRM and Strategic Human Resource Management', *Human Resource Management Review*, 23(1): 18–36.

O'Connell, P., Russell, H., Watson, D. and Byrne, D. (2009), *The Changing Workplace: A Survey of Employees' Views and Experiences*, Dublin: National Centre for Partnership and Performance.

Paauwe, J. (2009), 'HRM and Performance: Achievements, Methodological Issues and Prospects', *Journal of Management Studies*, 46(1): 129–152.

Renwick, D., Redman, T. and Maguire, S. (2013), 'Green Human Resource Management: A Review and Research Agenda', *International Journal of Management Reviews*, 15(1): 1–14.

Shanks, R., O'Neill, N. and O'Mahony, A. (2013), *Closing the Skills Gap in Ireland: Employers at the Heart of the Solution*, Dublin: Accenture, available from: <http://www.accenture.com/ie-en/Pages/

insight-solving-skills-paradox-seven-ways-close-critical-skills-gaps. aspx>.

Smith, D., de Leon, D., Marshall, B. and Cantrell, S. (2012), *Solving the Skills Paradox: Seven Ways to Close Your Critical Skills Gap*, London: Accenture, available from: <http://www.accenture.com/us-en/Pages/insight-solving-skills-paradox-seven-ways-close-critical-skills-gaps.aspx>.

Stone, D. and Dulebohn, J. (2013), 'Emerging Issues in Theory and Research on Electronic Human Resource Management (eHRM)', *Human Resource Management Review*, 23(1): 1–5.

Strohmeier, S. (2013), 'Employee Relationship Management – Realizing Competitive Advantage through Information Technology?', *Human Resource Management Review*, 23(1): 93–104.

Taylor, S., Osland, J. and Egri, C. (2012), 'Guest Editors' Introduction: Introduction to HRM's Role in Sustainability: Systems, Strategies and Practices', *Human Resource Management*, 51(6): 789–798.

Townsend, K., Wilkinson, A. and Allan, C. (2012), 'Mixed Signals in HRM: The HRM Role of Hospital Line Managers', *Human Resource Management Journal*, 22(3): 267–282.

Ulrich, D. (1997), *Human Resource Champions: The Next Agenda for Adding Value and Delivering Results*, Boston, MA: Harvard Business School Press.

Ulrich, D., Younger, J., Brockband, W. and Ulrich, M. (2013), 'The State of the HR Profession', *Human Resource Management*, 52(3): 457–471.

Van De Voorde, K., Paauwe, J. and Van Veldhoven, M. (2012), 'Employee Well-Being and the HRM–Organisational Performance Relationship: A Review of Quantitative Studies', *International Journal of Management Reviews*, 14(4): 391–407.

Index

Note: References to figures are indicated by 'f' and references to tables by 't'.